D1001261

Images of Society

GIANFRANCO POGGI

Images of Society

ESSAYS ON THE SOCIOLOGICAL THEORIES OF
TOCQUEVILLE, MARX, AND DURKHEIM

STANFORD UNIVERSITY PRESS
STANFORD, CALIFORNIA
LONDON: OXFORD UNIVERSITY PRESS
1972

Stanford University Press
Stanford, California
London: Oxford University Press
© 1972 by the Board of Trustees of the
Leland Stanford Junior University
Printed in the United States of America
Stanford ISBN 0-8047-0811-8
Oxford ISBN 0 19 690400 5
LC 79-183892

to the memory of my father
ENRICO POGGI
(1897-1970)

Acknowledgments

I am indebted to a number of colleagues for comments and criticisms on drafts of the essays that follow, and for general advice and encouragement concerning the project as a whole. I should like to thank in particular Tom Burns and Dennis Wrong. Much guidance was afforded by student audiences at Edinburgh and at Victoria, B.C., by way of feedback from lectures in which the content of nearly all chapters was tentatively expounded.

To my wife, Pat Poggi, I am indebted both for moral support and for pertinent and penetrating comments on all chapters, as well as for keeping at bay our daughter Maria, whose contribution to the enterprise was nearly as substantial but not nearly as direct.

Mrs. Barbara Vold, of the University of Victoria, B.C., cheerfully produced an excellent typescript. Miss Violet Laidlaw, of the University of Edinburgh, had previously, over a number of years, assisted in the chore of typing drafts and variously helped to keep the project going.

G. P.

Contents

Introduction

These essays have emerged from my experience of teaching one-year courses in sociological theory to honors students and beginning graduate students in sociology. These courses have generally included a sequence of lectures dealing with a few sociological greats (chosen from Tocqueville, Marx, Durkheim, Weber, Simmel, and Pareto) and a somewhat shorter sequence dealing with selected authors, "schools," or issues in contemporary sociological theory. Each year the first group of lectures has seemed to provide the greatest interest and inspiration for myself as well as for my students. In this book, therefore, I have pursued a rewarding subject by elaborating some of the insights to be gained, in particular, from a close reading of some major writings of Tocqueville, Marx, and Durkheim. I hope to reemphasize the importance of these writers by showing what a substantial contribution they can still make to many problems that are (or should be) major theoretical issues in today's sociology. The proof of this particular pudding, of course, cannot be given in an Introduction; it lies, if anywhere, in the individual essays and in the book as a whole. Here, I shall only indicate the approach I have adopted, which is much like the one used in my lectures.

My approach has certain definite limitations. Above all, this book is not intended to be an exercise in the history of social thought. Such an effort would involve sketching the historical and biographical context of an author's works, tracing the evolution of specific concepts in those works, and other "philological" concerns. Many of these are quite beyond my abilities and interests, let alone my very finite capacity for taking pains. Choosing a less structured approach, I have sought, as it were, to install myself within some particular writings of each author, and to convey to the reader (as to my students) at least something of what I have learned from those writings. But even this process has been considerably limited, and the reader should be aware of the constraints I have accepted.

First of all, I have not sought to survey and synthetize the thought of these authors in its entirety. This has been done (or rather, attempted with varying degrees of success) many times before. Moreover, the greats (or, if one prefers, the classics) are such precisely because they do not lend themselves to comprehensive, exhaustive readings. Rather, they should be visited and revisited, always with new questions in mind—or even better, with a willingness to let *them* formulate new problems, raise new issues, and suggest new insights. There is treasure in these writers; but all too often those who try to seize it at one go come up with very little, or at least with nothing that previous explorers have not long since gained.

At any rate, I have attempted not a comprehensive and authoritative rendering of these sociological classics, but an interpretive reading focused on individual books and on relatively circumscribed problems. As a consequence, the reader will find that the treatment of each writer ignores various writings of his and leaves out certain central concepts and themes. The Tocqueville section, for instance, does not discuss the "tyranny of the majority" or the so-called Tocqueville hypothesis (which explains why revolutions occur where and when they are least expected by those who have not read Tocqueville). In the Marx section, very little is said about class, ideology, or surplus value. The section on Durkheim barely mentions anomie, and religion only enters the last part of the chapter dealing chiefly with *Elementary forms of religious life*. Though I must agree that there is something perverse about these omissions, I hope that the delight I have admittedly taken in thus "staging Hamlet without the prince" has not led me entirely astray. The problems that I have addressed in the individual essays that follow do not strike me as peripheral with respect to either the authors' own thematic concerns or the current preoccupations of sociological theory.

Another limitation of my approach has been a concentration on what appears to me valid and viable, or at least distinctively suggestive and forceful, about a given author's treatment of a given theme. The fact that I have usually disregarded or glossed over what struck me as irrelevant or wrong-headed is another reason why my readings do not amount to balanced appraisals of the various authors (singly or in comparison with one another). Only in dealing with Durkheim have I broken this *nihil nisi bonum* rule and devoted a short chapter to some criticisms of his thought; but even this section is not intended as a balanced appraisal.

Furthermore, I have only occasionally made use of the secondary literature on each author. I am not, of course, claiming that I have conducted pristine readings of the works under consideration. My understanding of Durkheim, for instance, probably reflects even more than I am aware the interpretation advanced 35 years ago by Parsons in *The structure of social action*. My approach to Tocqueville is influenced by Bendix's. And my antideterministic reading of Marx echoes a line of Marxological thinking well established in Europe (though by no means unchallenged), which stresses the continuity between the idealistic dialectical tradition and Marx's thought, as well as the continuity within the latter. I have also availed myself here and there (especially in the section on Marx) of secondary literature supporting my own interpretations, but mostly without going into the related exegetical issues. In any case, I have not dealt systematically with the massive and ever-growing body of scholarship (sociological and other) that exists for each author, having decided quite early that the time and energy required for doing so would be far too much and the gains not quite proportionate to the effort.

This does not mean that the following essays contain only material derived from the authors; indeed, judging from some readers' reactions to early drafts of these essays, I seem to have read *into* these authors many of the arguments constructed upon their writings in the chapters that follow. This is probably most clear in the section on Tocqueville. Having concluded rather early that the historical referent of his ideal type "aristocracy" was the European Ständestaat, I have used in my reconstruction of that type a few twentieth-century discussions of the Ständestaat. Similarly, in discussing democracy I have drawn upon some post-Tocquevillian interpretations of the characteristics and dilemmas of this sociopolitical system, perhaps in order to partially offset my disregard of other features that have already been expanded on by Tocqueville and his previous commentators.

But on the whole, I am not inclined to agree that I have read too much into these authors. The novelty of my treatment, if any, lies in my having focused each essay on some problem that I feel was definitely of interest to the author involved and to which he had a distinctive contribution to make, but which somehow has not usually been given this privileged "focal" status by sociological commentators. I have thus made it my business to read Tocqueville with an eye mainly to the typological contrast of aristocracy and democracy, to indicate what Marx would have made of the central problem in Parsons' *Structure of social action*, to identify the strategic location of religion within Durkheim's general theory of social institutions, and so on. Given these and similar problems (which, as I have argued, are not peripheral to either those authors or modern sociological theory) my treatment takes the form of collating, selecting, and rearranging (sometimes quite extensively) the main contributions of a given author to the solution of a particular problem.

Unavoidably, this operation involves a certain arbitrariness, or (more positively) inventiveness, and can also require the introduction of concepts and arguments not directly or exclusively derived from a given author's works. This has probably happened most frequently, again, in the section on Tocqueville, whose analyses I have restated in more modern terms than he uses and arranged into a general argument that (hopefully) develops more clearly than his. There is a considerable change in the sequence of topics (Tocqueville's sequence sometimes follows no easily discernible line of argument), and I have taken the liberty of inserting into that sequence notions that were inferred from Tocqueville's own text rather than immediately derived from it. (These insertions, incidentally, are specifically indicated as such in the text only when they are particularly sizable or particularly inferential.)

More generally, I have as a rule given little attention to elements of an author's thought that fitted poorly with what seemed to me the main burden of his treatment of a given problem. So far as I can tell, I have done so only after exercising due care in determining that burden. Of course there is, again, an ineliminable "judgmental" component in any such operation; but then, to paraphrase Nietzsche, "When you go to the classics, bring along your mind." Abiding by this command is a liability if one's reader wants nothing but a "philologically" correct rendering of this or that classic work, *or* if the account given of an author's treatment of a given problem is intrinsically defective or untenable. I have already suggested that the philologically minded reader is probably looking at the wrong book; and I leave to those otherwise minded the problem of whether the following essays are in fact faulty or irrelevant, that is, whether or not they add to his understanding of what Tocqueville, Marx, and Durkheim were doing.

It should be quite clear from the foregoing that these essays are not intended to spare the reader the "trouble" of making direct contact with the writings of Tocqueville, Marx, and Durkheim. On the contrary, it will be quite useful if the reader is already acquainted with these authors; and if he is not, my efforts will hopefully encourage him to become so. He will gain not only theoretical insight of the kind I have attempted to convey in these essays, but also other intellectual rewards that in my judgment no amount of exposure to contemporary sociological writing can equal. For one thing, all three authors are talented writers (although their literary abilities are sometimes obliterated by particular translations). The richness of their imagination, the profundity of their reasoning, and the width of their learning never outrun their powers of expression, which allow them to reach the reader in the most effective way. Moreover, even a slight acquaintance with the lives and work of these authors will reveal that none of them were "academic" people in the pejorative sense of the term (which, as it happens, applies to nearly all their modern imitators). They were passionately committed to their diverse (indeed, contrasting) moral and political values, in the name of which they led their whole existence and also played their part as scholars.

Finally, the scholarly work of Tocqueville, Marx, and Durkheim, besides revealing their ethical preoccupations more openly than is today deemed respectable, cuts boldly across the boundaries of several disciplines, revealing a catholicity of interests and a breadth of learning that has no equal among today's sociologists. In the writings I will discuss speculative insights are provocatively interspersed with empirically grounded analyses, historical argument blends with sociological, and economic reasoning alternates with the critique of ideology. Even when it is possible (as it is often with Marx and almost always with Durkheim) to assign particular works primarily or exclusively to a single discipline, one is impressed by the number and variety of disciplines across which these writings range, at once acknowledging the distinctiveness of each discipline and rejecting its tendency to constrain a scholar's imagination within its own themes and approaches. I have no doubt that all three authors would have agreed in finding utterly preposterous the way in which a great American publishing house sought to promote an introductory sociology textbook in the late 1950's: "This text focuses on the structure and changes of society. All other concerns—whether psychological, economic, or even anthropological—have been avoided."

I have had, regrettably, little or no chance to convey these "extratheoretical" aspects of my authors' thought in the essays that follow. They have been mentioned only as added gains the reader may expect if, motivated by the success or failure of the essays themselves, he seeks out or returns to a direct acquaintance with the authors I discuss.

ALEXIS DE TOCQUEVILLE

SOURCES

As far as possible the research for this section has been conducted using original language editions of Tocqueville's writings. The most important of these are referred to throughout the section in abbreviated form, as indicated below:

D. *De la démocratie en Amérique*, 2 vols. (Paris: Genin, 1951). The two volumes are indicated respectively as D/I and D/II. After each page reference to this edition the italic numbers following the semicolon refer to the corresponding paging in *Democracy in America*, translated by George Lawrence, 2 vols. (London: Collins, 1969). The division of the material between the two volumes corresponds to that in the French edition, but in this translation the paging is consecutive between the two volumes.

A. *L'ancien régime et la révolution*, edited by G. W. Headlam (Oxford: Clarendon, 1904). The italic numbers here refer to *The old regime and the revolution*, translated by Stuart Gilbert (London: Collins, 1969).

All translations in the text, unless otherwise indicated, are my own.

1. *The Aristocratic Order*

Modern sociology emerged largely as one intellectual response to the "great transformation" that swept through European society after the mid-eighteenth century, rendering the nature (and perhaps the very survival) of that society acutely problematical.[1] Particularly in its early phases, sociology took the form of a protracted and concerned, though not always self-conscious, examination of the causes and consequences of two main components of the transformation: the Industrial Revolution and the French Revolution.[2]

Alexis de Tocqueville (1805-59) considered the second component by far the more significant of the two. And he devoted most of his scholarly work to establishing that the French Revolution had deeper roots in history, a wider geographical field of action, and a greater overall significance for the social and political ordering of nineteenth-century European society than had generally been acknowledged. In his view, the revolution and its aftermath signified first the breakthrough in Europe, and then the progressive, irresistible advent throughout Western Christianity, of a wholly new kind of society. Tocqueville called this society democracy, and felt that its general nature and tendencies had to be explored. Among the many valuable contributions that he made to this theme, those on which I intend to focus my own sociological discussion of his two masterpieces, *Democracy in America* (1835-40) and *The old regime and the revolution* (1856), are the typological contrast of aristocracy and democracy developed in the former (to be discussed in this chapter and the next) and the "case study" of the French transition from aristocracy

---

[1] See Karl Polanyi, *The great transformation* (Boston: Beacon, 1957).
[2] This viewpoint has lately been taken (and perhaps somewhat overstated) in Robert Nisbet, *The sociological tradition* (New York: Basic Books, 1967).

to democracy that Tocqueville presents in the latter (to be discussed in Chapter 3).[3]

The first part of *Democracy* (1835) followed the rather limiting procedure of analyzing the concrete features of the American republic, and only occasionally did it raise a more general question by attempting to distinguish what was democratic from what was American. In the second part (1840), however, Tocqueville pursued the larger question consciously and systematically. To this end, he worked out two contrasting, comprehensive, and internally consistent ideal types: aristocracy and democracy. And democracy was portrayed as intrinsically, entirely, and irreversibly different from aristocracy.

Since these two constructs were essentially no more than a device for generating insights into the nature of the French Revolution, Tocqueville never took the argument further to ask, for instance, what elements the two types had in common and what invariant relationships, if any, obtained between corresponding elements of each. His emphasis was exclusively on the magnitude and importance of the differences between aristocratic and democratic society. For the same reason (that is, because his whole analytical effort was directed to analyzing the nature of modern society) both types referred exclusively to large-scale, territorial, sociopolitical groupings. Within these units, of course, Tocqueville often worked down to smaller, less complex groupings, and some of his statements are applicable

[3] So far, most sociological interpretations of Tocqueville have somewhat disregarded *The old regime* and concentrated on *Democracy in America*, a source of perceptive comment on the society, politics, and culture of the early American republic. Various students have sought to establish the extent to which the features emphasized by Tocqueville have persisted or been modified in modern America. See, for example, the many references to Tocqueville in Seymour Lipset and Leo Lowenthal, eds., *Culture and social character* (New York: Free Press, 1961). Others have sought insights into the general tendencies of sociopolitical development in a democracy; for example, J. P. Mayer, *Alexis de Tocqueville: A biographical study in political science* (New York: Harper & Row, 1960), a previous edition of which bore the title *Prophet of the mass age*. Of greater analytical relevance is the work of authors who seek out Tocqueville's ideas on the social conditions necessary for the persistence and effective operation of representative government. See Seymour Lipset et al., *Union democracy* (Glencoe: Free Press, 1956), particularly pp. 74-76. My own sociological interpretation draws its inspiration mainly from the example set by Reinhard Bendix in *Nation-building and citizenship* (New York: Wiley, 1964).

to collective units on any scale; but in principle his discourse was confined to units on the scale of the national state, and was not directly applicable to families, small groups, tribal societies, or formal organizations, however large these might be.[4] (Incidentally, this is perhaps one reason why Tocqueville is not, as it were, a "sociologist's sociologist.")

Each of Tocqueville's two constructs is a conceptual assemblage of traits, characteristics of the society in whole or in part that are held to be typically associated with one another (although it is not assumed that in any real historical society all these traits ever did or ever will occur together).[5] Tocqueville's own selection of traits is extensive: constitutional features of the political systems, the status of domestic servants, the aesthetic tendencies associated with each construct, and so on. I have found it necessary to be more selective in my own formulation of his ideal societies, and have organized this formulation rather differently from Tocqueville's. He proceeds, chapter by chapter, to show how aristocratic and democratic societies differ in each separate aspect of social life; I have chosen instead to work out a reasonably complete picture of one type, or at least of selected aspects of that type, before proceeding to an analogous discussion of the other type. As will be seen, I have also sought to clarify Tocqueville's own distinction between two subtypes of democracy and have attempted to spell out their characteristics.

For these reasons, as well as because I have frequently introduced considerations that Tocqueville did not present and referred to sources that he did not or could not use, my own presentation of Part II of *Democracy* does not closely follow Tocqueville's discussion. I have tried, however, to remain faithful to its main theoretical inspiration and to convey what I regard as its persistent sociological importance: to wit, its contribution to the understanding of the "great transformation."

[4] Tocqueville is explicit about this limitation: "I am speaking here of democratic government as applied to a nation [*à un peuple*] and not to a small tribe." D/I 328; 256.

[5] For a general discussion of such devices in sociological theory, see Reinhard Bendix and Bennett Berger, "Images of society and problems of concept formation in sociology," in Llewellyn Gross, ed., *Symposium on sociological theory* (Evanston, Ill.: Harcourt, Row, 1959), pp. 92-120.

Aristocratic Society

Although Tocqueville does not make the point explicitly, it is useful to think of the characteristics that compose each of his types as being clustered around one master characteristic that by itself can identify a given society as either aristocratic or democratic. The master characteristic that tells us what an aristocratic society *is*, before telling us *what it is like*, lies in the joint occurrence, within a large-scale sociopolitical system, of three conditions.

First, an aristocratic society, in Tocqueville's terms, is a dualistic system; that is, it is sharply divided on several dimensions (education, opportunity, degree of involvement in the larger society, etc.) between the mass of the populace in the lower tier and a small, privileged minority in the upper tier; and in principle the gap between the two is unbridgeable. The minority, which typically culminates in a paramount ruler, may also be internally differentiated on a variety of dimensions, but none of these differentiations is as substantial as those marking off the total minority from the populace.

Second, each individual or collective component of the privileged minority enjoys its privileges by right, and not (as one might say in a formulation taken from Roman law) *vi, clam aut precario*—that is, neither by dint of force, nor clandestinely, nor on a ruler's sufferance. The privileged have an established right to their respective advantages in the sense that they may legitimately resist any encroachment on those advantages, even from the ruler himself. Their rights rest on an understanding that affects and limits the ruler's powers, establishing around the privileged a variously defined but inviolable sphere of immunity, a franchise.

Third, among the rights enjoyed by the privileged are some that allow the privileged to exercise governmental powers (that is, powers involving if necessary a legitimate recourse to coercion) over certain sections of the populace or over members of the privileged collectivities themselves. Thus the governance of the society as a whole is to a greater or lesser extent dispersed among the various sections of the privileged minority, as part and parcel of their privileges; and it is to be carried out by each privileged group within its own sphere and on its own behalf, rather than by a unified agency operating in a distinctive, overriding, *public* sphere and on behalf of a generalized, all-comprising polity.

Tocqueville does not explicitly state, as I do, that these features of an aristocratic society are the most distinctive; but he does emphasize them repeatedly, as in the following passages:

In countries organized aristocratically and hierarchically, power never addresses itself to the governed as a whole (D/II 259; *759*).

[In historical examples of this type] the national power did not exist directly before the eyes of the individual citizens: each of them was aware only of his duty of obedience toward a given man; only through the latter, as if automatically, were all others reached (D/II 320; *802*).

The ruler was not exclusively responsible for governing and administering the citizens: he was obliged to leave this responsibility in part to the members of the aristocracy. . . . For the most part, those who acted in his place owed their power to their birth and not to him; they were not continuously in his hands. The ruler could not advance them or destroy them from one moment to the next (D/II 441-42; *904*).

This characterization of Tocqueville's aristocratic society suggests that his discussion is concerned with a rather restricted class of sociopolitical systems—specifically, to the sovereign powers of Western Europe during a period bounded at one end by the consolidation of relatively large and unified territorial units and at the other end by the French Revolution and the diffusion of its impact. Naturally, the area and the period in question are both wide enough to cover a variety of social arrangements; but at the appropriate level of abstraction all these arrangements do seem to possess an essential sameness of structure, a collection of basic traits like those outlined.

If Tocqueville's main concern is in fact to point up the magnitude and significance of the French Revolution and its European ramifications, it is hardly surprising that the example he chooses to contrast with post-Revolutionary European society should turn out to be a unique sociopolitical system from the same context: the Western European *Ständestaat*.[6] So far as one can determine from *Democracy*,

---

[6] The best contemporary sociological treatment of the Ständestaat is probably that presented briefly in Bendix, *Nation-building and citizenship*. Probably the best previous treatments are in Max Weber, *Economy and society*, edited by Guenther Roth and Claus Wittich (New York: Bedminster, 1968), and in Fritz Oppenheimer, *Der Staat*, 2d ed. (Stuttgart: Fischer, 1964).

it was certainly his intellectual and emotional familiarity with the
Ständestaat that provided him with the empirical base for his construct of aristocratic society. Of course, the material on which a
scholar bases his abstractions need not set ultimate limits for the
analytical use of those abstractions. Tocqueville himself perhaps expected his construct to make sense of historical conditions other than
the Western European ones from which he had evolved it; and it was
possibly with this end in view that he did not include in his ideal type
of aristocracy some features that did obtain throughout Western Europe (e.g., the privileges held by corporate bodies other than the
nobility, in particular by the Catholic Church and by many cities).

However, it is hard to see to what other historical settings Tocqueville's notion of aristocracy might be applied. Archaic Greece and
Rome may appear to be suitable candidates. But both were city-
states, whereas the type envisages, as I have said, territorial units
more on the scale of the national state. Moreover, the dualism of an
aristocratic society is not the dualism of master and slave. Finally,
Tocqueville's picture of aristocratic society has very few of the traits
associated with "archaic" societies in general. In fact, judged by the
master characteristic of aristocratic society that I have proposed, even
Eastern European societies do not fully qualify as aristocratic. In
Tsarist Russia, at any rate, not even the nobility, let alone the Church,
cities, or guilds, ever enjoyed the autonomy of the Western European
Stände, for the Russian principle of Imperial autocracy came before
all else.[7]

Before going on to some of the other characteristics that make up
Tocqueville's ideal type of aristocratic society, let us look very briefly
to the unique historical entity that was both the empirical base and
the target of his formulation. That entity was not the Europe of
"heroic" feudalism, where a few weak centers of political power
were interposed between the supranational powers of Empire and
Church and the locally based powers of the warrior class, the feudal
lords. Tocqueville's referent, I repeat, was the Ständestaat, a later
entity resulting from a long, geographically diversified but concep-

[7] See Dieter Gerhard, "Regionalismus und ständisches Wesen als ein Grund-
thema europäischer Geschichte," in Gerhard, *Alte und neue Welt in vergleichen-
der Geschichtsbetrachtung* (Göttingen: Vandenhoek & Ruprecht, 1962), pp. 13-
39.

tually unitary process that widened the powers of sovereign territorial rulers (generally royal dynasties) and narrowed those held by the feudal class.

In developing, the Ständestaat restricted, and finally eliminated some of the traditional rights of the feudal class, most significantly the right to wage "private" wars and feuds. But it left only slightly modified other rights with great economic, political, and status significance. In particular, the feudal class retained various jurisdictional and governmental powers over itself and over most of the populace, and these were inextricably bound up with its seigneurial rights and its status prerogatives; at the same time, such powers became more diverse and circumscribed, and were clothed in more technically formulated, more ritually imposing juridical forms (D/I 3; 6).[8] Furthermore (although Tocqueville did not include them in his model), the Ständestaat also retained or established similar prerogatives for the Church, certain religious orders, cities, universities, and other groups.

Thus the Ständestaat was a unified, sovereign political entity whose governmental functions were performed not only by the ruler and his own administrative apparatus but also by many other groups with overlapping authority (A 42; 62). The feudal lord, as head of a lineage, presided over his own landed estate and its villages, and also sat in a regional assembly of his peers. The craft and the trade guilds ruled their members and their members' families, and indirectly affected their customers. The Church held power over its own personnel, and over all people where certain relationships were concerned. A city's authority encompassed its own citizens, visitors to its market, and to some extent people living or traveling in the adjoining countryside. There were also independent regional and municipal courts.[9] And so on. The picture becomes even more complicated if one considers regional variations within each country and the multi-

---

[8] On this process see Gerhard, "Regionalismus und ständisches Wesen." See also Otto von Brunner, "Vom Gottesgnade zum monarchischen Prinzip," in *Das Königtum: Seine geistigen und rechtlichen Grundlagen* (Lindau: Thorbecke, 1956), pp. 279-305.

[9] The most significant contributions to the sociological categorization of these various authorities are probably those made by the German historian of legal and political institutions Otto von Hintze, now mostly collected in his *Staat und Verfassung* (Göttingen: Vandenhoeck & Ruprecht, 1962). Tocqueville's own *Old regime* is also helpful.

ple relations within each major jurisdiction: for example, the relation between a parish and a bishopric, and that between the latter and the local governing bodies of religious orders; or the ramifications of the lord-vassal relationship affecting land tenure. All of these jurisdictions and interrelationships, moreover, could change with the passage of time.

If it is to retain its distinctive usefulness, a typological approach to such a complex historical reality must naturally abstract from most of these complications. And Tocqueville's aristocratic model presents us with a highly streamlined Ständestaat that lacks many of the dimensions of variation found in that "historical individual." For instance, Tocqueville disregards the difference between countries like Britain, whose nobles form a permanent, country-wide assembly of their own, and countries like France, where no such body exists. Above all, he purposely ignores the fundamental long-run change that all Ständestaaten actually experienced: the steady growth of monarchical power at the expense of the autonomous jurisdictions or estates of the realm.[10] He designs his model (and this also holds, to a lesser extent, for his model of democratic society) with a view to emphasizing the internal consistency and potential stability of the system.

This strategy is so clearly inherent in the nature and purpose of the typological approach that I have no hesitation in adopting it here —indeed, with a vengeance, since as I have indicated my account will perforce be even more selective than Tocqueville's own discussion. In organizing my argument, I will employ a distinction frequently used by Tocqueville himself, that between "political" and "civil" society. I do so with some misgivings: one could argue that whereas the distinction is fully pertinent in a democracy it is not applicable to aristocracies, where private and public, civil and political, are closely bound together and essentially inseparable.[11] However, if the distinction is here taken purely as a device for organizing an argument and facilitating the comparison of aristocracy with democracy, I cannot

[10] Hans Jacoby, *Die Bürokratisierung der Welt* (Neuwied: Luchterhand, 1969). Part I, "The rise of the modern state apparatus," is a good elementary discussion of this phenomenon.

[11] On this problem see Jürgen Habermas, *Strukturwandel der Öffentlichkeit* (Neuwied: Luchterhand, 1965).

see any harm in employing it. And as we shall see, it also applies to my later discussion of *The old regime* (Chapter 3).

The Political Society

As we have seen, the aristocratic society is a large-scale territorial unit with a paramount ruler, who is typically a member of a privileged minority, the nobility. And since the other members are his peers, he has both claims on them and obligations toward them. Basically, he is entitled to their counsel, their aid, and their loyalty; and he is obligated to respect their privileges, to recognize that they hold those privileges by right and not at the ruler's own pleasure. A ruler's title is typically lifelong and hereditary, being vested not so much in his own physical person as in his dynasty. And since the same holds for all members of the nobility, one could say that the system of claims and obligations actually connects the ruler's and nobles' respective lineages, resting on a compact entered at some point in the distant past and now vested with the sanctity of tradition.

As the head of the overall sociopolitical unit (i.e., the state), the ruler is primarily responsible for the conduct of foreign affairs (including vital decisions on wars and alliances) and for the preservation of peace in his domain. He meets these responsibilities not only with the assistance of the nobles but also through the services of a body of officials who, unlike the nobles, derive their powers from him, owe him a personal submission not expected of the nobility, and can in principle be removed at will. (This is the "patrimonial-bureaucratic" component in the rule of a Ständestaat, to which Tocqueville pays little attention in *Democracy*.)

The ruler can enact legal norms (*leges*) and is not himself bound by them. In an aristocratic society, however, there is a great deal more to the law (*jus*) than such enacted norms, which typically regulate only limited matters and are valid only if they are compatible with the basic framework of the law.[12] And the framework itself is not valid because of enactment, since no secular, visible power can endow its own decisions with the law's majesty. The law of an aristocratic society, then, is not in principle a body of enacted rules; rather it ap-

---

[12] This notion is emphasized in Brunner, "Vom Gottesgnade zum monarchischen Prinzip."

proximates a situation formulated in ideal-typical terms by Weber.[13] (Tocqueville himself does not discuss either the aristocratic or the democratic legal system in these terms.)

All law exists primarily in the form of rights, i.e. of specific, differentiated, legitimate claims vested in given individual or collective subjects (D/II 395; 867). These rights have the backing of religion and tradition, and they are ultimately sanctioned by their holder's power of claiming them for himself, by force if necessary (D/II 422; 889). The two mottoes of the British monarchy, *Dieu et mon droit* and *Nemo me impune lacessit*, convey very clearly what is involved. A noble lineage possesses its own right and its own law (the duality of meaning of the French *droit* is significant); God is the ultimate guarantor of these prerogatives, and whoever encroaches upon them can expect prompt retribution. In principle, these mottoes apply to any noble lineage, not just to the ruler's.

All rights manifest themselves not as possessions enjoyed because the abstract requirements of some enacted rule have been met, but as self-justifying claims that receive their validity, like all the law, from the sanctity of tradition. Rights appear as privileges, as the diverse "liberties," "franchise," and "immunities" that pertain to a given estate (*Stand*) and thus to all lineages and groupings belonging to that estate (D/II 318; 799-800). A legal system that approximates this model, that does not predate rights but is coeval with them, necessarily leaves little room for legislation in the modern sense of the term. It does not contain the basic assumption that any secular agency operating in the present can *create* law, can impart the validity of law to decisions by the simple device of observing certain formal procedures in reaching those decisions.

To the many activities of the nobility that might be called political, we can apply a distinction that Tocqueville formulates in another context (distinguishing between government and administration): some activities pertain to the governance of the country as a whole, or large regions of it, whereas others have a purely local scope. Normally, the nobles engage in large-scale activities not as individual heads of lineages but as members of corporate bodies that meet periodically. These assemblies may offer the ruler advice on his current

[13] See Weber, *Economy and Society*, especially p. 1099.

political concerns, restate the boundaries of the law (constituted mainly by the nobles' own rights), and deliberate on their collective reaction to the ruler's policies. It is probably misleading to think of these activities as involving the kind of political activity—that is, political participation—that a democracy allows, in theory, to all its citizens.[14] And the assemblies of nobles in an aristocratic state are not at all like democratic representative law-making bodies.

In the first place, the democratic notion of participation involves the merging of individual wills in novel, self-validating decisions that transcend those wills. It is assumed that each participant is equal, and that each will constitutes an ad hoc formed judgment on the best way to pursue a universally shared interest. By contrast, when a number of aristocratic estates offer their counsel to the ruler, each of them is expected to "stand on its rights," to voice its own traditional prerogatives and thus safeguard its own differentiated standing with respect to the ruler and to all other estates.[15] In the second place, representation in the modern, democratic meaning of the term is not involved. In principle, each nobleman represents only himself, or rather, his lineage; and each estate likewise represents only itself. Neither is supposed to speak for a wider constituency.

The nonparticipatory, nonrepresentative nature of aristocratic political activities may justify a general statement: if by politics we understand an activity intended to shape new authoritative decisions and involving competition for the support of a general constituency, then there are no politics in the typical aristocratic society. Indeed, no general constituency exists in a society where political rights are only an aspect of the ascriptive privileges enjoyed by an exclusive minority, and where the populace has no political standing in the larger society but entertains only locally based and typically unproblematical relations of independence toward its "betters." To use the terminology of contemporary political science, under such conditions there is no "political demand" on the part of the populace; and the estates

[14] This same conclusion is reached, also with reference to Tocqueville but by a somewhat different argument, in A. Pizzorno, "Introduzione allo studio della partecipazione politica," *Quaderni di Sociologia*, XV (1966), No. 2, p. 238. See also Guido De Ruggiero, *Storia del liberalismo europeo*, 5th ed. (Bari: Laterza, 1949), pp. 2-3.

[15] See Gerhard, "Regionalismus und ständisches Wesen," p. 29; Oppenheimer, *Der Staat*, p. 563.

of the nobility could not act to process the demand even if it existed.

It is probably a matter of definition (and not one that Tocqueville's argument directly raises) whether one can state, as I have done, that under these conditions the aristocratic society knew no "politics." There is no doubt that the management of this society involved the issuing and enforcing of authoritative decisions both nationally and locally, and that the nobility, mainly through its corporate bodies, was involved in those decisions even at the national level. Tocqueville emphasizes that noble bodies, exactly because they do not have to spend time courting the favor of constituencies, normally tend to give very careful consideration to the matters they deliberate; as a result, the product of their deliberations is likely to be mature and responsible. The statutes the ruler issues on the advice of nobles are likely to be well pondered, phrased in technically precise language, and mindful of the diverse contingencies of their application. Of course, being the product of a narrow, privileged body, their content may well be reprehensible; for example, it may reinforce the prerogatives of landowners with respect to tenants, or impose overly harsh penalties on criminals (D/I 360; 286). More generally, in Tocqueville's view, the role played by noble estates in policy formation often gives the policies of aristocratic societies some unique qualities: steadfastness of purpose, maturity of deliberation, a keen awareness of the interests of future generations, and a persistent preoccupation with the continuity of governmental action.

There is nothing so committed to its own view as an aristocracy. The mass of the population may be seduced by its ignorance or its passions; one may catch a king unaware and lead him to change his mind; and in any case no king is immortal. However an aristocratic body is too large to be taken in and too small to yield without resistance to the impact of unreflecting feelings. An aristocratic body is comparable to an enlightened man who is steady in his purpose and undying (D/I 358; 284).

Individual noblemen may become involved in national and regional political activities otherwise than as members of aristocratic bodies, usually by being called to assist the ruler on a more regular basis—as members of his privy council, as judges in his courts, or as supervisors of the administrative activities carried out by commoners whom the ruler has put in charge of a given sphere of affairs. These

official positions are eagerly sought because of the prestige and influence they carry; but they are not pursued as doggedly and shame-
lessly as they tend to be when they confer social worth on a man who
has none of his own. Normally, the nobles appointed to high administrative posts will be men whose lineage, wealth, and education confer on them a high standing independently of their offices (D/II 124;
641), men whose motivating ambition is to seek glory for the realm
and for their own lineage (D/I 332; 259), to experience command and
responsibility rather than to enrich themselves (D/II 204; 711). Men
of this kind, Tocqueville feels, are less likely to use their offices for
corrupt ends and personal gain; and their very indispensability to the
management of the ruler's affairs will tend to restrain the ruler and
his officials from encroaching on the prerogatives of the nobility.

As I suggested in my first characterization of aristocratic society,
the nobility exercises governmental powers not only through its cooperation with the ruler's national or regional government but also
on a local basis, as an indispensable dimension of each nobleman's
superiority over a section of the populace that is generally determined
by the landholdings of his own lineage. The basic principle is one
somewhat overstated by the French legal formula *chaque baron est
roi dans sa baronnie* (each baron is king within his own barony). Each
nobleman, that is, within the framework of the law, has ruling powers over the population of his territory: he polices the territory, he
raises troops within it, he levies taxes, he adjudicates quarrels, and
he punishes crimes; he also oversees the maintenance of roads, assistance to the sick and the poor, and the management of the parishes
in his domain (D/II 413; 883). He does all this in a private capacity
and not as an official of the ruler, although from time to time his
levying of taxes will reflect not just the demands made by his own
style of life but also those of the ruler's foreign policies and administrative needs. Normally, in fact, even the implementation of national
policies, which in principle are the primary responsibility of the ruler,
devolves *by right* upon the nobleman in the exercise of his own governmental powers.

The interaction between the national and local levels of government, and their intersection in the governmental responsibilities of
the nobleman, are nowhere as clear as in the management of military

affairs. Typically, an aristocratic army naturally draws its leaders from the nobility. The command of military operations is simply another expression of the nobleman's generalized position of social advantage (D/II 361; 838); it is his right and responsibility to raise and equip troops on his own territory and out of his own resources, and to lead them in the field himself. Thus the troops fight under the standards of individual noble lineages, and quite often the proceeds of their operations (occasionally territory, more often booty) accrue to the patrimony of the lineage.

An aristocratic army, therefore, does not have a professional officer corps, since normally even the lower positions of command will go mostly to the nobleman's dependents. Most noble officers get little specialized military training, and they may even command armies when they are scarcely more than adolescents (the Great Condé, for example, was only 22 when he won the battle of Rocroi). The chain of command normally parallels the hierarchy symbolized by the grading of the respective titles of nobility. For this reason, the ruler is normally the supreme commander of his country's army. But he cannot count on the immediate devotion of that army to the interests of the country and the glory of his own dynasty, or on the *direct* submission of all the troops; these things depend on the noblemen's loyalty to the ruler. Consequently, a recurrent and all too often unsolved problem in aristocratic armies is the strategic and tactical coordination of the major operational units, particularly those led by noblemen who are nearly equal to the king in aristocratic rank.[16] However, the same armies are normally spared the tensions caused by the jockeying of professional officers for promotion. Indeed, in aristocratic armies,

This man is naturally called upon to command a regiment, that man a company; these represent the boundaries of their ambitions, and they are content with having attained them. . . . The officer, independently of his army rank, occupies an elevated social position anyway. The former is in his eyes but a complement to the latter; if he devotes himself to the trade of arms, he does so less in response to ambition than out of a feeling of obligation originating from birth (D/II 362; 838).

[16] See Renate Mayntz, *Soziologie der Organisation* (Reinbeck: Rowohlt, 1963), p. 12.

For the same reason, to the rank and file of aristocratic armies "military discipline is only a prolongation of social servitude" (D/II 381; *854*).

If these are the essential features characterizing the political activities of the ruler and his nobles, the crucial point about the political role of the remainder of society—the great majority of the population—has already been made. The populace simply has no political role to play. This same point has recently been stated by a student of pre-Revolutionary French society:

The peasants ... before the beginning of the revolutionary disturbances, exercised no direct influence on policy. Admittedly in a sense they determined the history of France. They worked the land, which provided overwhelmingly the greater part of the national income. The primitive peasant economy was reflected in every aspect of the national life, including the court, which was of a kind that only peasant economies produce. Peasant needs and desires, however, were of no account. Policy was made by the ruling groups.[17]

The political insignificance of the populace, of course, was only another aspect of its social insignificance—of the fact that it existed only in territorial "slices," each locally bounded and each incorporated, for the purpose of the general social and political process, in the figure of its noble governor and superior (but, as I have suggested, not *represented* by him) (D/II 320; *802*). Under these conditions, the populace was simply not part of the larger society, which was coextensive with the circle of the privileged, where the populace was, as Tocqueville phrases it, "neither heard nor seen" (A 2; *24*). The fact that the populace was purely the object and never the subject of political activity was but one barely distinguishable aspect of its all-encompassing situation of dependence, which ultimately stemmed from the fact that the people had no military or economic resources of their own; at most they possessed unenforceable, though often recognized, claims to their masters' benevolence (D/I 8; *11*). Hence there was a drastic difference between the disenfranchised populace on the one hand and the enfranchised minority of the privileged on the other, however internally differentiated the latter may have been.

[17] C. B. A. Behrens, "Looking for Louis," *New York Review*, XV, No. 2, pp. 18-19.

I emphasize this point, the dualistic nature of aristocratic society, because there still persists (and is stated by Tocqueville; see D/II 137; 653) a popular belief that this society was held together by many convergent and *continuous* "chains of dependence," all built on the feudal relationship of lord to vassal and all together spanning the whole distance from ruler to serf. In reality, even the true feudal society had a sharp discontinuity in this vertical chain, which corresponded to the difference between relationships primarily of "seigneurie" and relationships primarily of "feodalité."[18] And a comparable two-tiered structure was maintained in the Ständestaat. This discontinuity cannot be satisfactorily conceptualized in terms of the familiar dimensions of stratification, that is, purely as the juxtaposition within the same society of "men very great and men very small, men very rich and men very poor, men very enlightened and men very ignorant" (D/II 453; 914). The populace simply did not inhabit the same society as the nobles; for they enjoyed no immunities with respect to the privileged groups, and the enjoyment of immunities was the essence of belonging to the society at all.

I am not arguing that commoners had no claims whatever on their lords. But what claims they had were still those of dependents—claims to the lord's protection and benevolence, which could not be upheld, as the lord's own claims could, either by the claimant's appealing to a court of his peers or by his resorting to legitimate "self-aid," to the forcible seizure of his rights. This view is confirmed *a contrario* by the occasional violent and short-lived attempts of sections of the populace (typically, the peasant *jacquerie*) to rise against their betters. The usual aim of these revolts was not to enforce claims or achieve citizenship in the larger society; rather, the rebels sought to abolish the larger society in order to set up strictly local enclaves of love and brotherhood.[19] For this very reason some notable students of these uprisings refuse to characterize them as political.

My discussion so far has outlined the political aspects of aristocratic society, largely from the standpoint of Tocqueville's own discussion but with occasional reference to contemporary work on the

[18] I interpret in this sense Robert Boutruche, *Seigneurie et feodalité*, 2d ed. (Paris: Aubier, 1968).
[19] See Eric Hobsbawm, *Primitive rebels* (New York: Norton, 1965).

Ständestaat. We must now relate this characterization to Tocqueville's most urgent moral concern: the presence or absence of restraints on the central government's tendency to increase its own prerogatives indefinitely and to concentrate all governmental functions in itself (D/I 401; *872*). Clearly, by virtue of the political features we have considered, such restraints do exist in an aristocratic society (D/II 442; *905*); and to this extent and in this sense such a society is typically a free society. Tocqueville himself qualifies this statement by saying that freedom is not conferred on an equal basis, as a right, on all members of the society but is always "bound up with the notion of immunity and privilege" (A 126; *142-43*).

Schematizing Tocqueville's thought on this point I would suggest that the freedom typical of an aristocracy (i.e., the restraint placed on the activity of the central government) rests on two overlapping principles, which we can label "cultural" and "structural."

Cultural principle. There exists, over the society as a whole, a "firmament of law,"[20] ultimately guaranteed by the Deity and endowed with the majesty of tradition (D/I 8; *10*). Since this firmament legitimizes the powers of both the ruler and the privileged minority, it binds both kinds of power indissolubly together. Therefore, any serious attempt by the ruler to interfere with the prerogatives of a section of the minority threatens his own legitimacy and deprives him of any title to the support (or acquiescence) of all other sections of the minority.

Structural principle. As we have seen it is basic to an aristocratic society that within it there exist "nearly independent individuals or groups on which it falls to administer justice, to raise and equip troops, to levy taxes, and often even to formulate or interpret the law" (D/II 413; *883*). These "intermediate" powers sustain freedom in the larger society (D/II 441; *904*) because the following assumptions can be made about them (although Tocqueville does not spell them out):

1. As a rule, intermediate powers have an interest in exercising and defending their governmental prerogatives, since these prerogatives are an essential component of the general position of social advan-

---

[20] I borrow this expression from R. I. MacIver, *The web of government* (New York: Norton, 1965).

tage they enjoy (D/I 134; *117*). The revenues of a typical member of
the privileged minority, the noble landlord, rest to a greater or lesser
extent on his ability to command unpaid labor, to exact tributes, to
monopolize certain services and levy tolls for their use, to demand
the delivery of certain amounts of produce, and so on. In non-
Tocquevillian terms, the transfer of surplus from the direct producers
to the upper social stratum, in an aristocratic society, takes place
largely through political means, and the members of the upper stratum have an obvious interest in preserving these means. Some prerogatives, one may note, and in particular police and judicial powers,
often benefit the populace without being directly profitable to the
nobles who exercise them; but the exercise of these prerogatives is
one way of securing the continued allegiance of a noble's dependents.

2. As a rule, the intermediate powerholders are factually *able* to
exercise their governmental prerogatives and to resist interference
from the ruler (D/II 442; *889*). As we have seen, the typical privileged
nobles are wealthy landlords, who can normally use their revenues
to raise and equip troops loyal to themselves, and who can control
the flow of part of the surplus produce (if any) toward the ruler's
treasury. Furthermore, individual noblemen can generally rely on the
solidarity of their peers, since they enjoy most of their rights not as
individuals but as members of an estate (D/II 443; *905*). This applies
even more clearly to the Stände that Tocqueville does not discuss,
such as cities and guilds. The individual member in those groups is
quite powerless, and the Stände's power rests directly on the fusion
of the individuals into corporate bodies.

The coexistence of the structural and cultural principles insures
that the management of a great many governmental affairs will remain decentralized. This differentiated structure of highly autonomous powers is for the ruler a source of both support and resistance.[21]
The collaboration of the intermediate powers is indispensable if the
whole society is to back the undertakings of the ruler. That collaboration, however, cannot be constrained. It must be duly requested
and justified by the ruler, and will normally be granted only condi-

---

[21] For the crucial significance, ideological justification, and legal construction
of the power to resist, see the discussion in Fritz Kern, *Kingship and law in the
middle ages*, translated by S. B. Chrimes (Oxford: Blackwell, 1939), Part I.

tionally, the most likely condition being that the prerogatives of the intermediate powers be enhanced or at least respected.

If the peculiar equilibrium between central and intermediate powers that characterizes an aristocratic society is maintained, the society will be capable of great accomplishments, particularly in its external relations. The steadfastness of political action resulting from the continuity of a ruling dynasty, the interest of both the ruler and the noblemen in increasing the glory and fortunes of their respective lineages, the loyalty they can normally evoke from their respective dependents, and above all the firm collaboration between the central and intermediate powers—all these factors commit aristocratic nations to great designs and inspire them to seek military might, conquest, and empire (D/I 9, 347ff; *11, 273ff*).

The Civil Society

In those parts of *Democracy* where Tocqueville considers the features of aristocratic *society* rather than aristocratic government he has very little to say about the lower tier of that society, the populace. The many and varied insights he presents on the daily existence, tastes, intellectual tendencies, and moral preoccupations prevalent within that society refer almost exclusively to its privileged minority, and most specifically to the nobility. There are a number of reasons for this. Tocqueville, himself the scion of an aristocratic lineage, may have naturally identified with his own ancestors and their peers.[22] It may also be argued that the limitations of the available historical record encourage the student of pre-Revolutionary European society to emphasize the nobility over the populace. As a fictional seventeenth-century chronicler conjured up by Alessandro Manzoni remarks, history, that "illustrious war against Time," has consistently busied itself with "Princes, Potentates, and qualified Personages," to the neglect of "mechanick people of little consequence." Even an analytical reinterpretation of the historical record must inevitably reflect this bias.

Perhaps the crucial reason lies in two closely connected points I have made. If the essential characteristic of the aristocratic society is the strict fusion of political significance with social privilege, and if,

[22] There is an indication of this in D/II 453; *914*.

as a consequence, the populace really is not a constituent part of the larger society, then an analysis focused (as Tocqueville's is) on the aristocratic society as a comprehensive, supralocal sociopolitical system, must make the holders of political power the protagonists of its discussion of nongovernmental matters as well. In this respect it is appropriate that Tocqueville should focus on the nobility alone, disregarding the ruler, the Church, the cities, and the guilds.

Only the nobility, indeed, is a visible, nationwide social group, a social realm with distinctive rules and preoccupations. The ruler is too unique, except to the extent that he and his household conform to the pattern of noble existence; the Church is too cosmopolitan at its upper levels (the hierarchy) and too local at its lower levels (the parish clergy); the cities and guilds are too rooted in single localities, too vernacular, to form by themselves a nationwide continuum of social existence. Only the members of the nobility systematically entertain social relations on a national or regional basis and share a distinctive pattern of existence. It is natural that this pattern of existence should be the constant referent for Tocqueville's discussion of social life in an aristocratic society, and that non-noble social groups (especially domestics and craftsmen) should come into the discussion solely by virtue of their close association with the nobility, in whose life they are not only an indispensable support (this would apply to most of the populace) but also a visible and constant complement (D/II 67ff, 237ff; 597ff, 740ff).

Typically, the noblemen are large landowners in an economic system where land is by far the dominant form of wealth and agriculture the predominant economic activity (D/II 422; 889). There is no true market in land, and in a sense the estate does not belong to the nobleman but to his lineage. A close relationship, a kind of identity between the noble lineage and its estate is sanctioned by legal principles that make the estate indivisible through inheritance and place it *extra commercium*. Also, a noble family typically resides on its own land, and the names of the two coincide (D/I 77; 61). In spite of this, the nobleman himself is not directly involved in the management of his estate, which is entrusted to dependents and carried out according to patrimonial rather than commercial criteria. The land is not seen as a capital asset in which other resources may be invested.

What is expected of it is that it provide the noble household with the wherewithal to maintain an appropriate standard of living, both by keeping the family stores replenished with produce (part of which may be sold on a market operating mainly as an adjunct to the estate) and by providing the family with the governmental and semi-governmental powers that are typically associated with a title to land.

Like all of aristocratic society, the aristocratic family exhibits a strongly hierarchical pattern. The noble is unmistakably the master of his family; his relationship to his wife and children is formal and aloof, and emphasizes his superiority (D/II 259; 758). There is also a marked ranking among the children, with the firstborn son in a clearly favored position, since he will one day assume the title to the family estate and the headship of the family (D/II 262; 760). Accordingly, he is expected to associate more closely, though not necessarily more warmly and spontaneously, with his father, and to receive an education that will prepare him for his future position of leadership.

Since the advancement of a noble family's fortunes cannot normally be expected to come from the management of its estate, given the criteria for that management, it is sought, if at all, by seeking to add to that estate. This may be done through war or through rewards for special services to the ruler; but more commonly, estates increase through inheritances and dowries. As a result, the marriages of the nobility tend to be arranged by parents rather than entered freely. Hence the husband-wife relationship is often cold and emotionally detached, and "society" may come to look permissively on a nobleman's extramarital liaisons—but not his wife's, since these are a direct threat to the integrity of the lineage (D/II 278-82; 770-75).

As can be seen, a principle of ascription operates in close association with the principle of hierarchy in structuring aristocratic family relations. Both principles extend well beyond the sphere of family life, and characterize the aristocratic social structure as a whole. As a result of both, the aristocratic civil society is a harmoniously and visibly structured social space; and each individual in that society holds a comprehensive, diffuse status whose various dimensions will vary closely with one another. The position of a nobleman in the army, for instance, depends closely on his general rank. More generally, a man's title of nobility is a good "predictor" of the wealth he can be expected to possess, of his style of living, of the number and nature of the jurisdictional prerogatives he enjoys, and of the kind of men he will choose to associate with.

This structuring of social status gives the individual nobleman's self-image two distinctive qualities, which I will call security and aloofness. The first, being closely related to the ascriptive principle, probably characterizes not only the members of the privileged minority but also certain sections of the populace, particularly those who have a close relationship of dependence with the nobility (D/II 226; 731). However, only in the higher reaches of the society will security acquire the significance that Tocqueville emphasizes: that of giving the individual a firm feeling of identity, of leading him to take his own worth for granted, of making him feel assured about the rightness of his own behavior. Particularly in the most privileged individuals, the heads of the more ancient and exalted lineages, this strong feeling of intrinsic, inalienable worth can engender what I have called aloofness: that is, a tendency for the individual to emphasize his distance from all others, including his own peers, a disdain for mundane and acquisitive concerns, and a keen feeling of identification with one's own ancestors (D/II 308-9; 743). The spaciousness of the surroundings in which a privileged individual moves and his willingness to spend time on his own or in the sole company of domestics and animals are visible manifestations of this way of conceiving the self.

An "aloof" conception of the self often finds expression in a particular attitude that I would characterize as loftiness (D/II 61-62; 591-92). The nobleman devotes himself to pursuits conceived as fitting because they presuppose a superiority, a detachment from the petty concerns of everyday life and of common people (D/II 296; 784). These pursuits—the strenuous practice of hunting and other sports, the cultivation of learning, or the exercise of leadership in war and diplomacy—are engaged in not as a means of *acquiring* status but as a way of *expressing* it, as a projection of one's innate qualities. This understanding of the trials to which an aristocrat may subject himself is sustained by a conviction that had already been voiced by Pindar, the loftiest poetic voice of the Hellenic aristocracy: "True value attaches only to him who was born to glorious worth.

The one who merely grasps what he has himself attained, faltering shadow of a man, will never tread with a firm foot, and his immature spirit must go content with merely touching on a thousand lofty things" (*Nemean Odes*). Some of these noble pursuits, especially hunting and warfare, develop in the typical nobleman a detachment from creature comforts (D/II 171-72; *684*) and train him to a familiarity with solitude, danger, and the company of lowly, rude people. They can be interpreted historically as part of his heritage from early feudal ancestors, in whose life hunting and warfare played an indispensable part (D/II 319; *801*).

Loftiness, however, finds expression in a complementary characteristic of the nobility: its commitment to the cultivation of manners and taste (D/II 301; *787*), to the pursuit of aesthetic refinement and disinterested intellectual concerns (D/II 61-62; *543*). The elaboration and maintenance of standards of attainment are a continuous moral concern of the nobility, and they are expressed in many areas of social life—from the practice of useful crafts to scholarship and the arts (D/II 68, 79-80; *598, 605-6*), from sociable intercourse to the conduct of international relations. Noble existence as a whole, notes Tocqueville, is so styled as to suggest "a natural loftiness of feelings and thoughts, a delicacy and harmony of taste, an urbanity of mores." Although these formal, exterior aspects of noble existence are often contradicted by the actual conduct of individuals, they are nevertheless such as to inspire in the observer "a noble pleasure" (D/II 301; *787*).

In any case, a keen, exacting sense of *form*, an awareness that an appropriate mode of expression creates and enhances value, is characteristic of the noble pattern of existence (D/II 80; *606*). But this does not mean that noblemen prefer overall uniformity and sameness, since they keenly discriminate among a large variety of objects and substantive pursuits, each of which possesses its own style, standards, and form. Aesthetic taste, intellectual orientations, conceptions of self, value preferences, patterns of consumption—all these things are the objects of distinctive, exacting standards, which can impart to life a diversified outlook and appearance (D/II 313; *795*).

Each major collective unit in the aristocratic society, each estate, has its own material and mental artifacts, and its typical pursuits and

preoccupations (D/II 67; 597). As a consequence, standards maintain both a "differentiated uniformity" within the existence appropriate to each major station in life and a consistent, hierarchically
ordered diversity between stations (D/II 238; 740-41). This structural
principle, as we have seen, applies to the aristocratic legal system,
which emphasizes ascriptive rights over enacted legal rules. And
Tocqueville notes, in discussing "honor," that the majority of moral
norms are also specific to single positions within the social structure,
since they are formulated and enforced within distinctive groupings
rather than throughout the society (D/II 317-26; 798-807). Aristocratic society, then, appears not as a collection of equal individuals
but as an ordered array of externally heterogeneous and internally
homogeneous groups (D/II 220; 725); within each group collective
action is regularly and easily engaged in (D/II 136; 653), and individual members possess a firm feeling of identity.

Everybody knows exactly where he stands on the social ladder; he does not
seek to climb further and is not afraid of sliding down. In a society thus
organized, men of different castes communicate little with one another; but
should chance throw them together they are willing to deal with one another, without either hope or fear of becoming confounded with one another. Their relationships are not based on equality, but they are not constrained (D/II 226; 731).

Behind these controlling principles of social existence in an aristocracy, it is easy to detect another factor that probably has the
greatest overall significance: traditionalism. There is a reverent attitude toward the past, a feeling that history justifiably sets boundaries
to action in the here and now, a sense that timeworn practices and
attitudes have an intrinsic wisdom and sacredness (D/II 101; 621).
These are perhaps the ultimate moral and intellectual foundations of
the aristocratic society as a whole. They are reflected again and again:
in the priority of rights over legal rules; in the inalienability and in-
divisibility of landed estates; in concern for the continuity of a lineage, which finds expression in genealogy and heraldry (D/II 136;
652); in the ascriptive mechanisms of role allocation (D/II 326; 810);
in the emphasis on custom in socialization; in the social guidance
exercised by the aged; in the view that craftsmen and artists prove
themselves by pursuing an ideal of attainment set by the old masters;

in the low prestige of economic activities, such as industry, that systematically reward innovation; and finally, in a stratification system that attempts to maintain itself unaltered. "The memory of what has been, rather than a preoccupation with the existent" (D/II 259-60; 758), is the guiding force for all activity. An aristocratic society views itself as the continuation of tradition into the present (D/I 332; 260). In this firm commitment lies its chief strength; and the weakening of this commitment, as we shall see, fatally weakens the society.

A Final Note

In this reconstruction of Tocqueville's model of the aristocratic society, I have opposed the widespread tendency to view such a society as a continuously stratified pyramid. Aristocratic society is above all dualistic, with a basic discontinuity between the privileged minority and the general populace. One may wonder, however, what provides the overall "vertical integration" in such a society. What, if anything, holds it all together and keeps the discontinuity from becoming an irreparable fission?

Let me note in the first place that empirically speaking the problem is not as urgent as it may seem. An aristocratic society required only a low level of overall vertical integration. In the normal run of things, the populace lived in self-enclosed communities where custom and the writ of the noble lord covered all aspects of existence. The problems of sheer physical survival preoccupied most individuals and families, narrowly circumscribing the scope (and the "vertical reach") of their awareness and activity. Within this pattern of dependence and subordination the components ultimately reaching up to the national level were few and weak, and were normally closely intermingled with those originating at the local level.

And yet this is not the whole story. The aristocratic society as Tocqueville conceives it is, after all, a unified, large-scale sociopolitical system, not an agglomeration of adjacent, structurally similar but totally self-enclosed communities. Concretely, each Ständestaat of pre-Revolutionary Europe was in fact a *state*, a sovereign, comprehensive system of rule that somehow *did* span the whole distance between the king and the lowliest villein. One might suggest that although the villein, like a cat, *could* look at a king, he did not normally bother to do so. But the king's sight did occasionally fall on the villein's bent back. What, then, allowed such top-to-bottom relations to come about, however infrequently?

Tocqueville's answer is straightforward. "Since some men had a hold on other men, [the king] could limit himself to leading the former. The others would follow" (D/II 259; 758). This is perhaps not the whole answer, for one should recognize the significance of more strictly cultural methods of vertical integration, as well as the structures that implemented these methods (in the case of the Ständestaat, the Church was very important from this standpoint). It is nonetheless quite appropriate to reemphasize the role of the nobility, who were well suited to the task of leading others. Before we examine Tocqueville's democratic model, it may be useful to sum up the attributes of a noble estate that allowed it to perform this integrative function.

1. The specific nature of the nobility's relationship to the populace gives the lord powers and privileges, but also responsibilities (such as adjudication and the keeping of order) that have a particular integrative significance (A 39-40; 60).

2. Each nobleman has strong interests in a specific territory because of his role as landlord; but at the same time he typically maintains corporate, associational, and kinship relations with other noblemen and also with the ruler (D/II 147; 664). He is thus a uniquely effective link between the local and national levels of government.

3. The nobility is a *conspicuous* social group. The consistency of its status attributes and its emphasis on form and style, in the eyes of the populace, are highly effective symbols of the majesty of aristocratic rule and the intrinsic validity of the cultural system (D/II 101; 621).

4. The nobility holds a monopoly of land, the strategic economic resource (D/II 207; 714). And its control of land, as I have emphasized, also generates noneconomic powers (A 36; 57).

5. The nobility is a leisure class (D/II 203-4; 711). As such, it is also a *classe disponible* (Turgot), a class that is free to exercise its superiority over all aspects of existence. Thus it can carry out at the local level the public initiatives that are taken at the center of the system, and can do so with a minimum of supervision by the ruler.

2. *The Democratic Order*

I have suggested that the aristocratic society of Tocqueville's typology has a definite historical-geographical location. By contrast, no comparable boundaries can be assigned to his democratic model. The first, in Tocqueville's judgment, is clearly a thing of the past; the second is an incipient and evolving reality (D/II 440-41; 903). Democracy is obviously destined to supplant aristocracy everywhere, and it will probably triumph even where aristocracy has never established itself. Moreover, democracy is inherently an enduring system once it is established, and Tocqueville's typology leaves no room for a viable large-scale sociopolitical system other than aristocracy or democracy. The future of democracy cannot be predicted, precisely because it is a continuously evolving phenomenon. Its past and its present merely indicate the diverse outcomes its development may have, not what kind of outcome will appear in a specific place.

The empirical base of Tocqueville's ideal democratic model is drawn from his close analysis of two systems he considers democratic: France after 1789, and the United States of America (D/I 15; 17). However, these are not just two instances of democracy as such; each also exemplifies one of two varieties of democratic development, which together set the boundaries of this development in the foreseeable future (D/I 85; 67). Because democracy is a continuing reality, and because Tocqueville's empirical base for his analysis of it is far narrower than that offered by the rich historical record of the Western European Ständestaat, the analysis itself is not only a simple empirical description of democracy and its variants but also a concerned and sometimes troubled speculation on the promises and threats of the future. Thus Tocqueville's discussion of democracy is to some extent a political blueprint or scenario, with a much larger "prescriptive" component than his discussion of aristocracy (D/II 400; *871*). He attempts to apprehend the future shapes of societies and states; he articulates his fears and hopes (D/I 16; *17*) rather than just conceptualizing what he has empirically established; and he leaves the reader in no doubt of his own preference between the alternatives of French "despotic" democracy and American "republican" democracy (D/I 308; *241*).

In the following discussion, while attempting to give full weight to the despotic/republican alternative, I shall ignore the "prescriptive" nature of many statements that Tocqueville makes about democracy as such and about that alternative. Instead, I shall reconstruct his type of democratic society as a straightforward parallel to his type of aristocratic society: that is, as the comprehensive, integrated conceptualization of a large-scale sociopolitical system.

Democratic Political Society

The basic characteristics of a democratic society are diametrically opposed to those of an aristocracy. In a democratic system membership in the society—i.e., citizenship—is bestowed equally on all men who have a certain factual and objectively verifiable relationship to the society itself (as a rule, those who are born in its territory).[1] Status differences between citizens may exist, and may acquire legal recognition; but the law does not attach them to specific ascriptive affiliations or corporate memberships. Finally, the status characteristics that exist do not as a rule embrace governmental powers; these are exercised not by individuals or groups operating on their own behalf, but by a unified political agency (however differentiated its organization) (D/II 413; *882*).

Several features of the political and legal systems will normally be associated with these major characteristics of a democracy. The legitimacy of the system rests on the collective sovereignty of its members (D/II 395; *868*), who are coextensive with the society. The ultimate justification for the existence of the system, in fact, is the will of the people (D/I 88ff; *68ff*)—a rather more secular justification

---

[1] The best sociological discussion of the development of citizenship is T. H. Marshall, "Citizenship and social class," in his *Class, citizenship, and social development* (Garden City, N.Y.: Doubleday, 1965). See also Bendix, *Nation-building and citizenship*, Part I.

than that typical of aristocratic systems, which generally emphasize the sanctity of tradition and possess a religious legitimizing myth.

In a democracy the law is first and foremost a body of rules, not an assemblage of ascriptive claims. The citizens may possess rights (and varying rights at that); but these rights presuppose the validity of the law under which they are held, that is, of enacted general commands. The enactment of law is the governmental activity *par excellence*, and the ultimate source of law is the will of the people. Since this will is a secular reality that continually finds new expressions in the here and now, lawmaking itself is potentially a continuous activity that reacts to changing needs and orientations.

Each democratic law is typically a formal, impersonal command, uniform throughout the territory of the state and addressed equally to all its citizens (D/II 394; 867). Normally, it gives rights or duties to certain individuals or groups only to the extent that these citizens fall within the abstract terms of the law itself. In the political sphere, the most significant rights generally establish each citizen's title to participate to a greater or lesser extent in the expression of the people's will, and thus, indirectly, to enact laws. Participation can be diversely regulated, and ranges from voting rights in national legislative referendums to the right of access to local public bodies.[2] Titles to more extensive participation in public affairs are generally vested in citizens who are elected to lawmaking bodies or appointed by such bodies to specific governmental posts; the powers thus acquired do not attach to individuals as such but to the offices themselves (D/II 343; 823).

The powers of democratic officials cannot be exercised arbitrarily, nor purely within the constraints of custom and good faith; they are attributed for specific public purposes, and the manner of their exercise is closely regulated. Officials themselves are not entitled to the personal loyalty of citizens, but only to a respectful compliance with commands to the extent that these are duly and competently issued. However, citizens do owe their society as a whole a diffuse loyalty and attachment. Tocqueville calls this attitude patriotism, and he

---

[2] On the historical development of rights of political participation, see Bendix, *Nation-building and citizenship*, Part I. On the significance of political participation in general, see Pizzorno, "Introduzione allo studio della partecipazione politica," pp. 235-87.

claims that it is absent in aristocratic societies (D/II 320; *802*). Often, patriotism is focused on the figure of a king, who is the state's highest official and the symbol of the country as a whole (D/II 435; *900*); but the ultimate ruler of any democracy is supposed to be the citizenry itself.

Another critical right, pertaining to both the political and civil spheres, is each citizen's claim to the protection of his legitimate interests by the state, and particularly by the courts. This right is shared equally by all citizens, but its enforcement recognizes the other, differing rights that citizens acquire in their private capacities. For example, the courts and the law enforcement agencies can prohibit one person from interfering with another's possessions, or with the other's peaceable pursuit of his own interests; and they can restore to citizens any rights that have been violated.

The right to participate in public affairs (mainly through voting in elections) and the right to acquire private rights are the essential aspects of democratic citizenship in Tocqueville's characterization. However, these rights can be variously implemented in different democratic systems, both by law and by informal arrangements or practices; and in some cases they may be restricted almost to the vanishing point. As we shall see, a democratic system must create and maintain a rather complex and fragile configuration at both the political and the social level if its two basic rights are to retain their significance.

The central powers in a democracy acquire an importance that they do not possess in an aristocracy (D/II 394; *867*). They assume tasks that in an aristocracy are performed by the intermediate powers. Moreover, the demand for public action is typically greater in a democracy (D/II 427; *893*). The central government not only becomes the sole center of rule, but also deals with many concerns that are not the object of public action in an aristocracy. As a result, "The unity, the ubiquity, the omnipotence of social power and the uniformity of its rules, are the salient traits" of the democratic political system (D/II 396; *869*). For this reason governmental offices are much sought after.

Since offices (with the frequent exception of the monarchy) are elective or appointive (D/II 141; *658*), not hereditary, they are competed for; and the chief means of competition are such tactics as winning over the public by demagogic promises, obliging those who have powers of appointment, and manipulating public opinion by doing favors for those who can influence it (D/II 124; *640-41*). As a consequence, offices often go to corrupt men, or to men not particularly suited for the peculiar responsibilities of leadership, mediocrities with whom a large section of the citizenship can somehow identify (D/II 310-14; *242-44*). Such officials will most likely pursue their own private advantage and will favor their supporters at the expense of the public (D/I 344-47; *271-73*). They may lose office if these actions are noticed; but the damage they have done will not be undone, nor is there any guarantee that they will be succeeded by more honest and competent officials. Furthermore, frequent changes of those in power tend to aggravate the tendency toward discontinuity of public action that commonly afflicts democracies, which is particularly detrimental in the field of foreign relations.

The democratic political process is what we today understand as "politics." It often involves an appeal to the broad masses of the citizenry, and it aims mainly at the formation of new rules and the implementation of new policies. It presupposes the possibility of replacing those who hold office, and thus generally takes the form of a contest between organized groups (parties) of actual or potential leaders and their supporters. The welfare of the population at large is the generally acknowledged standard by which past public action and the merits of the contending political groups are supposedly assessed. But this standard lends itself to different interpretations because of the varying interests that characterize different sections of the population (D/I 175; *145*); hence the definition of public welfare is often at issue, and the whole political process is intrinsically open-ended and controversial, continuously generating new issues and inviting the confrontation of alternative solutions to them.

The operating expenses of a democracy generally compel the government to exact from the population a continuously increasing share of the wealth produced by the nation's economy (D/II 418; *885*), often with the net result of transferring resources from the wealthier to the poorer sections of the population. The fact that public officeholders control extensive resources that they have no direct hand in producing is of course one reason why the manning of gov-

ernmental posts is the key issue in the political process, and why that
process generates greed and invidiousness.

The claim of a democratic state on the patriotic loyalty of each
citizen, the pervasiveness of government in all spheres of social life,
the unitary character of the state and its control of a large share of
the nation's resources—all these make it possible for a democracy to
command massive efforts from its people. Democratic politics, by
contrast, tend to produce discontinuous policies, which often unfairly
favor one set of interests over another, creating envy and discontent.
Only in situations of obvious danger for the country as a whole can
a democratic government command the undivided loyalty of its citizenry and carry out authoritative, consistent policies (D/I 347ff;
273ff).

Democratic Civil Society

As the basic characteristics of a democratic sociopolitical system imply, strong, unified groups have no part in its civil society, and the
individual acquires an unprecedented importance. Not only is he in
principle the sole holder of political rights; he also tends to be the
sole center of initiative in social affairs at large. His actions are supposed to be oriented primarily by a concern for his own private welfare (D/II 167; 680), and he is expected to rely primarily on his individual resources. The individual can be visualized as an isolated point
in an infinite and homogeneous social space; he is not part of a wider
collective entity held together by distinctive shared rights and interests and integrated with other such entities in a hierarchical order.
"The men who inhabit a democratic country, having no superiors,
inferiors, or habitual and necessary associates, fall willingly back
upon themselves and view themselves in isolation" (D/II 339; 871).

This does not mean, however, that in a democracy individuals normally have a strong sense of their own distinctiveness and uniqueness,
or that they are each characterized by very personal traits. Quite the
contrary, according to Tocqueville: as a rule the individuals making
up a democratic population display a remarkable (indeed, disquieting) sameness of motives, tastes, concerns, thoughts, and patterns of
action (D/II 101-2; 622). All too frequently, in accounting for this
sameness, Tocqueville chooses to invoke purely cultural factors, pri-

marily the upsurge of a somewhat mysterious "passion for equality." In fact, one may treat various aspects of the sociopolitical constitution of a democracy as independent variables that generate, or at any rate maintain, sameness.

For instance, although the law of the state addresses itself to each of its citizens instead of resting on the established rights of corporate units, it offers only abstract and general commands, without giving anyone particular rights or obligations that would allow him to sustain a feeling of uniqueness. Although most of the business of society is carried out on the initiative of individuals, each of them is expected to guide his actions by the desire for advancement and security, which all his fellow individuals are also expected to feel (D/II 176; 688). Most social undertakings require an intense commitment by several individuals; but this commitment is generally expressed by the individual's willingness to interact with others as an abstract entity, to make his own action calculable by leaving as little leeway as possible to the specifically individual aspects of his own personality (D/II 315; 796).

In spite of the sameness of motives, tastes, and concerns among members of a democratic society, it is not easy for these members to cooperate with one another. The shared motives are basically invidious, and thus in principle divisive; as a rule, they lead to only a strained, suspicious, and temporary cooperation. Because individuals acquire at birth (or legal maturity) all the universally shared rights of citizenship, they naturally focus their attention on the advantages that they do *not* share with all. But these advantages are only held on a factual basis: precisely because they can be acquired, they can also be lost (D/II 173; 685). Moreover, the significance of advantages to those who enjoy them is continuously eroded by comparisons with the advantages that other individuals have gained (D/II 181; 692). Since the advantages of an individual are not determined by his membership in a cohesive group that has its own distinctive rights and life style, it is quite possible that he will hold comparatively more advantageous positions on one dimension of status (e.g., income) than on others (such as prestige or political influence). Such discrepancies render the democratic individual painfully uncertain of his own standing—indeed, of his own worth and his very identity. Men are under constant pressure to measure their own advantages against those enjoyed by others; they strive to achieve a precarious consistency of status and fear to be overtaken by others.[3]

Envy caused by status insecurity is thus the dominant passion of a democratic society (D/II 174; *685-86*), and it forces all citizens into frantic acquisitive activities (D/II 69; *598*). Typically, these are carried out as commerce and industry (D/II 206ff; *713ff*); agriculture no longer dominates the economy, and in any case land is also managed according to commercial criteria (D/II 210; *716*). Landholdings tend to be smaller than those in aristocratic societies, since democratic legislation breaks up landed estates through its own inheritance rules (D/II 69; *598*). Cultivation is intensive, and both land and agricultural produce are marketed. All adult citizens are as a rule engaged in gainful work, either on their own or as employees; there is no leisure class (D/I 82; *65*. D/II 203; *711*).

The compounded effect of all this is that under democratic conditions the economic system produces more and more wealth. More objects are available to increasing masses of consumers, new technological devices appear, and basic commodities tend to become cheaper (D/II 68-71; *597-600*). These economic developments, together with the tendencies of public action already mentioned, affect the stratification system. The lower strata benefit most, constantly improving their relative position. Thus both extreme poverty and extreme wealth tend to disappear, and an intermediate condition comes to be enjoyed by the majority of the population (D/II 344-45; *824*). Moreover, the whole stratification system becomes fluid (D/II 12; *550*), not just because no *legal* boundaries between statuses exist, but also because it has become factually possible for individuals to move upward or downward within the system according to their own

---

[3] A basic formulation of the problem of status consistency is offered in Gerhard Lenski, "Status crystallization: A non-vertical dimension of social status," *American Sociological Review*, XLV (1954), No. 4, pp. 405-13. For a recent reassessment of the problem see Pizzorno, "Squilibri (o incongruenze) di stato e partecipazione politica," *Quaderni di Sociologia*, XV (1966), No. 2, pp. 372-86. To some extent, it may be claimed, the relations between Stände in an aristocratic society are invidious. But in principle, as I have emphasized, each estate "stands on its rights," views its own advantages as legitimate components of a fundamentally immutable status system that embodies a universally acknowledged hierarchy. To the extent that such ideal-typical conditions obtain, it cannot be said that the relations between Stände are invidious in the sense that those between democratic individuals are.

success or failure in acquisitive activities (D/II 173; 684). Under these conditions, even people who occupy the same broad stratum at a given time find it difficult to undertake sustained solidary action, since each expects to improve his own situation more by his own exertions (or through the benevolence of the government) than by cooperation with his status equals.

From time to time, observers and critics have suggested that a democratic population, being a mass of equal but atomized individuals, is perennially threatened by anarchy. Tocqueville disagrees: in his judgment, anarchy is possible but not likely, for a number of reasons. To begin with, the strength, pervasiveness, and effectiveness of the central government's action would tend to produce the opposite condition to anarchy: a totally centralized, omnipotent government superimposed on a totally docile society. Second, the universal desire for well-being and security prompts democratic individuals to guard against the possibility that the invidiousness of their typical relations may lead them to employ force and fraud against one another. The calculating, matter-of-fact view of life predominant in a democracy, and the prevalent commercial and entrepreneurial attitudes, convince them of the benefits of orderliness and predictable actions (D/II 175ff, 315; 687ff, 796). Finally, the individuals are disposed to accommodate one another (D/II 223; 729) and enter obligatory relations because they are very much like one another. They all feel individually weak, unable to exercise much pressure on one another (D/II 235; 738). And they have common bonds in their duties toward the state (D/II 231; 736), in the citizenship rights they all possess, and in the objective similarity of their living conditions. All these factors allow them to overcome the disruptive centrifugal potentialities of their atomized condition, and to create among themselves a network of peaceable relations.

Tocqueville does not develop a comprehensive, abstract portrait of typically democratic social relations; but such a portrait can be easily pieced together from his scattered examples, integrated with concepts from other sources. The result can be presented as a contrast with the social relations typical of an aristocratic society. These, as we have seen, are relations between unequals. They entail a multitude of reciprocal expectations and affect many interests of both parties. They are regulated by preestablished, traditional norms that rigidly determine behavior and minimize the use of bargaining and ad hoc accommodations. They are often established ascriptively, without a specific act of will, and they are long-term arrangements. Finally, the obligations that aristocratic practice assigns to each side of a relationship are often incommensurable, since they assume one party's intrinsic superiority and the other's intrinsic inferiority.

The relations typical of a democracy, by contrast, show features that sociologists have learned to label *Gesellschaft*-like.[4] They are, in principle, freely entered between equals, neither reflecting nor establishing a relationship of intrinsic superiority and inferiority (D/II 262-67; 744-48). If one party does not fulfill his obligations, the other can do no more than withhold his own action; he himself has no means of punishing the defaulter or forcing him to act. However, once these relations are duly entered, they are backed by the law, which is superior to both parties and operates according to general, impersonal rules. To form a social relationship the would-be parties do not have to carry out any narrowly specified, solemn formalities; but they must *consciously* wish to associate themselves with each other, and they must agree on the terms of their relationship (D/II 243; *145*).[5]

Given these characteristics, the terms of a democratic relationship normally reflect the objective strength of the parties' respective bargaining powers (D/II 244; *750-51*). Normally, the relationship will not involve a great many aspects of the parties' existence, and it will neither presuppose nor engender any general feelings of loyalty or mutual attachment (D/II 244; 745-46). The typical social relations of a democratic society result from the pursuit of only one specific interest, which can be objectively measured (most often in monetary terms); they develop all their effects the instant they are entered, or do so over a limited and presumably short period (D/II 251; *752*). The obvious example is a business transaction involving money. With its objectivity, the universality of its uses, its mobility, and its equalizing power, money in democratic society is a critical facility, through which men relate to one another, values are allocated, alternatives are assessed, and sanctions are enforced.

[4] See Ferdinand Toennies, *Community and association*, C. P. Loomis, ed. (London: Routledge, 1955).

[5] This is the sociological import of the controversial juridical concept of the "legal autonomy" of parties to a contract.

The men who live in a democratic age have a variety of passions, but most of these either lead to the love of wealth or are engendered by it. This is not caused by the pettiness of these men's souls, but by the fact that the actual significance of money is greater than in aristocratic societies. When the citizens are all independent of and indifferent to one another, one can only obtain the assistance of one's neighbor by paying for it. Hence wealth acquires an infinity of uses and its significance is enhanced (D/II 314; 795).

I have suggested that democratic relations do not imply or establish a condition of superiority and inferiority, except on a purely factual and temporary basis. However, the specific relation of employer and employee, especially in industry, seems to be a major exception to this rule.[6] The submission of the employee and his obviously permanent condition of inferiority are so apparent that Tocqueville is moved to speculate on whether one should view employers as a "new aristocracy." The worker, he feels, "is in a condition of continuous, narrow, and inescapable dependence on [his master], and seems born to obey as the other is born to command" (D/II 215; 719). However, this relationship between "poor and rich" is actually different from that obtaining in aristocracies. In a democratic society the rich do not make up a corporate group because they have "no sense of belonging together, no common targets, no common traditions, and no common hopes" (D/II 216; 720). Moreover, even the employment relationship has too many characteristics of Gesellschaft to be called aristocratic:

There is no true tie between the poor and the rich. They are not perpetually attached to one another, and from one moment to the next their respective interests may bring them together or force them apart. The worker is dependent on masters in general, but not on any specific one. These two men see one another in the plant and ignore one another elsewhere; they come together on one point, but on all others they are far apart. All the industrialist demands of the worker is his labor, and all the worker demands are his wages. The former does not engage himself to protect the latter, nor the latter to defend the former. They are not permanently connected by either habit or felt obligation. . . . Between worker and master there are frequent relations, but no true association (D/II 217; 721).

[6] Around 1900 Continental legal scholarship had great difficulty establishing a viable juridical conceptualization of the employment contract. See Ludovic Barassi, *Il contratto di lavoro nel diritto positivo italiano* (Milan: SEL, 1901).

Not only the role of industrial employee but all occupational roles in a democracy tend to leave on their occupants' personalities a fairly deep imprint (D/II 361; 838-39). However, when dealing with democratic social relations in general, Tocqueville stresses rather their fluidity and impermanence, the many contracts that they lead the individual to enter with a minimum of formality (D/II 68, 238; 598, 732-33). He sees aristocratic social relations, with their broad, well-marked, durable ties, as having been entirely replaced by a multitude of narrow, transitory relations (D/II 136, 294-95; 653, 783). As he says in a passage where he stresses the fact that every link between certain individuals to some extent marks them off from all others: "In aristocracies, men are separated from one another by high, immovable barriers; in democracies, they are divided by a multitude of small, nearly invisible threads, which are incessantly broken up and shifted about" (D/II 295; 783).

Family ties (and sometimes friendships) are significant exceptions to the general run of democratic social relations. Although family life under democratic conditions is not like that of aristocratic families, it does not fully conform to the Gesellschaft pattern either. Democratic marriage, to begin with, is normally entered freely; but the partners are typically moved by warm, spontaneous feelings of attraction, not by the calculation of advantage (D/II 281; 771). Such a marriage is a partnership between equals, each seeking comfort in the other's affection (D/II 260-64; 758-62). Democratic succession laws are seldom concerned with differences in birth-order or sex among the children of a marriage, who are encouraged to associate freely with one another and with their parents. A concern for the continuity of the family traditions and patrimony is rarely present (D/I 78; 62); and the single family no longer regards itself primarily as the present incarnation of a lineage (D/II 136-37; 652-53). Given the tempo of change in the larger society, the family plays only a minor role in training children for their adult status; as Tocqueville says, with some exaggeration, "Each new generation is a new people." On the whole, the democratic family operates as a refuge from the tensions of occupational life, political concerns, and status competition. It gives its members emotional security—a feeling of personal, irreplaceable value that Gesellschaft relations cannot produce.

It is the proper locus for the expression of affection and intimacy, for the cultivation of disinterested virtue and the maintenance of one's self-respect.

Like the family, other institutions of the aristocratic society show vastly different traits in a democracy. Intellectual pursuits, for instance, place much greater emphasis on the elaboration of general concepts and theories covering wide ranges of phenomena (D/II 23-28; 560-64). In literature and the arts strict stylistic canons that assign different modes and levels of expression to different themes have disappeared (D/II 82; 607-8).[7] Religion may still be cultivated, but in a new spirit that minimizes the intervention of the deity in daily affairs, restricts the importance of ritual, and obscures the distinctive theological characteristics of different sects. In general, the democratic mind is pragmatic, questioning, self-reliant, and open to change. It is steadfastly oriented toward the present and the future rather than the past; indeed, it tends to disregard the latter and is suspicious of tradition (D/II 12; 549-50). Finally, the democratic individual is far more aware of what all men have in common than was his counterpart in an aristocracy (D/II 25; 562).

The Democratic Dilemma

So far, my characterization of democracy has concerned only traits that Tocqueville treats (explicitly or implicitly) as common to two basic variants of democracy: despotic democracy, and republican democracy. These two variants, however, differ not only in peripheral characteristics but in fundamentals; what they have in common as democracies is not, to Tocqueville, any more significant than are the traits peculiar to each. In this sense, any construct dealing only with democracy in general is analytically truncated. Democracy as such is an open-ended reality, and any concrete democratic system must face one primary problem: whether the central government should be, in Tocqueville's terms, arbitrary or moderate; whether it should ignore or acknowledge restraints on its actions, oppose or allow the existence of nongovernmental centers of power.

It should be noted that this is exclusively a *democratic* dilemma. In

[7] Erich Auerbach, *Mimesis* (Princeton, N.J.: Princeton University Press, 1954), discusses the gradual abandonment of these canons.

aristocratic societies the central government is restrained by basic characteristics of the type. All established rights, including governmental prerogatives, rest on a body of law that the government must respect if it is to preserve its legitimacy; in addition, there are many intermediate powers fully able to resist any encroachment on their rights. In a democracy, however, all law is government-made, and there is no significant legal ground on which to challenge governmental actions carried out within that law. Moreover, in principle no public powers are vested in any bodies other than the government and its agencies.

One might suggest that democracy, while casting off aristocratic restraints on the power of central government, has evolved two restraints of its own: the principle of the equality of all citizens before the law, and the principle that the people are the ultimate source of all power. Tocqueville, however, argues that neither principle can effectively restrain the central government unless it is sustained by specific institutional arrangements. Otherwise, both principles can be worse than ineffectual: they can actually be used to justify an arbitrary, all-engulfing despotism (D/II 130; 647-48).

In Tocqueville's judgment, the basic principles of democracy *must* be interpreted and institutionalized as effective restraints on government. If not, they will inevitably allow that government to escape all restraint (D/II 393; 865). Tocqueville's view of the democratic dilemma is pessimistic to the extent that it does not attribute equal probabilities to the two outcomes. The despotic outcome in his view follows of itself, through the inertia of democracy's basic institutional tendencies, *unless* action is taken that favors the republican outcome. Boundaries on the action of democratic government must be purposefully engineered and kept in operation (D/11 403; 874); they do not spontaneously evolve (D/II 149; 665). Because Tocqueville considered despotism the most likely outcome, I will discuss this variant first, thus pointing out the tendencies that must be counteracted if the less likely alternative of republican democracy is to evolve.

Despotic Democracy

The primary characteristic of despotic democracy—that is, the lack of legitimate restraints on the action of the central government—is obviously concerned with political society. But despotic democracy also displays its peculiarities at the level of civil society, and we may begin here to characterize it. If unchecked by institutional engineering (or, as we shall see, by underlying cultural factors), many features of democratic civil society engender in the population a moral tendency that we may call the *privatization of individual concerns*. Let us see how this tendency develops, and how it operates to nullify the democratic principle that all power belongs to the people.

In a democratic society many factors conspire to throw the individual entirely upon his own resources. The democratic intellect, with its empirical, skeptical bent, discredits or ignores all traditional sources of authority (at least in secular matters); in their place appears the sole authority of the individual's own powers of observation and reasoning, which are assumed to reside equally in all men. As a consequence, says Tocqueville, "Everybody shuts himself tightly into himself, and from there claims the right to judge the world" (D/II 13; 550). In the same sense there operate many factors (the continuous pressure of change, the loss of educational functions by the family, the rapid social mobility) by which in a democratic society "the woof of time is unceasingly broken" (D/II 137; 653) and the sense of continuity with the past diminished both for the individual and for society at large. Also, democratic social relations may compel the individual to view himself as the only significant point of reference, since they emphasize his own capacity for performance rather than his membership in ascriptive groupings; in any case, they are diverse, confusing, and constantly shifting.

The democratic individual, who has learned to consider himself the measure of all things, is also encouraged to consider other individuals as actual or potential opponents in a competition for personal advantage (D/II 173; 685). This is the outcome of several other features of democratic civil society: the primarily industrial-commercial nature of the economy; the fact that many possessions are sought only as means of distinguishing their owners from other men; the uncertainty and inconsistency of status differentials; and the fact that most social relations are expected to arise from bargaining. I have suggested that normally this competitive outlook does not bring about a war of all against all; but it does engender acquisitive, invidious attitudes, especially when poverty is widespread and the competition for advantage accordingly sharper.

As we have seen, moral habits of self-denial, responsibility for others, and awareness of other people's interests are typically nurtured only within the narrow circle of one's family and friends. Unless these attitudes are strengthened by religion, so that they can apply to less "private" concerns, they cannot be relied on to counteract the tendency that Tocqueville calls individualism: "a feeling that disposes each citizen to isolate himself from the mass of his fellows and draw apart with his own family and friends; having thus created a smaller society for his own use, he willingly relinquishes the greater society to itself" (D/II 135; 652).

These words spell out the bearing of individualism (i.e., the privatization of concerns) on that democratic dilemma. By definition, a democratic society is one that extends membership in the larger society, and thus in the political system, to all individuals. However, it also encourages an apolitical outlook, a tendency to invest very little energy in public concerns. The connection between these two characteristics is less paradoxical than it may seem. In aristocratic society, as we have seen, the right to exercise governmental power is only one of many inseparable rights belonging to certain individuals or groups; as a result, one need not step out of one's private capacity into a public one in order to exercise this right. The typical citizen in a democracy, however, is trying to augment his basic rights of citizenship by acquiring a structure of rights that pertain to him in his private capacity (D/II 185; 645); the exercise of a public role, for him, is thus a diversion from his most persistent and burning concerns (D/II 188; 677). The fact is that the distinction between private and public affairs truly applies only in a democracy.[8] Only in a democracy, therefore, is it possible that the concerns of the large majority of the citizenry will become, as I have put it, wholly privatized.

The privatization of concerns, if it occurs massively and persistently, can easily nullify the principle that all governmental action depends on the citizens' will (D/II 399; 871). On the basis of a number of scattered remarks by Tocqueville, I have distinguished three ways in which this happens.

First, the actual participation of a "privatized" citizenry in public

---

[8] On the problem of private versus public concerns, see J. Habermas, *Strukturwandlungen der Öffentlichkeit* (Neuwied: Luchterhand, 1965).

affairs will be quantitatively and qualitatively weak (D/II 188; *647*). The electoral turnout will probably be low, public issues will be meaningless to the man in the street, and the information on which voters base their decision will be scarce and unreliable (A 5; *27*). Under these conditions, it is more likely that unworthy men will be elected, and that small, committed factions will control the outcome of elections. The electoral process as a whole, together with all other channels for public participation, may soon be dominated by a minority bent on increasing its own power and advantage; and by the manipulation of elections and other processes, such a group will be able to legitimize its own irresponsible and arbitrary governmental actions (D/II 463-64; *901*). These outcomes are all the more likely when most of the populace is poorly educated.[9]

Second, privatized citizens will tend to take one of two attitudes toward governmental action, both ultimately favorable to despotism. In countries or within social strata characterized by relative affluence and flourishing business conditions, individuals may feel that the government should direct all its efforts toward maintaining "law and order," so that the economy can operate smoothly and private citizens can enjoy the profits of their acquisitive pursuits (D/II 180, 400; *698, 871-72*). Another attitude is more common in countries or within social strata characterized by relative economic insecurity and deprivation. Citizens in this condition, instead of expecting the government to maintain "business as usual" (which would favor the more fortunate socioeconomic groups), will feel that it should intervene positively on behalf of underprivileged groups, favoring them through its taxation and spending, and shifting resources toward them (D/II 340; *820*). These two attitudes, however incompatible otherwise, both express what may be called a consumer's view of politics, a view that emphasizes the private use of public action (D/II 363-64; *839-40*) and discourages any involvement in public affairs by citizens beyond the point strictly necessary for securing private advantages however defined. And either attitude will favor an effec-

---

[9] As is the case with practically all the propositions I have formulated, the analytical relationship here is a circular one: lack of political awareness on the part of the citizenry leads to massive apathy; apathy may render the electoral process less and less effective; and the resulting frustration of the electorate may produce further ignorance and apathy.

tive monopoly of public affairs by some small group of "strong men" or demagogues (D/II 189; 698).

The third dire effect of privatization, and the one most emphasized by Tocqueville, is that it hinders the formation within the civil society of associational groupings powerful enough to oppose the central government's innate tendency to expand its own power. Democracy proclaims the equality of all individuals and at the same time throws each of them upon his own resources. But the individual is almost helpless before the state, the only legitimate collective unit operating in a democracy. He is weakened by his isolation, by his status anxiety, by his doubt of his own worth in a society where money is the sole yardstick of value, by the pettiness of his aspirations, by his incomplete knowledge of the increasingly complex society he lives in, and finally by his very awareness that the social body is overwhelmingly more powerful than he is (D/II 345; 868). The individual citizen can accomplish something, particularly in the public sphere, only to the extent that he joins with others and acts collectively. But a thoroughgoing privatization of concerns makes such a development very unlikely. The following vision of democratic despotism, toward the close of *Democracy*, is particularly depressing.

As I try to imagine the novel conditions under which despotism may develop in the modern world, I envision a vast multitude of similar and equal men, all unceasingly engaged in activities intended to procure petty and vulgar enjoyments with which to glut their existence. Each of them stands apart, as if the destiny of all others were of no concern to him, and as if his family and his closest friends formed for him the totality of the human species. As for his fellow citizens, he is close to them but cannot see them; he touches them without feeling them; he exists only in himself and for himself; he may still have a family, but he no longer has a country (D/II 432-23; 898).

This extreme disintegration of social ties is *not*, in Tocqueville's view, a direct and necessary result of democracy. True, democracy destroys the broad, durable ties of aristocratic society and replaces them with limited and transitory relationships; but in principle it also allows the formation of more permanent groupings that encompass large numbers of like-minded individuals. These groupings may generate so much sustained, well-integrated activity, and attract so many intense individual commitments, that they become de facto agencies for the conduct of public affairs and thus limit the expansion of governmental activity (D/II 140ff; *657ff*). As I have suggested, however, this can happen only if the inertia of the despotic tendencies inherent in democracy is overcome through purposeful action. A thoroughgoing privatization of individual concerns hinders such action and thus creates in the civil society a vacuum of initiative, awareness, responsibility into which rushes the overwhelming pressure of centralized government. The result is foreshadowed in a passage immediately following the one just quoted:

Above this multitude [of citizens] there stands an immense and tutelary power, which takes entirely upon itself the task of ensuring their enjoyments and watching over their fate. It is absolute, intricate, uniform, farseeing, and mild. If its goal were to prepare men for their coming of age, one might liken it to a father's power. But on the contrary, it seeks to keep men forever in their infancy. It is all for the citizens having their enjoyments, provided they think of nothing else. It willingly operates for their happiness, but wants to be the only agent and arbiter of it. It affords them security, looks ahead to cater to their needs, makes their pleasures easier, manages all important business for them, directs their industries, regulates the distribution of their possessions after their death, and divides up their inheritances (D/II 433; *898*).

This passage makes clear the "circular" nature of the relationships between some of the variables I have discussed. The privatization of concerns may remove certain restraints from government; and government is then able to take actions that strengthen privatization, smothering the social forces and cultural currents that might challenge the priority of private concerns in the citizens' minds (D/II 140; *657*). For example, the government may prevent the diffusion of impartial information about public affairs (D/II 408; *878*); it may make religious bodies subservient to itself (D/II 416; *884*) or otherwise prevent them from proclaiming the individual's moral responsibilities toward his fellow citizens; or it may publicly emphasize the status advantages held by some individuals, thus increasing the envy and insecurity of its citizens. Once a government has acquired an effective monopoly of public affairs because there are no large collective groupings to challenge it, it may use this monopoly to make the emergence of any such groupings more and more unlikely. "A despot ... brands as subversive and unruly spirits those men who seek to join their efforts in the interest of the common welfare, and alters the natural meaning of words by calling those who keep strictly to themselves good citizens" (D/II 140; *657*).

A passage from *The old regime* makes clear this interaction between the tendencies inherent in democratic civil society and the government's effort to manipulate and strengthen those tendencies:

Since men are no longer attached to one another by ties of caste, class, corporation, and kinship, they naturally tend to concern themselves only with their particular interests, to think only about themselves and to withdraw into a narrow individualism that smothers any public virtue. Despotism, far from opposing this tendency, makes it irresistible: indeed it takes away from the citizens all shared commitments, all mutual needs, all necessity of attuning themselves to one another, all opportunity to act together; it immures them, so to speak, within their private existence. They naturally tend to stand apart from one another, and despotism seals them from one another; their feelings toward one another were already cold, and despotism freezes them (A 7; *27*).

According to Tocqueville, a democratic despotism acts under only one restraint: it must respect the universal ideal of equality among individuals. However, within the despotic context this restraint does not operate to produce freedom or justice (D/II 130-34; *648-51*). There are, in fact, two ways for a state to establish the equality of rights among its citizens: it may attribute rights to everybody, or to nobody (D/I 84; *66*). The second method is that adopted in a despotic democracy (D/I 11; *13*. A 165; *179*). In general, a despotic legal system is almost the opposite of an aristocratic one. In an aristocracy, the law is made up primarily of rights, legitimate claims establishing an individual's or a group's autonomy vis-à-vis the state; in despotism, the law consists exclusively of rules for the operation of the state's organs, and these rules vest no rights in the citizens (D/II 609; *874*).[10] This ideal-typical condition is not discussed by Tocqueville,

---

[10] One could work out a useful model of the despotic legal system from the arguments put forward by the Italian administrative lawyer Enrico Guicciardi, who distinguishes between norms of relationship, which vest claims in parties, and norms of action, which merely regulate the activities of public agencies. In these terms, a democratic-despotic legal system is made up exclusively of norms of action. See Guicciardi, *La giustizia amministrativa* (Padua: Cedam, 1953).

but it is implicit in two features that he sees as essential to the judiciary policy of despotic democratic governments: first, the independence of judges who are expected to settle controversies between citizens is restricted to the vanishing point; second, the courts are deprived of any jurisdiction over claims that a private citizen may bring against the state, and these claims are decided by the state itself.[11] In both cases, the state is accountable to no power but itself (D/II 420-21; *887-88*).

There is no need to detail here the characteristic features of a despotic political society. These are discussed in a relatively systematic way in the final chapters of *Democracy*, and can also be identified *a contrario* from Tocqueville's (and my) treatment of republican democracy. I shall just point out that although tendencies inherent in the democratic condition as such make its despotic form more likely than its republican form, despotic democracy in an extreme form appears to negate some features of democracy as such. A despotic democracy loses the openness to change that Tocqueville ascribes to democracies (D/II 358; *836*); it hinders the flourishing of commercial and industrial activity, the assiduous search for well-being, that the early forms of democracy possess (D/II 187; *696-97*). In a sense, despotism is not an implicit goal of the inertial tendencies of democracy, but a degeneration.

Republican Democracy

The primary characteristic of a republican democracy is that the government, without losing any of the basic features it possesses as a democracy, is so "regulated and legitimized" that it actually "follows the wishes of the people and does not limit itself to ruling in the names of the people" (D/I 347; *273*). As a result, the political process is "tranquil" (D/I 315; *746*). In a despotism, by contrast, it can easily become unruly and violent, both because government is arbitrary and because political dissent can only be expressed through subversion and revolution (A 169; *183*).

The peaceable nature of republican politics and the "regulated"

[11] The standard example of this kind of semijudicial institution is the French Conseil d'Etat, which has frequently been condemned by conservative scholars. In fact, as has often been noted, the Conseil and analogous bodies in other countries have built up an impressive record in the defense of private rights.

character of republican government are of course a subject to which Tocqueville devotes much attention. But many of the explanations he proposes can be subsumed under a very general one: the extent and the sophistication of institutional differentiation in the political system. This differentiation reveals itself, in the first place, in the fact that a republican democracy places certain interests and values outside the political process, more or less explicitly declaring them to be exclusively private (D/II 149; 665).[12] For instance, all religious bodies are free to assert their beliefs and practice their cults under common law, without any encouragement or interference by the state.[13] Thus none of the intense emotional and intellectual commitments that are involved in religious belonging and heightened by the confrontation between creeds are normally placed at stake in the political process. In the second place, among the matters that republican democracy allows within the political sphere, various institutional arrangements make some issues a more frequent matter of contention than others, so that the whole configuration of the political system is seldom challenged at any given time. For example, a contest over who is to man certain government posts typically implies agreement among the contestants on the powers attached to those posts.[14]

Tocqueville emphasizes one particular institutional device that serves to place some social affairs outside the political sphere and to focus the contest within that sphere on a few of the issues encompassed by it. He posits a distinction between a small core of relatively stable laws and an extensive periphery of laws that are continuously being framed, abolished, or modified to take into account even minor and transitory changes in the situations they affect and in the states of opinion they embody. Given the democratic conception of law as expressing a secular and thus empirically ascertainable and intrinsically changeable will, no law of the republic can be taken as absolutely unalterable; but the state itself may set stricter requirements

[12] The importance of thus limiting the scope of the political process has been stressed by Raymond Aron, *Démocratie et totalitarisme* (Paris: Gallimard, 1965), especially Chapter 7.

[13] For the historical development of this phenomenon see De Ruggiero, *Storia del liberalismo europeo*, Chapter 4.

[14] See the distinction between the levels of the political community, the regime, and the authorities proposed by David Easton in *A systems analysis of political life* (New York: Wiley, 1965).

for the formation and modification of *some* laws, making other laws a more likely object of contention in the normal course of the political process (D/I 168-69; 122-23).

This is, of course, one way of conceptualizing the distinction between "constitutional" and "normal" legislation—precisely the distinction that Tocqueville found in the American Republic. To his mind, however, it is not only important that some features of the political system should be more stable than others; it matters just as much that the more stable features should be the right ones, those apt to limit the extent and the arbitrariness of governmental powers. Much of his discussion of republican democracy can be seen as an exercise in constitutional design, distinguished from the many other such exercises carried out by nineteenth-century liberal thinkers because of its greater awareness of the sociocultural underpinnings of a constitution. Before we discuss these underpinnings, however, we must note some other constitutional features of republican democracy as envisaged by Tocqueville, many of which reflect the principle of institutional differentiation.

In a republican democracy, as in any other, all political power proceeds from the people's will; but that power is exercised by a variety of highly differentiated and relatively independent public agencies. Thus the very structure of the state's machinery is provided with obstacles to the immanent trend toward concentration of power, for each agency can be expected to resist encroachments on its special preserve. In discussing this "checks and balances" arrangement, Tocqueville pays but little attention to the counterposition of legislative and executive powers, and emphasizes instead the importance of local government (D/I 93-118; 72-97) and of a strong judicial system (D/I 145-91; 120-79. D/II 444; 406-7).

His discussion of local government rests on a somewhat simplified distinction between "governmental" and "administrative" activities. The former concern public matters like the maintenance of a national currency or military defense, which affect the interests of the country as a whole; the latter may include the building and upkeep of roads of mainly local significance, the relief of the poor, or any other projects that affect primarily the people living in a certain locality. In an aristocracy, even the conduct of governmental affairs is to some extent decentralized; and at the other extreme, a despotic democracy centralizes even administrative affairs. A republican democracy, however, centralizes governmental affairs and entrusts administrative affairs to locally constituted public bodies (D/I 127-42; *105-19*).

Local powers in a republic are not independent in the sense that aristocratic intermediate powers are, since they have no autonomy in properly governmental affairs and cannot legitimately have recourse to "self-aid" against the central government. But within their sphere of competence they are accorded a large measure of autonomy, so that they become effective bodies for expressing public initiative. In principle, they are not subjected to discretionary inspection by the central government, but are primarily accountable to the citizenry of the locality in which they operate. They may not make general laws, but may issue local ordinances; and they also perform local services for the central government with little supervision, e.g., in conscription, taxation, or the conduct of national elections. Local bodies are, for the citizenry, a relatively familiar and visible setting, in which there takes place a distinctive political process that is often more meaningful than the national political process to the average citizen (D/I 137; *119*. D/II 142; *659*). For the same reason they become training grounds for participation in the larger process, nurseries that develop future leaders for the national parties. The existence of local centers of power means that aspiring politicians do not have to focus their ambitions exclusively on national politics; thus there is more opportunity for political involvement among the whole population. American federalism, of course, provides the most sophisticated and advanced example of this particular strategy of differentiation (D/I 165ff; *136ff*).

For Tocqueville, himself a member of the French judiciary for some years, a strong judicial system works in many ways to maintain the limits on government power that are the essence of republican democracy (D/II 420-21; *887-88*). Rules that give tenure to judges, that suppress the influence of the executive on judicial appointments and advancement, that clearly and inflexibly allocate jurisdiction—all these minimize the probability that judicial powers will be employed by the political leadership as a tool to punish its adversaries and reward its friends. Moreover, a properly engineered machinery of justice, manned by citizens imbued with the appropriate values and possessing high prestige in the public mind, is able to insure that the law—that is, the abstract, general expression of the people's will—can maintain its supremacy overall other manifestations of democratic power. It can hold public agencies accountable for the observance of the laws that establish them and regulate their activities; it can sometimes quash ordinary legislation that conflicts with the constitution; and above all it can bar any encroachment by public agencies on the duly acquired rights of private citizens (D/I 145-52; *120-26*).

Further beneficial effects of a properly constituted judiciary can be specified. For instance, the ceremonial formalities surrounding the judicial function impart majesty to the law in the eyes of the citizens, and may counteract the lack of respect for formality that is typical of a democratic people (D/II 13; *551*). Similarly, the conservative orientation typical of legal personnel (D/I 603; *327*) lends the courts an air of continuity with the society's traditions, counteracting the democratic tendency toward ceaseless innovation. In fact, in a republican democracy not only the judges themselves but the lawyers and all other men associated with the judiciary's operations will acquire great importance (D/I 401-10; *328-33*). The lawyers, in particular, will be a large, prosperous, and prestigious professional group, involved also in activities having no immediate connection with the courts; and they will often be called on to staff political agencies of many kinds.

The key principle of institutional differentiation finds expression not only in the relatively composite and decentralized nature of the republican governmental apparatus, but also in the fact that this apparatus confronts a citizenry itself possessed of rights having a political significance (D/I 369-70; *293-94*. D/II 449; *910-11*). Tocqueville's treatment of these rights is relatively sketchy,[15] since it gives prominence to only three: the right to take part in elections (D/I 88ff; *68ff*), freedom of association (D/II 485-86; *891-92*), and freedom of expression (D/II 151ff; *667ff*). Even the right to insure the defense of these

---

[15] An Italian legal scholar, Gino Gorla, has nevertheless constructed an elaborate "system of rights" from Tocqueville; see his *Commento a Tocqueville* (Milan: Giuffre, 1947).

and other rights through the courts is not explicitly stressed, perhaps because it is implicit in the notion of a strong, independent judiciary. Also, Tocqueville's consistent emphasis on the contrast between aristocracy and democracy kept him from seeing that the rights of republican citizens as he portrayed them, particularly freedom of association and freedom of the press, are in a sense an extension and a generalization of the aristocratic notion of right as a franchise.[16]

Thus, by construing citizenship rights as intrinsically similar to the rights of the privileged minority in an aristocracy, Tocqueville adopted too narrow a conception of citizenship, one too tied to the liberal view of the relationship between state and citizen.[17] Such a conception cannot encompass the quantitative and qualitative development of citizenship rights (and thus of the very notion of citizenship) over the last century.[18] Citizens are increasingly vested not just with franchises to express their will without interference by the state, but also with *positive claims* to the performance of activities and the supply of services by the public powers. Tocqueville saw the beginnings of this development, but did not view it as a legitimate complement of the liberal notion of citizenship. In fact, he opposed it,[19] since in his view it could only make the citizens more and more abjectly dependant on the state, increasing the arbitrary power of the latter. He did not allow for the possibility that citizens might claim the benefits of increased public activity as a matter of right.

Whatever its limitations, Tocqueville's notion of citizenship rights plays a critical role in his conception of republican democracy, since it necessarily implies the existence of boundaries placed on the action of government. Although the following formulation is not explicit in his discussion, we may say that in Tocqueville's view the legal system of a republican democracy is a compromise between one in

[16] This point has frequently been made, both with reference to Tocqueville and in more general terms. See Richard Herr, *Tocqueville and the old regime* (Princeton, N.J.: Princeton University Press, 1962), pp. 128-29; Walter Ullmann, *The individual and society in the middle ages* (London: Methuen, 1967), especially pp. 68ff.

[17] On this general question, see Giovanni Sartori, *Democratic theory* (Detroit: Wayne State University Press, 1962), Chapters 12-16.

[18] See Marshall, "Citizenship and social class."

[19] This is conclusively demonstrated in Seymour Drescher, *Dilemmas of democracy: Tocqueville and modernization* (Pittsburgh: University of Pittsburgh Press, 1968).

which all law is made up of rights vested in individuals or groups and one in which law is exclusively a set of rules for the operation of public bodies. In a republic the system of rules itself both *establishes* equal, ascriptive rights and *recognizes* differential, acquired rights. The component rights and the component rules continuously interact with and condition one another. In principle, the rules have ultimate priority, for only under the rules can rights be held and exercised. But if the rules themselves are to be valid, citizens must exercise their rights. "Every citizen, vested with rights, takes part within his own sphere in the process [*marche*] of government" (D/I 473; 383), a process that is primarily the making of rules.

This sounds reassuring. However, the relationship between rules and rights is far from simple. I have just stated, for example, that the rules are made valid by the citizens' exercise of their rights. But what requires them to do so? One would have to assume a kind of super-rule that connects the exercise of rights with the production of valid rules. And such a rule cannot owe its own validity to the exercise of rights, since in a democracy rights obtain only within and under the law, flow from the law rather than making it up. How, then, is our super-rule to be justified?

Furthermore, it cannot even be taken for granted that the rights of citizens will in fact be exercised. As I have suggested, to exercise his public rights the citizen must "go out of his way," step outside the boundaries of his private concerns; but as we have seen, many factors make it unlikely that citizens will do this very often or in great numbers. Moreover, what can guarantee that the exercise of citizens' public rights will be orderly in its form and enlightened in its content? Is it not more likely to occur as a multitude of uncoordinated, poorly articulated, narrowly selfish demands? What can guarantee that a rule issuing from the exercise of public rights will actually command the respect of the citizens, particularly those who have not bothered to take part in its formation, or those who have been outvoted or have otherwise failed to embody their particular demands in the rule?

Equally disturbing questions can be raised concerning the probability that a differentiated political system, with its checks and balances, will actually limit governmental power. Each locus of power may effectively operate as a check and a constraint on other loci; but it might also cooperate with other powerholders, so that each can extend its prerogatives at the expense of a citizenry within which apathy and atomization can be presumed to be endemic. Perhaps the very multiplicity of political agencies and magnitude of power built into the vast political machinery of republican government will diffuse and enhance ambition, sow political passion, and inject the spirit of faction into the citizenry at large.

Little comfort can be drawn from remarking that some of these possibilities (most of which are not explicitly articulated in *Democracy*) contradict one another. After all, as Tocqueville knew, republican democracy is besieged by dangers as varied as anarchy at one extreme and the complete regimentation of society at the other. Without attempting to answer each query directly, I shall attempt to form a general answer by moving this discussion of republican democracy to the level of the civil society. Only a proper configuration of the civil society can stabilize and maintain the effectiveness of republican political features. This does not mean that the significant influences all run in the same direction, from the civil to the political society; the relationship is rather one of interpenetration and mutual conditioning. But the analytical relationships involved will not be specified in the following discussion, which merely sketches some traits of the civil society typically associated with Tocqueville's conception of republican democracy.

The dominance of economic concerns in the civil society is particularly apparent in a republican democracy; but various factors counter its tendency to diminish a responsible citizen's participation in public affairs. The very intensity and earnestness with which the society attends to acquisitive pursuits will produce considerable and diffuse prosperity. Economic disparities between individual citizens may be great, but the population at large shares a relatively high degree of economic security and a relatively comfortable standard of living (D/II 344; 824). It thus shares a feeling of partaking, however diversely, in a vastly successful cooperative endeavor, an increasing mastery of the whole people over its environment.

Such an economic situation sustains the stability and peaceability of the republican political process. Since there are no visible signs of an economic deprivation affecting large numbers, no demagogic leader can draw on a reservoir of bitterness and dissaffection in order to disrupt the constitutional political process. Most of the people own property, or possess skills that are at a premium wherever new commercial and industrial undertakings maintain a high demand for labor. Thus they feel that they have a stake in the system, and are accordingly less responsive to subversive political appeals and more willing to take a hand in the running of public affairs (D/II 345; 825). The economic achievements of the more fortunate are widely considered a just reward for their efforts and constitute no title to privileges in the proper sense of the term; thus they do not excite the envy of the less successful and are often regarded with admiration. The very fact that the economic system generates a visible and widely beneficial "success story" encourages individuals to satisfy their wants through their own exertions, at the level of the civil society, and not primarily by addressing demands toward the political system (D/I 323; 252) or attempting to direct public action to their own egoistic interests (D/II 342; 822). In particular, there is no widespread demand for political offices, which are in any case numerous and varied enough to accommodate whatever political ambitions may exist.

The manner in which the people go about their acquisitive pursuits, as well as the aggregate outcome of widespread prosperity, lends indirect support to republican political institutions. This manner is characterized by Tocqueville as *interêt bien-entendu*—in the standard English translation, "enlightened self-interest" (D/II 163-67; 677-80). Enlightenment, maintained by public education and the free circulation of ideas (D/II 151-52; 667-68), and exercised primarily in acquisitive pursuits, sets boundaries to ambition and curbs the tendency toward a "no holds barred" search for personal advantage. Individuals are attuned to each other's wants; at least for the near future, they can perceive the benefits of cooperation. Holding these views, they are less likely to bombard the political agencies with personalized demands, whose fulfillment might dangerously increase those agencies' hold on the civil society.

Only where enlightenment is diffuse can the average citizen "look after his private interests as if he were alone in the world, and the next moment commit himself to some public cause as if he had wholly forgotten those interests" (D/II 190; *698*). Only enlightenment allows him to transcend his private concerns and exercise the prerogatives and responsibilities of citizenship, to make appropriate, discriminating choices as a participant in the political process (D/I 460-66; *372-77*). That process can, so to speak, stay republican only because it is sustained by a condition of the civil society. But of course the relationship runs both ways, since public policies on education largely determine the degree and nature of the population's enlightenment.

Another critical resource of republican civil society, itself resting to a large extent on enlightenment, is what Tocqueville calls "the science of association" (D/II 150; *666*). Many citizens possess the moral qualities and technical skills required to organize voluntary groupings, which pursue in an orderly fashion the various interests shared by particular sections of the citizenry. This process opposes the atomizing tendencies of democracy and the central government's tendency to overexpand its powers (D/II 145ff; *662ff*). Each major association is an accumulation of social power: "A political, industrial, or commercial association, even a scientific or literary association, is like an enlightened and powerful citizen whose will cannot be bent or repressed by stealth and who, while defending his own specific rights against the demands of power, preserves the common freedom" (D/II 433; *905*). Like local public agencies, voluntary groupings offer the citizens a training ground in which to practice participation and acquire the skills of leadership. They circulate information concerning the general political process and facilitate the discussion of it. And they also allow their members to cultivate intimate, relaxed relations, to experience feelings that are otherwise typical only of families or very narrow circles of friends.[20]

Voluntary associations can accomplish all this, it should be noted, while still embodying the basic features of democratic social relations. They are typically oriented toward a single purpose or a set of closely related purposes. They are voluntarily established, joined,

---

[20] This line of thought has been pursued and analyzed by the proponents of the pluralist theory of democracy. See Seymour Lipset, *Political man* (Garden City, N.Y.: Doubleday, 1960).

and dissolved. They also respect, at any rate formally, the ground rules of a democratic political system: elected officials, the sovereignty of properly enacted rules over executive action, the accountability of officials to the rank and file, and so on. However, organizations with such intrinsically democratic features are not themselves *naturally* engendered by the democratic civil society (D/II 147; 665). They must be established by the concerted, persistent efforts of many individuals; and these efforts can be sustained only by a relatively high level of education among the populace, by the public recognition of freedom of association and freedom of expression as citizens' rights, and by a basic attitude of trust between citizens.

This last requirement is presupposed, rather than made explicit, in most of Tocqueville's discussion; however, interpersonal trust is probably the moral orientation that most needs to be diffused among the people if republican society is to be maintained (D/I 439; 355). The institutional machinery of society, both political and civil, can help to maintain a generalized attitude of trust. For instance, since good fences make good neighbors, a strong and efficient court system that can exact swift, visible, and proportionate retribution for violations of trust is itself an indispensable support of trust. But this and other structural guarantees of trust must be supported by a cultural patrimony, something approaching, in Tocqueville's words, a *consensus universalis*. Ultimately, the interactions of the autonomous individuals making up the society must be controlled by a shared orientation to one coherent set of compatible values, by a feeling of belonging together in a common undertaking.

Democracy indicates (again, not as explicitly as I am doing here) two aspects of this cultural patrimony, one secular and one sacred. The first, more directly related to the level of the political society, is a particularly intense patriotism, a conscious commitment to the welfare of both the nation and the smaller collectivities making up the nation. Such a sense of common destiny embraces all members of the society and imposes moral restraints on their dealings with one another (D/I 364-68; 290-98). The second cultural requirement is more immediately relevant to the civil than to the political society: a firm, relatively unchanging set of values (D/II 351; 824-25) sustained by a set of elementary beliefs about the nature of the deity, including the belief that the divine will is the criterion of all good and must transcend individual wills (D/II 33-34, 191-96; 569-71, 700-705).

Tocqueville insists on the primary significance of the second orientation, and thus on the functional indispensability of religion as the institution directly involved in creating and diffusing common values in a democracy. Naturally, religion must adapt itself to the general characteristics of the democratic setting. Typically, there will be a plurality of religious bodies, none of them dominant or officially sanctioned (D/II 15, 196; 552, 705); and all of these will deemphasize their distinctive (and possibly divisive) beliefs and cultural practices (D/II 37-38; 572-73), emphasizing the simple, universally valid understandings of what is true and proper that they have in common (D/II 170; 683). Under these conditions the several religious confessions will help maintain republican democracy by cultivating in the minds of the faithful a commitment to the "anchor values" on which republicanism ultimately rests.

I must therefore qualify my previous suggestion that the tendencies of democracy as such to evolve toward despotism can be countered by institutional engineering. In fact, the disquieting questions I advanced above imply that the effectiveness of engineered guarantees cannot be taken for granted. As Tocqueville himself emphasized toward the end of his life, institutional arrangements must be grounded on shared values if a democracy is to avoid the abyss of despotism. But these value commitments cannot be purposefully engineered. True, they are not ultimate in an absolute sense, not biologically rooted in a people (D/II 227; 732. A 154; 169) or given to it by the gods. But in connection with the probability that a democratic system will remain republican, they must be treated as givens, as parameters of the setting. Purposeful public action can seek to uproot them or diminish their hold on the public mind (a faction bent on despotism, for example, might attack or attempt to manipulate the churches); but they cannot be replaced at will with alternative orientations.

Thus, as we compare the supports of freedom in a democracy with those typical of an aristocracy, we find a mixture of contrasts and analogies. The "structural" support typical of the aristocracy, the intermediate powers and estates, is paralleled in a republican democracy by institutions that are produced by purposeful social engineering: a differentiated machinery of government, the existence of legal rights, and a multiplicity of voluntary organizations (D/II 149; *665-66*). The "cultural" support, however, is quite similar in the two situations. The aristocratic "firmament of law" must be closely paralleled by a set of values and beliefs that ultimately support democratic institutional arrangements.

3. The Old Regime

The types (and subtypes) I have derived from *Democracy in America* in the previous two chapters are so constructed as to emphasize the internal consistency and the stability of the sociopolitical systems they describe. Thus they do not easily lend themselves to a description of development and change within the systems concerned. In *Democracy*, however, developmental problems are continuously present under the surface of the typological discussion. For instance, Tocqueville sometimes attaches the adjectives aristocratic and democratic not to a *society* (or other generic term), but to particular *ages* or *centuries*; and he clearly suggests that democratic ages follow aristocratic ages. At other times he abandons his triadic scheme (aristocracy and the two variants of democracy) and speculates on intermediate and transitional types. "I have been describing two extreme conditions; but nations never move in just one step from the first to the second; they attain the latter only by stages and through infinite graduation" (D/II 83-84; 609). Also, Tocqueville frequently suggests that the past of a democratic country has a great bearing on whether a despotic or republican orientation will prevail within that country; and that much depends on whether the country did or did not possess proper aristocratic institutions before it became a democracy.

The diachronic problems thus raised are purposefully attacked in Tocqueville's second masterwork, *The old regime and the revolution* (1856), which provides the starting point for this chapter. Accordingly, I will treat that book as an exploration into the dynamics of change of large-scale sociopolitical systems. But it should be noted that Tocqueville, in making the transition between *Democracy* and *The old regime*, lowered the level of generality of the analysis. *The old regime* is not a book that one could today subtitle "A theory of political development" or "Patterns of transition from aristocracy to democracy." It is essentially a case study, since it deals with only one major instance of transition: the development of French society between Louis XIV and the Revolution.[1]

Tocqueville might have had various reasons for abandoning the relatively high level of generality that he had adopted in *Democracy* (especially in its second part). Perhaps what moved him to restrict his focus was the renewed urgency of his moral concern with the history and destiny of his own country. In fact, he wrote *The old regime* during the reign of Napoleon III—that is, so far he was concerned, very much *patriai tempore iniquo*, at such an anguishing moment in his country's history that he was unable to look beyond his country's boundaries even in his scholarly work.[2] One could also suggest that in concentrating on France alone he was expressing his intellectual diffidence and his aesthetic distaste for hastily conceived "systems of general ideas," which he regarded as a dangerous predilection of democratic scholarship (D/II 118-22; 635-39). Even when writing *Democracy*, however, Tocqueville had constantly held his own country before his eyes; and this had not prevented him from advancing broad, generalized ideas. I feel, then, that the adoption of a case-study approach in *The old regime* was simply a methodological result of his shift from synchronic to diachronic problems. This shift necessarily forced him to restrict the generality of his argument, and to emphasize the historical uniqueness and specific location of the events he described.

In his second book, then, Tocqueville seeks to establish the nature of a particular historical event, the French Revolution; and he tries to account for the fact that it took place, when it did, in France and not in another European country. As he pursues these objectives, however, he often advances propositions whose intended or poten-

---

[1] In fact, *The old regime* was conceived as but one section of a wider work, which was to discuss the impact on Europe of the French Revolution; only fragments of the other sections were completed, some of which are now collected in *The European revolution and correspondence with Gobineau*, translated and edited by John Lukacs (Garden City, N.Y.: Doubleday, 1959). As in the previous chapters, however, my discussion will be mostly confined to the ideas developed in the single book I am concerned with.

[2] The genesis of the book is extensively discussed in Herr, *Tocqueville and the old regime*.

tial analytical significance goes beyond the case at hand. The factors
he brings into his explanations are often specific values of variables
whose other values can, and often do, produce other results. The very
fact that Tocqueville is continuously, though not always self-con-
sciously, concerned about the *future* of France and other countries
makes his discussion something more than an ex post facto reconstruction of unique events. Tocqueville's own awareness of this is
hinted at in the opening passages of *The old regime*, for he says that
the book is intended not as a *history of* but as a *study on* the French
Revolution (A 1; 23).

Thus one can still read *The old regime* with an eye to analytical
rather than historical content, can look beyond the peculiarities of
the case and consider the implicit or explicit substructure of assumptions, concepts, and theorems regarding the nature of change in large-
scale sociopolitical systems. I intend to pursue this possibility here,
but only halfway; for I feel that one must still sacrifice some degree
of generality in order to discuss social change of this nature.[3] Accordingly, I will not be concerned, as Tocqueville was, with explaining
the specific geographical and temporal location of the Revolution
(A 4; 26) and the sequence of events precipitating it;[4] but at the same
time I will regard his book as illustrating only *one* path that sociopolitical systems may follow in the transition from aristocracy to
democracy. On the one hand, I will discuss *The old regime* with the
typology I have derived from *Democracy* very much in mind; on the
other, I will not try to adopt the level of generality that seemed
proper in discussing the earlier book.

If one were to formulate the theme of this chapter in the simplest
way, "How did France move from aristocracy to democracy?" the
most likely answer, on the strength of Tocqueville's own argument,
would have to be that it did not. The *ancien régime* of the book's
title actually denotes a prolonged transitional stage, a specific type
of sociopolitical entity that developed from aristocratic conditions

---

[3] This methodological thesis has been often advanced by Reinhard Bendix; see
his "Concepts and generalizations in comparative sociological studies," *American
Sociological Review*, XXVIII, No. 3, pp. 530ff.

[4] For an appraisal of *The old regime* as a work of history in the light of subsequent historical scholarship, see: Herr, *Tocqueville and the old regime*, Chapter
10; Alfred Cobban, *Historians and the causes of the French revolution* (rev. ed.
London: Historical Association, 1958), pp. 14-17.

and bore the seeds of a certain kind of democratic development; but it was itself neither aristocratic nor democratic in the proper sense of those terms. The general significance of the specific historical experience that Tocqueville described is simply that there can be no *one-step* transition from aristocracy to democracy, for two reasons: first, and more obviously, because a change so momentous cannot take place overnight; second, because the nature of the transition can vary, and when it does the *outcome* of the transition will also vary.

The French manner of effecting the transition is characterized, in Tocqueville's account, by two concurrent developments: the progressive degeneration of the aristocratic social and political order, and the ascendancy and triumph of monarchical absolutism.[5] In reconstructing the argument of *The old regime*, I will treat these two developments successively; and for the sake of exposition I shall consider the first as occurring in the civil society and the second as occurring in the political society.

The Civil Society

The starting point for my discussion is a general statement that is found in neither *Democracy* nor *The old regime*, but is nonetheless indispensable to a meaningful analysis of the latter book: ultimately, the long-term persistence of an aristocratic sociopolitical order depends on a relatively static techno-economic system. A society can operate on aristocratic principles only as long as its strategic economic resources are basically inelastic, as is the case with land; moreover, the technical and managerial devices for exploiting these basic resources must be susceptible of no fundamental change (D/II 46; 580), and must yield a product at best marginally greater from one year to the next. Only under these conditions can the great bulk of the society's product be allocated in an orderly and predictable manner on the basis of the traditional, ascriptive claims that Tocqueville considers the basic components of the aristocratic legal system. Only under these conditions can social power be similarly allocated to various social groups.

During the century preceding the French Revolution these condi-

---

[5] On the second phenomenon, see Heinz Lubasz, ed., *The development of the modern state* (New York: Macmillan, 1964), especially the articles by Ritter, Chabod, Lousse, and Lefèbvre.

tions were progressively undermined, in France and in other European countries, by a process that can be labeled "commercialization," which affected both rural and urban economic activities.[6] Tocqueville devotes little sustained attention to the workings of the French economy during this period; but what he does say indicates that commercialization was a major component of the overall transitional process (A 179-81; 192-94), although he might have hesitated to give it priority among the components operating at the level of the civil society. He repeatedly notes that under the Old Regime France was undergoing a rapid and extensive process of economic development, which drastically affected the landed nobility (who by and large lost ground economically) and the bourgeoisie (who generally gained from the process). And he occasionally notes qualitatively new features of the economy that had a powerful degenerative effect on aristocratic society.

This economic change may best be traced by looking (rather more closely than Tocqueville himself does) at the greatly increasing significance of money during the process of commercialization. Money, as we have seen, is the medium *par excellence* of typical democratic social relations; and for this very reason it is a formidable destroyer of the aristocratic social fabric. By reducing all resources and services to one common denominator, money allows the calculation and evaluation of an infinite variety of new productive factors and goods. Thus it implicitly refutes the basic assumption of the aristocratic economic system: that only certain combinations of resources and certain patterns of possession or consumption are appropriate. At the same time, money provides a store of deployable economic values, a large and potentially increasing supply of free-floating, unascribed resources that can be manipulated at will and will normally yield a considerable surplus. The allocation of this new surplus is not provided for by the traditional ascriptive claims, and is thus an inevitable source of conflict and disruption in the society.

In France, as money came to control the destination of larger and larger portions of the economic facilities and rewards of the society,

---

[6] On the critical significance of commercialization in the countryside, see Barrington Moore, Jr., *Social origins of dictatorship and democracy* (Boston: Beacon, 1966).

it devalued the significance of the traditional bases and symbols of social prestige and imposed itself as the dominant standard of evaluation. The possession of money necessarily became the main immediate target of social competition by both individuals and groups. And the competition itself was of a new kind, since the abstract and quantitative nature of the new monetary standard challenged all the old criteria of intrinsic worth, inherited dignity, and traditional superiority. The possession of money gave previously subordinate groups and individuals de facto powers that were incompatible with their traditional rank (D/I 4; 7). At the same time, since the economic system had begun to operate on market principles, even the old kinds of resources were put to new uses—and these resources were inherently incapable of much expansion. The management of family estates on a traditional basis became less and less profitable, and the maintenance of old styles of life by the traditionally privileged groups grew more and more onerous (A 87-88; *105-6*). These and other aspects of commercialization were major forces in the disruption of the French aristocratic system.

Along with commercialization, there occurred cultural changes that profoundly altered the intellectual and moral horizons of the privileged groups. In the first place, the value patterns associated with the aristocratic social order were disrupted (particularly as far as the bourgeoisie was concerned) by the increasing importance of individualistic concerns. To all individuals in privileged groups, status advancement, rather than the exercise of their present duties and privileges, now appeared to be a legitimate, morally commanding goal of action (A 88; *106*). It now seemed appropriate that the individual, acting purely for himself (or at most for his immediate family rather than his lineage), should join in the widespread competition for advancement, and equally appropriate that economic or professional achievement should be the aim of that competition.

But there was a discrepancy between these changed perceptions of what was morally appropriate and the structures of society under the Old Regime. The traditional patterns, however weakened by commercialization and however morally discredited (at any rate in the eyes of the bourgeoisie), had not yet been abandoned. In particular, ascriptive criteria still governed the status system, in spite of the fact that this system, having lost its previous significance as the visible embodiment of a shared value hierarchy, now operated purely as a "cascade of contempt." A multitude of privileges of feudal origin, as well as restrictions and regulations of mercantilistic origin, still blocked the path to individual economic advantage (A 35; 55-56). This discrepancy between the emerging individualistic and achievement-oriented value system, and the still-extant traditional norms, further disrupted the pattern of group relations (A 185; 196). Witness Beaumarchais's Figaro: the bourgeois no longer simply bewailed the fate that had denied him noble birth; now he questioned birth itself as the criterion of one's dignity and the key to one's chances of advancement. With reason, the character was long banned from the stage by the French monarchy.

Even as moral values had changed, the intellectual horizons of the privileged groups had been transformed (A 148; 164). The scientific and philosophical advances of the seventeenth century had discredited the notion that the universe was a cosmic order in which God was always present and accessible to man (D/II 14; 551). The universe, no longer an ordered cosmos, became impersonal, unstructured, and infinite. God at first withdrew from it; later, in the eighteenth century, the death of God was first hinted at and then proclaimed, and man remained alone in the universe.[7] Tradition, the moral bedrock of aristocracy, was undermined by these advances; and the Church, as the chief institution upholding the notion of God and His ordering of the cosmos, came under attack.

A questioning, skeptical intellectualism became dominant; and although it led to impressive achievements in many disciplines and technologies, it eroded a great many traditional certainties, including those that had directly or indirectly upheld the general esteem for the aristocratic order (A 155, 145; 170, 161). But that order still existed, and its natural inclination was to suppress the acceptance of the new attitudes and minimize their impact on the status quo. As a result, the spokesmen of the new intellectual persuasions—the scholars and men of letters who argued for a rational reordering of society—were usually denied access to any position of public responsi-

[7] This progression is discussed in the first section of Lucien Goldmann, *Le dieu caché* (Paris: Gallimard, 1965).

bility. They became bitterly and uncompromisingly alienated, and, Tocqueville argues, contemplated much more shattering changes than they might at first have been content with (A 144-54; *160-69*).

The disruptive effects of the new intellectual climate are easily assessed. It was secular and anticlerical, largely because official religion had become a bulwark of the status quo (A 16, 157; *38, 177*). It was oriented primarily to the present (critically) and the future (expectantly); and by projecting a self-confident view of the future it implicitly denied validity and legitimacy to the current social order (A 183; *196*). It inspired in its own true believers a fervent sense of anticipation that could become, should the opportunity present itself, a violent attack on all that existed. Finally, it fostered an intense attachment to worldly goods and material well-being. A system of beliefs like this could only undermine a social order that was constructed on religious presuppositions, valued the past more than the present, invested little hope in the future, and reserved material advantages to a privileged minority.

All these changes in the economy, moral outlook, and intellectual horizons of the Old Regime, together with developments at the political level that will be discussed shortly, worked against the estate system of stratification, an essential component of aristocratic society. Since the equality of all men was increasingly proclaimed in the name of rationalism, and since men (at any rate those within the privileged minority) actually were becoming more and more similar (A 84-89; *103-7*), the traditional privileges marking them off from one another appeared increasingly arbitrary. The same result was unintentionally produced by such monarchical practices as the sale of offices (that is, of privileges previously allocated only on a hereditary basis) and the usurpation of powers previously vested in the nobility (A 51; *70-71*).

When the nobility is not simply privileged, but powerful, when it governs and administers, its peculiar rights may be at the same time more extensive and less easily perceived. In feudal times, one regarded the nobility more or less as one today regards government: one tolerated the burdens it imposed because of the guarantees it afforded. The nobles enjoyed privileges bothersome to the commoner and possessed onerous rights; but they ensured the public order, administered justice, saw to the execution of laws, succored the weak, and managed public affairs. To the extent that the nobility ceases to do these things, the burden of its privileges [on the people] appears greater, and its very existence becomes inexplicable (A 39-40; 60).

The ancient ascriptive rights that remained were those conferring economic advantage and those establishing a superior prestige and social worth (A 36; 57). In the changing society, the former appeared more and more exploitative to those who did not possess them and the latter more and more arbitrary and insulting. Tocqueville notes that economic privileges in particular were not only maintained by the nobility but were often increased even as the public powers of the aristocracy declined. He refers particularly to privileges deriving from ancient seigneurial rights on land now in the possession of commoners and to the exemptions from various taxes that were enjoyed by nobles (and sometimes by bourgeois) as officeholders (A 94-96; 111-13). Land rights were particularly irksome to the peasantry (A 39-40; 59-60), and formed serious obstacles to the operation of an effective land market and the profitable management of landholdings. And tax exemptions scarcely earned the approval of those who had to somehow make up for the tributes not forthcoming from wealthy but untaxable nobles. Ironically, these privileges, although they seriously affected the general reputation of the nobility, could not arrest the gradual economic decline that the nobility was suffering because of the commercialization of the economy (A 86-87; 104-5).

Thus the first component of the disintegration of the estate system of stratification was a deep fission between the more privileged noble strata and the less privileged bourgeois strata. The second major phenomenon was a progressive estrangement of *all* privileged strata from the unprivileged populace, and particularly from the peasantry (A 97-101; 114-18). The estrangement was, to begin with, physical. Nobles left their country holdings (even when remaining landlords and officials *in absentia*), moving to the court and the larger cities. The bourgeoisie, and sometimes even the more successful peasants, left the villages and flocked to the towns (A 98, 124-25; 115, 146). The countryside was thus deprived of its traditional leadership and its sources of enlightenment and moral guidance (A 127-43; 143-59). More and more, those in the cities and towns regarded the peasantry exclusively as an object for contempt and exploitation. The villages sank deeper into isolation, ignorance, and apathy, occasionally bursting out in protest.

Another phenomenon of the Old Regime was the progressive disintegration of the privileged groups themselves, which lost the ability to act as units (A 102; *119*). Status competition now took place not just between the major estates, but also between smaller and smaller subunits of those estates; eventually, every privileged individual came to regard all his peers as rivals (A 84; *103*). The defense of estate prerogatives, previously a matter of common interest, became for the individual a far less pressing concern than his anxious attempts to trace subtle and shifting lines of invidious distinction between himself and his associates.

In this competition, it should be noted, it was still possible to convert one's de facto advantages into publicly recognized privileges. The competitors, then, continuously sought to make their achieved gains a matter of ascribed, legal privilege. This made the advantages only marginally more secure, but it greatly increased their obviousness, and thus their divisive effect. In a given town, for instance, the richer bourgeois families might establish (possibly through a purchased royal concession) that they alone could hold certain municipal offices that had previously been open to all members of the bourgeoisie (A 56; *74*); at the same time, each member of this privileged group might compete intensively with his equals for one specific office, and try to outbid them in securing from the monarch an exclusive right for his own descendants to that same office.

Because of the universalization of status competition, and because it occurred between smaller and smaller units, more or less artificial lines of fission appeared throughout the society, and the whole social context was atomized. Tocqueville suggests the extent of the breakdown: "At the time of the Revolution one would have sought in vain, in most parts of France, ten men who as a matter of habit would act in concert on a regular basis and who would engage in their own defense on their own initiative" (A 211; *223*).

Thus the society of the Old Regime was one in which economic and cultural changes combined to impede the continued operation of the social relations typical of an aristocracy. At the same time, in spite of the increasing similarity of all privileged individuals, in spite of the generalization of new moral and intellectual views, the Old Regime was not a democratic society. It was still marked by visible and legally established differences, although these were more significant as symbols and tokens of competition than as frameworks for collective action by large numbers of men. Although acquisitive orientations had become widespread, the peaceable, systematic pursuit of productive activity was not encouraged and was often arbitrarily impeded. This was still a dualistic society that refused to acknowledge the equal worth of all its members; and it also reaffirmed, by its stress on style, form, and ceremonial precedence, the significance of the differences that persisted within the privileged groups. In the economy, the large holdings of the landed nobility, though often less productive than differently managed holdings, still accounted for a large share of the total product. The cultural consensus toward which a democracy tends did not exist; there was instead a deep rift between two hostile cultural orientations, the traditional and the modern (A 152; *167*).

Perhaps the most distinctive feature of this unstable social order was that privilege, now the goal of widespread ambition (A 98-99; *116-17*), had become less secure in its tenure and more uncertain in its significance (A 51, 108; *71, 125*). In particular, it had largely lost its political significance: it no longer insured that privileged groups and individuals would be able to carry out governmental functions, to stand up against the central government. The aristocratic system of privileges had built into the society many differentiated, highly localized centers of initiative and leadership, each rightfully entitled and factually able to summon, within its own sphere, a common effort in the pursuit of common tasks. Under the Old Regime, privilege no longer sustained this structure. Mindful of the feudal origins of the privilege system typical of the Ständestaat, Tocqueville formulates this point as follows: "Feudalism had remained the most important of all our civil institutions while ceasing to be a political institution" (A 41; *61*). This he considers the key reason for the instability of the Old Regime, and for the fact that it was intrinsically a transitional system. Such extensive dissociation between the civil and political societies, he felt, was ultimately fatal.

The Political Society

We may summarize Tocqueville's extensive discussion of political society under the Old Regime by distinguishing two critical phenomena. The first was a marked expansion of the powers of the central government under monarchical absolutism, always at the expense of the intermediate powers.[8] The process was one of centralization in the proper sense: that is, a progressive transfer of functions from the intermediate powers to the political and administrative machinery controlled directly by the ruler. At the same time, there was a tendency for a wider and wider range of social interests to become the object of governmental action (D/II 417; 884).[9]

The second phenomenon was that the power of the central government not only grew but also changed its very nature and methods of operation:

The monarch ... no longer has anything in common with a monarch of the middle ages. He possesses different prerogatives, occupies a different position, acts from different motives, and evokes different sentiments. The state administration, which expands everywhere amid the wreckage of the local powers ... the hierarchy of functionnaires who increasingly replace the government of the nobles—these new powers operate according to procedures and principles that the men of the middle ages either ignored or disapproved of (A 27; 49).

The chief manifestations of this phenomenon were a systematic disregard of and hostility toward tradition, an emphasis on the rational coordination of administrative effort from above, a preference for nonpublic procedures in forming and implementing decisions, and a contempt for requirements of form in the conduct of governmental and administrative action. In his discussion of the physiocrats, Tocqueville implies that these new patterns were a realization, at the level of the political society, of the rationalistic orientations whose effects on the civil society have already been mentioned (A 164-72; 179-88).

---

[8] Recent historiographical work maintains that a significant and partly successful movement to restore aristocratic political privilege took place in the second half of the eighteenth century.

[9] Tocqueville had made this distinction in the second part of *Democracy*; see D/II 420; 887.

Tocqueville discusses several concrete developments through which both the above phenomena found expression in the French example. First, the monarch's capital city became much more important (A 69-70, 79-84; *81-82, 98-103*). Paris asserted itself more clearly than ever before as both the headquarters of the absolutist state and the most important manufacturing, commercial, and intellectual center in the nation (A 82-83; *101*). Tocqueville stresses the political aspect of this development, whereby Paris became "the master of France" (A 84; *102*). From this city came detailed regulations and directives concerning the most trivial affairs involving the public interest (or alleged to do so) and concerning even the most distant villages (A 55; *75*). To it came reports from local officials of the central government, statistical accounts, and requests for a multitude of decisions.

Second, the machinery of the French government could increasingly be characterized as a bureaucracy. In particular, the functions of its various agencies were more and more clearly and narrowly defined; and the whole structure looked increasingly like a pyramid in which the activities of a great many offices were coordinated by the absolute submission of each office to those placed above it, and by the extensive use of written regulations and instructions from above.

Third, the bureaucracy as a whole operated increasingly as an autonomous legal system (A 43; *63*), according to substantive and procedural principles foreign to the traditional legal system.[10] The agencies of the central government were placed outside the jurisdiction of the judicial bodies typical of an aristocratic polity (in France, primarily the *parlements*); and the adjudication of claims resulting from the operation of these agencies was reserved to other state agencies operating in a semijudicial fashion and generally without any guarantee of publicity (A 61; *80-81*). The new "judicial" bodies, furthermore, effectively claimed what is called in German legal language *Kompetenz-Kompetenz*: that is, the prerogative of themselves declaring what affairs fell within their own prerogative.

Fourth, the central agencies, besides expanding their own preroga-

---

[10] The development of "public law" has not been adequately studied so far from any other perspective than that of legal scholarship; see, with reference to the Prussian case, Hans Rosenberg, *Bureaucracy, aristocracy, and autocracy, 1660-1815* (Cambridge, Mass.: Harvard University Press, 1958).

tives, often established their right to supervise and control the activities of the intermediate powers even within the latter's residual competences. The autonomy of municipal bodies, in particular, was severely restricted by the rapid development of what was later to be called *tutelle administrative* (A 50, 60; 70, 80).[11] That is, a locally based agent of the central government (under the Old Regime, the *intendant*) now had the right to overrule decisions taken by municipal bodies, checking on the administration of their finances and instructing them on the conduct of their own public business:

> The towns are unable to institute a toll, raise a tax, get a mortgage, sell their properties, go to court, farm out their goods, or dispose of their surplus revenue without first being authorized to do so by the King's council acting on the intendant's recommendations. Before any public works can be carried out, the council must grant its approval of the works' plans and estimates; the contracting out of the works is done under the supervision of the intendant or his subordinates, and normally they are to be carried out under the direction of the engineer or the *architect fiscal* (A 55; 74).

Finally, the central administrative machinery displayed a great dynamism, an eagerness to enter new fields, lay down new guidelines, establish and modify regulations—above all, to provide authoritative guidance on all manner of activities, subjecting them all to its own control (A 3; 25). Only the persistence of traditional restraints and the embryonic nature of the new state apparatus set limits to this dynamism (A 73-75; 92-94).

The causes of these changes in the nature of the central government's activities that can be derived from Tocqueville's discussion fall within two clusters: the extent to which the aristocratic system of government had broken down within its own traditional spheres of competence; and the emergence of new demands, of new tasks to be undertaken with political means, that by their very novelty transcended the competence of aristocratic government.

Tocqueville emphasizes primarily the first cluster of causes, and within this the central government's deliberate policy of eliminating or hindering its rivals. "The central power, having attained the destruction of all intermediate powers, and finding between itself and

[11] In the standard English version of *The old regime* (A: 70), the rendering of this expression as "paternal government" is somewhat misleading.

the individuals nothing but an immense and empty space, appears to each of these individuals as the sole operative center in the social machine, the sole and necessary agent of public life" (A 75; 94-95). Behind this policy, in addition to the government's inherent tendency to expand its own powers, lay the social composition of the personnel who staffed the absolutist administration.

Tocqueville suggests (though later research has considerably modified this view) that the officials of the central government under the Old Regime were mainly persons of lowly bourgeois or commoner origin, who had limited economic resources and relatively low social standing (A 43-45; 63-66). For such men, the ascendance of the governmental machinery they worked for was their only chance of overcoming a deeply resented condition of social inferiority. The typical agent of the central government had a personal investment in that government's attack on the autonomy of the traditional nobility and local corporate bodies; he was directly interested in asserting the supremacy of his own role and the roles of his colleagues. Moreover, because he held his post only at the discretion of his superiors, he was motivated to fulfill his duties aggressively not only by his hope of advancement but by his fear of demotion or dismissal. At all administrative levels, therefore, there were personal components to the dynamism displayed by the central government as a whole.

A further failing of the aristocratic order was the chronic financial need in which the government found itself, which in complex and often indirect ways contributed to paralyzing the intermediate powers (A 107-13; 124-30). Tocqueville argues, for instance, that financial difficulties led the French government to impose new taxes on the commoners and the bourgeoisie, insuring the nobility's complicity by exempting it from those taxes; and that this policy, in turn, embittered the bourgeoisie against the nobility, so that these two estates found it impossible to act together in defending their prerogatives from usurpation by the central government (A 95-96; 113). He also suggests that the same financial pressure led the government to adopt policies such as the sale of offices, the withdrawal of rightfully acquired privileges, and the repeated exaction of tributes originally established as extraordinary measures (A 51; 71). In the long run, these practices corrupted the very concept of privilege, made the privileges retained even more resented, and thus indirectly contributed to the paralysis of the estates, which could only function if their individual members respected each other and were able to cooperate.

The estate system was also paralyzed by factors (in my view not fully recognized by Tocqueville) that were independent of the government's actions and were rooted instead in trends within the civil society. Aristocrats whose view of the world had become thoroughly secular could not be as intensely committed to traditional values (even those concerning their governance of the population and their activity in public bodies) as their sincerely religious forebears may have been. And bourgeois entrepreneurs intent upon their acquisitive pursuits could not spare much energy for performing public functions that had largely lost significance for them. The privatization of individual concerns, which, as we have seen, is the bane of democratic societies, was already at work under the Old Regime; and it could only have a paralyzing effect on the traditional political institutions. Privatization engendered political apathy and absenteeism, and thus made the assumption of greater responsibilities by the central government unavoidable. As Turgot stated in a report to Louis XVI, which Tocqueville quotes:

The nation is a society composed of ill-joined corporate bodies and a people whose members have but few ties with one another; as a consequence nobody looks after anything other than his own personal interest. Nowhere can one detect a visible common interest.... In this perpetual contest of claims and undertakings your majesty is obliged to decide everything in person or through royal agents. One awaits your expressed order for contributing to the public weal, for respecting the rights of others, sometimes even for exercising one's own (A 114; *131*).

The second group of variables that modified the nature and extent of the central government's activities under the Old Regime were the variety of new tasks to which the government had to attend. Tocqueville refers to this in a chapter on the central government's policy of encroaching on the jurisdiction of the autonomous courts:

The times open up to the central government ever new fields of action where those courts will be unable to compete with it, since these fields concern matters for which no judicial precedents exist, matters foreign to the courts' routine. Society, which undergoes great progress, engenders at all moments new needs, each of which is a source of power for the central government, which alone can attend to them. While the sphere of action of the courts remains the same, that of the central administration continuously expands with the progress of civilization (A 67-68; 87).

Not only the ancient autonomous courts but other independent jurisdictions that the Old Regime had inherited from its aristocratic past were bypassed by the emergence of new needs.

What was novel about these new demands, what could not be handled effectively by aristocratic government, was not so much the nature of the demands as the way in which they were voiced. Functions such as poor relief, the maintenance of public order, and the building and upkeep of roads had been performed for centuries by intermediate powers. However, three aspects of these and other demands under the Old Regime account at least in part for the increasing role of the central government in meeting those demands: the expectation of uniformity in the satisfaction of a particular demand in the various parts of the country; the perceived magnitude of the need; and the perception that the traditional ways of meeting that need could be improved on. Tocqueville emphasizes the first aspect, and for this reason I shall treat it before making the other two more explicit than he does.

1. The governmental-administrative structure that the Old Regime had inherited from its aristocratic past was a very diverse one. Like all Ständestaaten, it involved a great number of crisscrossing jurisdictions (A 42; 62), each operating under its own traditional rules, jealous of its prerogatives, and strongly rooted in a specific locality. Thus the same public need could be met to widely different extents and in widely different ways, depending on the specific jurisdiction that saw to it. Under the Old Regime, this lack of compatibility between the public arrangements made for different sections of the population to meet identical needs began to appear harmful—as indeed it was, particularly from the standpoint of the growing business community. Contrasting public regulations that affected the conduct of the same business enterprise in two adjacent parts of the country, for instance, would reduce the mobility of economic resources and products, make it difficult to compare the profitability of different combinations of them, and arbitrarily favor some producers while dam-

aging others; transactions between businesses in different localities could only be uncertain.

If these and other negative effects of the lack of uniformity were to be eliminated, the responsibility for doing so obviously had to fall on a center of initiative that stood above the uncoordinated jurisdictions and could override their attachment to their own idiosyncratic arrangements—which meant, of course, that the regulatory powers of the central government had to be increased. "Throughout the eighteenth century one sees an increase in the number of decrees, royal pronouncements, and decisions of the [king's] council that apply the same rules in the same fashion throughout the realm. The idea of a legislation so general and uniform, the same everywhere and for everybody, arises not only in the minds of governors but also in those of the governed" (A 85; *103-4*).

2. The increasing magnitude of demands sometimes forced the central government into the picture, most obviously in the military sphere. The organizational and technological innovations of warfare under the Old Regime required the fielding of men and matériel on an unprecedented scale. Consequently, the operations of recruitment and training, and the procurement of military equipment, could no longer be handled by the old, aristocratic arrangements, which left these responsibilities to a hodgepodge collection of noble lords and corporate bodies. The conduct of military operations themselves now had to be coordinated to an extent impossible under the old system. Inevitably, the central government had to restrict the military prerogatives of the intermediate powers and play a greater part itself (A 46-47; 67).

3. Finally, even public needs that were not new or larger than before required increased intervention by the central government to the extent that new ways of meeting them were specifically demanded. A systematic search for improved ways of handling problems could not be expected of the intermediate powers, who often had a definite interest in carrying out their tasks in traditional ways. A guild, for instance, was not likely to abolish or restrict its members' profitable monopoly of certain economic activities; and a provincial court composed exclusively of noblemen was not likely to reduce the seigneurial rights to land that its own members had enjoyed for centuries just

because these rights had lately become particularly obnoxious to others. But if old needs were to be met on other than the old terms, the elimination of such long-standing arrangements was often necessary; and to the extent that it was, it required the central government's intervention (A 167; 181).

In general, a demand for novel patterns of public action as such must threaten jurisdictional powers that are inherently tradition-bound, and it can only be met by powers intrinsically disposed to innovation. Under the Old Regime, as depicted by Tocqueville, such demands for novelty were raised often and vocally. For example, to cope with the new opportunities and threats of commercialized agriculture, farmers increasingly asked the authorities to introduce new marketing arrangements, and to inform them of new agricultural techniques. Such a demand could only be satisfied if directed in the first place to the central authorities, since these, Tocqueville insists, were quite willing to adopt new procedures, issue new directives, and thereby acquire new powers (A 49-50; 69-70).

This eagerness of the central government to innovate (A 206; 218-19) was, in Tocqueville's judgment, a major reason for the radical character of the French Revolution (A 193-98; 206-11). The ultimate cause of the Revolution was the dissociation between the configuration of the civil society and that of the political society; but the institutional rearrangement that had to be made could have been less abrupt, drastic, and ruthless if the central government had not, by the extent of its governmental innovations, so clearly revealed the unworkability of the aristocratic system (A 185-98; 199-211). The central government's urge to reform wittingly or unwittingly robbed the old order (or what remained of it) of sacredness in the public eye:

Throughout his reign Louis XVI was continuously speaking of reforms to be carried out. There were few institutions whose elimination he did not see as impending, before the Revolution came to eliminate them in fact. . . . Some of the reforms that he himself carried out changed suddenly and without the necessary preparation customs that were ancient and respected; and he sometimes encroached on established rights (A 194; 207).

Thus was weakened, and finally destroyed, the hold of traditional institutions—indeed, of tradition per se—on the people (A 149-50;

165). There emerged a new conception of political action as a self-contained, self-justifying process capable of creating at will a workable new arrangement for society (A 163-73; *178-87*). The monarchy's arbitrary meddling with traditional social relations gave the strongest sanction to the feeling, already widely diffused in the civil society, that those relations had no intrinsic validity (A 193-98; *206-11*). The urge toward change from above exacerbated the instability inherent in a dissociated sociopolitical system.

I suggested in Chapter 1 that the aristocratic ruler finds in the intermediate powers both restraint and support. Thus the French monarchy's own efforts to elude and curb aristocratic restraints, as well as the internal corrosion of the intermediate powers, deprived it of reliable support (A 209; *221-22*). This was most dramatically shown when the Estates General, called in 1789 after a very long period when the monarch had preferred to rule without them, proved unable to function as Estates General and experienced an upsurge of radicalism. In the interest of centralization and innovation the central government had so disrupted the French aristocratic constitution that the whole society had become unable to answer the government's appeals in a coherent, responsible manner:

When, sixty years ago, the different classes into which France was then divided came into contact again after having been so long held apart by so many barriers, it was on their sorest points that they first made contact; and as soon as they reestablished contact they tore at one another (A 114; *131*).

[Almost all negative aspects of the Old Regime that have been discussed] owed their origin to the craftiness with which our kings had applied themselves to creating dissensions among men in order to rule over them more absolutely. But when the bourgeois was thus isolated from the nobleman and the peasant from the nobleman and the bourgeois, when the same process, carried on within each class, made of each a conglomeration of small, separate units nearly as isolated from one another as the classes were, it came to pass that the whole was simply a homogeneous mass whose parts were no longer tied together. No longer was there anything organized that could bother the government; thus there was no longer anything that could support it. So the whole edifice in which the rulers gloried came apart completely and instantly as soon as the society on which it was based began to stir (A 143; *158-59*).

Finally, according Tocqueville, the quantitative and qualitative changes in the central government's power that occurred throughout the Old Regime not only created a fatal imbalance in France and plunged it toward violent change, but also predetermined the *manner* and *direction* of that change (A 198; *210-11*). That is, they precluded a transition to republican democracy and set the Revolution on a course toward democratic despotism. The dynamism of the central powers engendered throughout the society an expectation that change could only be directed from above and from the center. The centralizing policies of the absolutist administration set the pattern for the autocratic actions of the French Republics and Empires:

> One marvels at the surprising ease with which the [Revolutionary] constituent assembly was able to destroy in one fell swoop the ancient French provinces, some of which were more ancient than the monarchy itself, and to divide the kingdom systematically into 83 distinct parts, just as if one were dealing with the wilderness of the New World. . . . It might have seemed that they were cutting up living bodies; but in fact they were merely dissecting cadavers (A 82; *101*).

> When a nation destroys the aristocracy within its own body, it sets out toward centralization. . . . The democratic revolution that was to destroy so many institutions of the Old Regime was bound to strengthen this one [centralization]; in the society built by the Revolution centralization found a place so easily that one could easily mistake it for a product of the Revolution (A 68-69; *88*).

The legacy of absolutism to later French history, in Tocqueville's judgment, was thus "a state stronger than society." The content of governmental action did change drastically between the Old Regime and the revolutionary and post-Revolutionary regimes. But those changes never really modified the relationship between the state and society that had evolved from the decay of the aristocratic constitution and the triumph of monarchical absolutism.

KARL MARX

SOURCES

As far as possible the research for this section has been conducted on original language editions of Marx's writings. The most important of these are referred to in abbreviated form, as indicated below.

F. *Frühe Schriften*, edited by H.-J. Lieber and P. Furth, Vol. 1 (Stuttgart: Cotta, 1962). After each page reference to this edition, the letter and italic numbers following the semicolon refer to the corresponding pages in one or the other of the following two translations (unless no translation is available).

B. *Early writings*, translated and edited by T. Bottomore (New York: McGraw-Hill, 1964).

E. *Writings of the young Marx on philosophy and society*, translated and edited by L. Easton and K. Guddat (Garden City, N.Y.: Doubleday, 1967).

W. Marx and Engels, *Werke*, Vol. XIII (Berlin: Dietz, 1962). The italic numbers here refer to the corresponding paging in *The German ideology* (Moscow: Progress Publishers, 1964).

S. Marx and Engels, *Selected Works*. 2 vols. (Moscow: Foreign Languages Press, 1962). Contains a useful selection of translations.

K. *Das Kapital*, edited by H.-J. Lieber and B. Kautsky, Vol. I (Stuttgart: Cotta, 1962). The italic numbers here refer to the corresponding paging in *Capital*, translated by E. and C. Paul (London: Everyman's, 1930).

G. *Grundrisse der Kritik der politischen Ökonomie (Rohentwurf), 1857-1858* (Berlin: Dietz, 1953). Where possible reference has been made (in italics) to the paging of the translation of a section of this book edited by Eric Hobsbawn, *Precapitalist economic formations* (London: Cohen & West, 1964).

All translations, unless otherwise indicated, are my own. In a few of them, I have omitted numerous italics of emphasis that were present in the original.

4. The Nature of Social Reality

It might be suggested, with only a little oversimplification, that all sociological theory addresses two basic problems: What is the nature of modern society? How is society possible? Both Tocqueville and Marx, to the extent that their works can be read as contributions to sociological theory, seem to deal primarily with the first question. But Marx, unlike Tocqueville, also offers a relatively comprehensive and consistent treatment of the second. Sociological students and critics of Marx have already devoted a great deal of attention to some elements of this treatment—particularly to the notions of class and ideology, to theories of conflict, and to the coercive components of the social order.[1] Other aspects of Marx's general thoughts on society, however, have been largely ignored by sociologists, who have left them to the attention of historians of social thought and philosophers.[2] It is to some of these aspects that I direct my attention in this chapter, deferring my reconstruction of Marx's thought on the nature of modern society to the next. As the title of this chapter indicates, I am here addressing myself to problems that go somewhat beyond sociology as such, involving highly speculative arguments. I have pursued these problems in spite of my own uneasiness, and in spite of an awareness that I could not do them justice, for two reasons.

First, some recent developments in sociology and anthropology in-

[1] On these questions, see: Reinhard Bendix and Seymour Lipset, "Karl Marx's theory of social class," in Bendix and Lipset, eds., Class, status, and power (Glencoe, Ill.: Free Press, 1953); Hans Barth, Wahrheit und Ideologie, 2d ed. (Zurich: Rentsch, 1961), Chapter 3; Ralf Dahrendorf, Gesellschaft und Freiheit (Munich: Piper, 1961), Chapter 9; Lewis Coser, Continuities in the study of conflict (New York: Free Press, 1967), Chapter 7.

[2] A good collection of articles (mainly in French and German) dealing with these ideas from a philosophical perspective makes up Volume III of the Annali dell'Istituto Giangiacomo Feltrinelli (Milan, 1965).

dicate an increasing concern with the philosophical, or speculative, underpinnings of these disciplines—assumptions about the nature of man, ideas of the relationship between nature and culture, and so on.[3] In discussing a "classic" author who has at times considered the same problems I feel I should not miss the opportunity to outline his views as a contribution to the current discussion. Second, and more important, I think that a great deal of what Marx has to say about "social reality" is implicitly shared by many scholars whose writings have contributed to the "sociological tradition."[4] This is not to say that other "classic" authors drew on Marx's work in forming their own assumptions about the nature of social reality; in fact, although most of them studied Marx, none seem to have known the early writings in which Marx most explicitly confronted the problems we are to discuss. Rather, Marx himself was articulating, in those writings, a view of man and his activities that did not originate with him, and the same view independently inspired the thought of other great sociological theorists (most notably Weber and Simmel).

There are, of course, significant differences between Marx's explicit views on the problems I will examine and the implicit views of other authors. Indeed, my assumption that similarities exist and are important would be difficult to establish in a critical sense. However, given this assumption, most of the differences appear to result from two overlapping factors: first, a great variation in ethical preoccupations and metaphysical assumptions;[5] and second, the varying degree of thoroughness and radicalness with which other authors drew their respective conclusions from compatible positions of departure. In both respects, Marx was certainly the odd man out when compared to all other originators of the sociological tradition.[6] The uniquely Marxian aspects of the argument I will pursue stem directly from Marx's revolutionary political commitment, materialistic metaphysics, and ruthlessness in pursuing the implications of his positions on the problems under discussion.

---

[3] This interest is reflected, for example, in Peter L. Berger, *Invitation to sociology: A humanistic perspective* (Garden City, N.Y.: Anchor, 1963).

[4] See Robert Nisbet, *The sociological tradition* (New York: Basic Books, 1967).

[5] This point is extensively (and to my mind satisfactorily) developed with reference to Max Weber in Karl Loewith, *Gesammelte Abhandlungen* (Stuttgart: Kohlhammer, 1960), Chapter 1.

[6] This much, at least, is clear from the arguments in Nisbet, *The sociological tradition*.

Leaving aside the ethical and metaphysical components of Marx's views (as I shall do, where possible, throughout this chapter), what position on the nature of social reality does he derive from various components of post-Renaissance Western thought and presumably share with other sociological greats? Put simply, he views social reality as *man-made reality*; it owes its origin and its configuration to the activity engaged in by concrete human individuals, is a product of that activity. The diversity of social reality, its variability in time and space, and its ability to coerce man as if from outside or above him (as Durkheim emphasizes), can ultimately be accounted for by the ways in which man goes about producing it. "The root is man" (F 497; B 52); one forgets the ultimate man-rootedness of social reality only at one's own peril.

But what does it mean to say that man *makes* social reality? And what must be true of man if he has this power? Oddly enough, a useful point of departure toward reconstructing Marx's answer to these questions can be found in the opening statement of the very first piece of his writing to come down to us: a composition that the seventeen-year-old Karl Marx wrote in 1835 as part of his passing-out examination (*Abitur*). The topic was "Reflections of a youth upon the choice of a calling":

Nature itself has determined for the animal the circle within which it is to move, and the animal unconcernedly covers this surface without striving to cross its boundaries, without even conceiving of a different circle. Also to man the Deity assigned a general goal, to ennoble mankind and Himself; but He left man himself to search for the means of attaining that goal. He left it to man to choose, within society, the position most appropriate to him, from which he might best advance society and himself. This choice is a great privilege that man enjoys over all other creatures, but at the same time an act through which he may ruin his whole life, thwart all of his plans, cause himself misery (F 1; E 35-36).

The views that Marx was to elaborate within a decade or so of his passing-out examination and remain faithful to throughout his work[7] are closely tied to this statement. But they differ on crucial points in conceptualizing the relationship between man and animal. Possibly

[7] The view that there is an essential continuity between the "young" and the "mature" Marx is quite controversial, and I shall not try to establish it here. For a persuasive argument, see Shlom Avineri, *The social and political thought of Karl Marx* (Cambridge, Eng.: Cambridge University Press, 1968).

the most critical modification is the elimination of the odd symmetry
between the couples Nature/animal and Deity/man, a symmetry that
entails an unresolved dualism of Nature/Deity and hence a dualism in all of reality. A unified reality would have to be ruled by a
single authority, either the Deity or Nature; and the post-adolescent
Marx resolutely opts for Nature, which rules both man and animal.[8]
Man is conceptualized, in the first place, as a part of Nature (K 208;
198), and more specifically as a part of living Nature. In this quality,
which he shares with animals and plants, man is both a passive and
an active being—a being endowed both with needs and with resources, which he can himself control, for meeting these needs (F 660;
B *207*). At the same time, like all the separate parts of Nature, his
existence is finite: as an individual living being he cannot escape the
organic cycle of birth, growth, and decay.

A second important modification of the 1835 ideas in Marx's later
thought was a widening of the realm of choice envisaged in his essay,
a widening closely associated with a thoroughgoing "socialization"
of the choosing subject. That is, choice now determines not only an
individual's occupational position within a fixed society, but also the
shaping of the society itself by some kind of collective subject; not
only a unit's positioning of itself within a given network of relations,
but also the gradual emergence and the determinate configuration of
the network. The concept of society is now "desubstantialized," since
society is viewed as intrinsically modifiable and not as a superindividual entity confronting the individual person. Paradoxically, this desubstantialized social reality at the same time acquires an even greater
power to constrain the activity of the collective subject.

One could synthesize a third modification of the 1835 statement by
suggesting that for Marx man is characterized vis-à-vis the animal not
by the absence of a "circle" that sets boundaries to his activity, or by
his ability to break through any given circle, but rather by the fact that
he cannot break through one circle without laying down another.
That is, man's ability to make choices does not mean that his activity
is intrinsically devoid of constraints, but that his activity itself is the
source of those constraints.

[8] On Marx's view of nature as the ultimate framework of reality see Alfred
Schmidt, *Der Begriff der Natur in der Lehre von Marx* (Freiburg im Breisgau:
Europäische, 1962).

Given these modifications of Marx's earliest views, where does the later Marx (both "young" and "mature") stand on the problem of man's distinction from the animal? Both man and animal are parts of living Nature and thus active as well as passive beings; and both unavoidably carry out their activity within limits. However, the limits, or circles, of the human species are incomparably more diverse and more variable in configuration than seems to be the case for any other species. This greater diversity and variability rests on man's ability to fashion the constraints within which he operates, thus imparting to them a variance in time and space that is wholly out of proportion to the relatively narrow variance of man's biological equipment. Apparently, though both man and animal can carry out activity, the modalities of man's activity are utterly unique (F 652; B 208).

The Marxian position as reconstructed so far is clearly in keeping with the concerns and orientations of the German idealistic tradition. Thus I do not feel it inappropriate to state man's uniqueness in the terms used by Schiller, an eminent representative of that tradition, in a statement strikingly similar to the previous Marx quote:

As far as plants and animals are concerned, nature does not limit itself to indicating a line of conduct but itself carries out such conduct. In man's case, on the contrary, nature indicates a line of conduct, but carrying it out is up to man. Only man has the privilege of breaking, by his own will, through the circle of necessity that animals find infrangible; only he can thus initiate a whole new series of events. To the act [*Akt*] through which he thus operates is appropriately given the name of action [*Handlung*].[9]

If action as such is the peculiarly human mode of human activity, what are its characteristics? There are in fact many, all more or less closely related. I shall simply list some of the characteristics that appear to me to play a significant role in Marx's own thoughts on human action, without attempting to order them in a comprehensive, rigorous manner.

Marx on Human Action

Nonimmediacy. This quality of human action is somewhat puzzlingly stated by Marx: "The animal is immediately one thing with its vital

[9] Quoted by Arnold Gehlen in *Der Mensch: Seine Natur und seine Stellung in der Welt* (4th ed. Bonn: Athenaeum, 1950), p. 39. On Marx's view of the idealistic tradition, see Helmut Klages, *Technischer Humanismus* (Stuttgart: Enke, 1964).

activity, it is not to be distinguished from it, it *is* it. Man makes his vital activity itself into the object of his will and his consciousness" (F 567; B 127). We have argued so far that man does not simply carry on activity within given circles, but actually creates those circles through his activity; this would suggest that he is more deeply involved in his own activity than an animal is in its. Yet Marx suggests that man somehow keeps his own activity at arm's length, somehow stands apart from it. How is this possible? That is, what human quality, unshared by animals, allows man to contemplate his own activity so that it becomes "action"?

Consciousness. The qualities mentioned by Marx are two: will and consciousness. Of these, consciousness is mentioned more frequently throughout his work and is probably the critical quality. Consciousness is simply man's ability to work out in his own mind the givens of a situation (to form an "image" of it, in contemporary language) and to "plan" the ways his activity will adapt to or modify that situation.[10]

Creativity. An element of creativity (or "freedom")—an ability to transcend the givenness of the situation and, in Schiller's terms, "initiate a whole new series of events"—is intrinsic to consciousness as Marx uses the term (although this creativity is by no means continuously evident in human activity). Both early and late Marxian texts convey this point.

[1844] Since all that is of nature must be born [*entstehen*], so *man* must also have his birth act, history, which is, however, a conscious [*gewusste*] birth act; and because it is a birth act with consciousness, it is a birth act that transcends itself. (F 652; B 208)

[1867] We refer to labor in a form that is exclusive to man. A spider performs operations that resemble those of a weaver, and the way in which a bee builds its wax cells puts to shame many an architect. But what from the beginning puts the worst architect ahead of the best bee is the fact that the former, before he builds his own cell in wax, has already built it in his head. At the end of the labor process there emerges a result that from its beginning was already present in the laborer's representations, already *ideally* present. (K 177-78; *169-70*)

---

[10] On the concepts of "image" and "plan" in human reasoning, see George Miller et al., *Plans and the structure of behavior* (New York: Holt, 1960), Chapter 2.

Selfhood. We can take a further step and suggest that what consciousness establishes is man's "selfhood," the mysterious platform from which man is able to view his own life and activity as objects, assessing his own situation and designing his own action. Through selfhood, man sets himself as the measure of all things (F 567; B *127*). The nature of this unique resource is very difficult to pin down, and for most authors some metaphor or other takes the place of a hard-and-fast definition. The twentieth-century social philosopher Ortega y Gasset, for example, visualizes selfhood as an ability to retreat within oneself toward a still center, a place of silence and intimacy; only this allows man to engage in diverse activity without becoming wholly submerged in it.[11] Marx seems to prefer the imagery I have used above, which portrays man as "standing back" from himself and his own activity. This, at any rate, seems implied in his suggestions that man can somehow "split himself up," that he can "have relations with himself" (F 568-69; B *128-29*).[12] Characteristically, Marx seems to be much more interested in exploring how selfhood and consciousness develop than in discussing their elusive nature. Two points concerning this problem of development deserve extended analysis, both because they can be seen as further characterizations of action and because they convey something distinctly Marxian within the framework of the idealistic tradition.

Sociability of the subject. The first point pertaining to the development of selfhood has already been mentioned: the radical "socialization of the subject." Throughout his work Marx continues to assume that the characteristic human ability to engage in action resides in individuals—that is, all action must ultimately expend a physical and mental effort that only individuals can deploy (e.g., K 177; *169*). Selfhood as such is unavoidably a property of the individual, but to Marx it is just as inevitably a product of social relations. Marx did not possess the analytical tools needed to argue this point satisfactorily (indeed, only Freud and G. H. Mead were to develop them); but he established several points to his own satisfaction:

1. The crucial support of selfhood is consciousness; but conscious-

[11] José Ortega y Gasset, *The dehumanization of art* (Garden City, N.Y.: Anchor, 1958), p. 112.
[12] The Bottomore translation does not convey the idea that man "splits himself up" or "doubles" himself.

ness, in turn, is a social product, since it can only be expressed through the unequivocally social reality of language (W 30; 42).

2. The awareness of selfhood, the consciousness of individuality, can only arise when the subject enters relations with others whom he recognizes as both similar to himself and yet irreducible to himself, a point best stated in a footnote to *Capital*: "Since the human being does not come into the world bringing a mirror with him, nor yet as a Fichtean philosopher able to say 'I am myself,' he first recognizes himself as reflected in other men. The man Peter grasps his relation to himself as a human being through becoming aware of his relations to the man Paul as a being of like kind to himself" (K 25; 23). In an earlier text, Marx suggests that man can relate to himself only through the relations he has to other men (F 567; B 129).

3. Marx consistently criticizes the liberal-utilitarian belief in the absolute autonomy of the individual, and two aspects of that critique have a special bearing on the social nature of selfhood. First, Marx asserts (as Durkheim was to do independently) that the autonomous individual, whom liberal-utilitarians regard as the starting point of social development, is on the contrary a very late product of it (G 391, 396; 90, 96). Second, he claims that even when the individual so conceived is placed in a proper historical framework, his very image (as conceived, for instance, by the classical economists) is intrinsically arbitrary and false: "The economists put it this way: Every man cares for his private interest and his private interest only. . . . But the point of the matter is that the private interest is already a socially defined interest, and it can be achieved only within conditions that have been set down by society and through means that have been supplied by it" (G 74).[18]

With these arguments (whatever their inadequacies in modern terms), Marx establishes that the individual, that inescapable center of all human action (W 540; 658), is in fact a social product.

---

[18] Considering how consistently Marx held this position, which opposes the utilitarian tradition, it is odd that he is often treated as a representative of that tradition. This is the case in Talcott Parsons, *The structure of social action* (2d ed., Glencoe, Ill.: Free Press, 1949), pp. 107ff; the same view appears in Percy Cohen, *Modern social theory* (London: Heinemann, 1968), p. 79. For a critique, see Coser, *Continuities in the study of conflict*, especially p. 149.

There is another aspect to what I have called Marx's "radical socialization of the subject": the belief that the true historical actors, those who actually determine the setting of action, are ordinarily groups. The single, isolated human being is viewed by Marx as more receptive than creative, more passive than active, more a consumer than a producer (e.g., W 355; 329-30). The momentous historical task of changing the context of human activity is beyond his ability; to the extent that he is forced, or chooses, to act alone, he can only adjust himself to existing conditions or idly fancy that he is somehow changing them through heroic but intrinsically ineffectual action. The Marxist philosopher Georg Lukacs has phrased this point as follows:

The individual cannot ever become the measure of all things. Objective reality, indeed, presents itself as a set of rigid things that he finds ready-made and unmodifiable before himself, and which he can only acknowledge or reject through his subjective evaluation. Only the class . . . can undertake to reverse the totality of reality through praxis. . . . For the individual, the thing-like character of reality and the associated determinism brought about by thought as it establishes necessary connections among things are unsuppressible.[14]

I shall not pursue this point, since it has been extensively discussed by both sociologists and Marxists (with special reference, of course, to the concept of class). But if the role of groups as "true" actors is to be consistent with the "desubstantialization" of the concept of society that I have attributed to Marx the groups themselves must be construed as the products of a set of relations, each involving the activity of individuals. Although many of Marx's more significant texts actually adopt this construction of the "collective actor," other texts, and perhaps most texts by Marxists, come dangerously near to "substantializing" it. This can happen for several reasons besides a simple failure to apply the strategy of desubstantialization rigorously. For one thing, a certain economy of discourse is implicit in hypostatizing the collective actor. Marxists are also pressed by moral and strategic considerations; it may be wise, for example, to view the working class as a concrete superindividual in order to actually evoke the unity of action this concept presupposes. Finally, the relationship

[14] Georg Lukacs, *Storia e coscienza di classe* (Milan: Sugar, 1967), p. 254. The original work is in German.

of individual to collective actor is often given a "dialectical" construction in which the collective actor at first emerges from individual lines of action but then goes on to subsume individuals and form them in its own image (see W 74-75; 92-93).

Praxis. The second major aspect of Marx's ideas on the genesis of selfhood is the concept of praxis, the union of theory and practice. The key Marxian insight here is again one that has only in this century found a more articulate demonstration (if not a more cogent formulation), particularly in the works of Freud and Dewey. Essentially, Marx holds that thought, "discursive consciousness," and knowledge emerge from the ongoing confrontation between man and the intrinsically practical problem of sustaining his own existence, and not from primarily "contemplative" preoccupations. Consciousness is, in other terms, a facility of action, a resource by which man mediates his relationship to nature; it does not develop in a realm of its own and occasionally descend to relieve man in practical tasks that are themselves purely animal. Consciousness does not "realize itself" through action, but is itself an activity, intrinsically (though not directly) connected with man's sensuousness, needs, and disposition to tinker with reality.

A non-Marxist philosopher, C. I. Lewis, expressed views that appear, on the face of it, quite similar to Marx's concept of praxis. "The primary and pervasive significance of knowledge lies in its guidance of action: knowing is for the sake of doing. . . . A creature which did not enter into the process of reality to alter in some part the future content of it could apprehend the world only in the sense of intuitive or aesthetic contemplation; and such contemplation would not possess the significance of knowledge but only that of enjoying and suffering."[15] However, as Marx recognizes, consciousness, in spite of its origin in the pragmatic confrontation of man with reality, can sometimes delude its possessor into viewing it as placed outside and above reality; the contents of man's mind appear to possess independent significance as historical forces, and somehow to use men to make history rather than being used by them in the same task.

[15] C. I. Lewis, *An analysis of knowledge and evaluation* (La Salle, Ill.: Open Court, 1946), p. 1.

Objectness. Having set forth some of Marx's views on the origin of selfhood and consciousness, we may now consider a new way in which he characterizes action as man's unique mode of activity. Action possesses the property of "objectness," in that it always eventuates in objects (F 567-68; B *127-28.* K 182, 193; *173, 183).* This is particularly obvious in the case of productive labor (which is, indeed, the prototype of action). Labor can fill the subject's world with bits of reality that were not present in Nature (F 648; B *205-6.* G 208). The subject's activity fixates itself in these objects, which he can employ as means to future activity (as tools or raw materials); they somehow stand as both a bridge and a screen between man and raw nature, and they become a point of reference in intersubjective relations.[16]

Man's action also eventuates in two classes of less palpable objects: ideas (representations, concepts, linguistic structures, theories, symbolic complexes) and relations. The objectness of ideas is declared by Marx in his polemic against the conception of consciousness as a transcendental reality divorced from the plane on which man manipulates material objects on behalf of his own interests. He points out that language itself, the medium of consciousness, is suffused with the materiality of those aspects of physical nature (sound waves, the material media of writing) in which it must ultimately embody itself if it is to function as language (F 605; B *164).* (Various modern social scientists have formulated and elaborated this concept independently.)[17]

Intersubjective relations are also objects resulting from man's actions, and their objectness is crucial in Marx's thought. It is difficult to argue this point without bringing in the concept of alienation, which is more appropriate to a later stage of my discussion. But it is worth noting that according to Marx the social significance of material objects themselves is grounded on the relations built around them. "A Negro is a Negro. Only within determinate relations does he become

[16] This point has been emphasized by the Czech Marxist philosopher Karel Kosik, in a book that I know only in its Italian translation, *Dialettica del concreto* (Milan: Bompiani, 1965).

[17] See, for example: Leslie White, "Four stages in the evolution of minding," in Sol Tax, ed., *Evolution after Darwin* (Chicago: University of Chicago Press, 1960), II, 239ff; Hannah Arendt, *The human condition* (Garden City, N.Y.: Anchor, 1959).

a slave. A cotton-spinning machine is a machine for spinning cotton. Only within determinate relations does it become capital. Taken out of such relations it is as little capital as gold is money, or as sugar is the price of sugar" (K 930; 849-50). From this standpoint, it would seem that only the objectness of relations actually establishes the nature of material objects.

A serious difficulty in analyzing Marx's statements on relations is the fact that he tends to use the word as a primitive term needing (or admitting of) no articulation through other concepts; hence he fails to develop the concept analytically. A few passages hint that relations are of a perceptual nature (W 30, 346; 42, 396); that they are sets of expectations located in a subject's intellect and pertaining to the bearing of another subject's activity on the expectant subject's own activity. However, Marx's recurrent polemic against idealistic interpretations of action commits him to emphasizing that somehow those expectations, like all expectations, are only a part of reality, and rather than determining it are determined by it (e.g., W 63; 70. K 49; 47). In the present context, the point to be stressed (and on this Marx is unequivocal) is that relations are *made*: "They are produced by man exactly as cloth, linen, and such are,"[18] and action as much eventuates in them as takes place within them. Both these properties seem to me to imply that relations are ultimately *objects*.

Negativity. Objectness stands in a rather cryptic relationship to another characteristic of action: negativity.[19] Action is intrinsically negative for two reasons. First, since it implies a choice, it involves the denial of all those alternatives that are not chosen. Second, it normally takes place within the context of the results of previous action, which we can visualize as a set of objects. The root of the word "object," in both English and German (*Gegenstand*), implies the notion of resistance, of an obstacle. Thus action, if it is to affect the situation, must somehow overcome the resistance of already created objects; it must negate them. I have suggested that only by laying down new circles can the old ones be transcended; contrariwise, only by negating the old circles can new ones be laid down.

[18] Quoted from Lukacs, *Storia e coscienza di classe*, pp. 62-63.
[19] This property has been particularly stressed by Herbert Marcuse in *Reason and revolution: Hegel and the rise of social theory* (New York: Humanities Press, 1954).

This notion of negativity may appear abstruse and of little import. But it clearly connects with two previous points: the impotence of the isolated individual; and the ineffectuality of disembodied, contemplative, autonomized ideas. The requirement that the old circles bounding man's activity be negated means that collective actors must act upon ideas. Furthermore, the same notion connects with a point I will discuss below: the necessity that action be strictly related to whatever is acted *on* (indeed, acted *against*). If action could take place by simply asserting novelty without changing the givens of the situation, neither the manner nor the results of human activity would be constrained by limits arising from its context. But since every action is determinate in its results (the first meaning of negativity), every subsequent action must counter those results (second meaning). In a sense, the given thus sets boundaries to the possible action that will negate it (e.g., W 35; 47. K 523-24; 527).

"Acting back." I shall conclude this list of Marx's characteristics of action (one among the many that could be elaborated) by mentioning a concept as elusive and intriguing as that of negativity. Human action *acts back* on its subject to an extent and in a manner that animal activity does not. It does not simply "maintain" or "reproduce" the subject, but modifies him, crucially affecting his activity, passivity, needs, and resources. The selfhood of the subject can indeed be conceptualized as an ability not only to retrieve the outcomes of action but also to develop from these a further ability to engage in qualitative new action.

In many passages, Marx states that action necessarily modifies the subject himself. For example, discussing economic activity:

In the act of reproduction itself, not only are the objective conditions modified—e.g., a village becomes a city, a desert becomes cultivated land —but the producers themselves are also modified, in that they draw from themselves new qualities, develop themselves in production and are transformed, acquire new powers and new representations, new modes of relation, new needs and new speech (G 396; 93).

What is in question here is something more than the fact that man objectively "evolves" in the sense that he is different now from what he was earlier. The crucial point is that this evolution is mediated by man himself, through the purposive action of concrete individuals—

an action that itself changes qualitatively. The relationship between acting and being acted upon is ultimately mediated through consciousness, and this again sharply distinguishes man's evolution from the animals, which is a concatenation of purely naturalistic events. "Both the generation and the satisfaction of [man's] needs are themselves historical processes that one would seek in vain in the sheep and the dog. . . . Sheep and dogs are undoubtedly, in their present situation, the products of an historical process, but *malgré eux*" (W 71; *87*).

The fact that the uniqueness of man's evolution rests on consciousness does not mean, however, that evolution involves only man's spiritual or mental qualities. Since consciousness, as we have seen, is an instrument in the total confrontation of concrete man with reality, the evolution mediated by it (which we call history) affects *all* of man's being. History is the process of man's education in all its aspects, sensory and motor as well as mental (F 600-601; B *159-61*).

Alienation

The remarks of a contemporary Marxist philosopher, Karel Kosik, suggest that Marx shared with other representatives of a broad Western tradition many of the views outlined so far.

Marx and Hegel, in the construction of their work, develop one shared symbolic motif that was widely diffused in the cultural setting of their time. This motif, to be found in philosophical, literary and scientific writings, is the "odyssey." The subject (the individual, the individual's consciousness, the spirit, the collectivity) must go on a pilgrimage through the world and know the world in order to get to know itself. The subject can acquire knowledge only to the extent that it acts upon the world; the subject knows the world only by actively intervening in it, and only by actively transforming the world does it get to know itself. The self-knowledge of the subject coincides with its knowledge of its activity in the world. But the subject that returns home after its pilgrimage through the world is different from the subject that undertook the pilgrimage. The world it has traversed is also different, is a changed world, because the very pilgrimage of the subject through it has modified the world itself, left traces upon it. In turn the world manifests itself to the subject in a different manner at the end than at the beginning of the pilgrimage, because the experience acquired by the subject has modified its vision of the world.[20]

[20] Kosik, *Dialettica del concreto*, pp. 202-3.

Suggestive as the metaphor of the pilgrimage may be, it needs to be significantly qualified if it is to provide insights into Marx's view of action and social reality. In the metaphor a unique, pristine, self-originating subject traverses a virgin world for the first time, freely charting his path through it; and at the end of his journey all the modifications the world and himself have undergone are the result of his own free actions. Such a metaphor is applicable to historical experience only if the pilgrimage is comprehensive of all history and the subject coextensive with all of mankind, since all of history by definition can only happen once, and since the collective subject includes all possible actors. To deal with other, narrower, historical experiences, the metaphor must be modified. The subject does not spring, armed only with his subjectivity, from nowhere. He never traverses a virgin world, for the path he follows is to some extent laid out in advance for him, and the experiences that modify himself and the world around him are never simply his own experiences. Countless other pilgrimages have shaped the reality he confronts; his own subjective reality, in fact, is largely a product of those pilgrimages, and to this extent predates and limits his pilgrimage. As Marx put it: "Individuals have always started out from themselves [*gingen immer von sich aus*], but naturally from themselves within the given historical conditions and relations, not from the 'pure' individual as the ideologues conceive of him" (W 75; 93).

It is only on the strength of this fact that something more than a purely individual pilgrimage, or a helplessly repetitive pilgrimage, can take place through history—or that history itself can take place at all.

Because of the simple fact that every successive generation finds itself in possession of the productive forces acquired by the preceding generation, which serve it as the raw material for new production, a coherence arises in human history, there is formed a history of humanity which is all the more a history of humanity since the productive forces of man, and, therefore, his social relations have become more developed (S 442).

By the same token, as the past opens up new possibilities for the present, it forecloses others. Because "every productive force is an acquired force, the product of previous activity," men are not the free arbiters of their actions. Not only to the extent that they avail themselves of the results of past achievements, but also to the extent that they act to get rid of those results in order to fashion anew the setting of their own activity, men are constrained to confront the past in its own terms.[21]

Much of what I said earlier about the creativity, or freedom, of action implies an inherent open-endedness such that it is necessarily impossible to predict exactly what direction action will take. The open-endedness, however, reaches deeper than that, and it is more than the simple presence of "creativity" in the shape action will take. Man may, indeed, *not* act at all. The characteristics of action that have been listed are only potentialities, and they need not be present in all of man's activity. Man *can* break through circles to fashion new ones, but he need not. He may, instead, accept whatever circle surrounds him and simply move inside it, "without even conceiving of a different circle." He may never actually avail himself of his selfhood in order to stand away from his own situation, never confront his own activity as an object, and never realize the unity of theory and practice. He may never start out on the pilgrimage, may fail to leave traces on the world, may never return home, or may return home unmodified, having learned nothing about the world and himself. He may conduct himself in a merely affirmative fashion instead of negating the givens of his situation by acting. In all these cases, man's existence fails to realize his essence (F 567; B 127).[22] In sum, his activity may simply "lose the name of action."

Unfortunately, this important point is never explicit in Marx, perhaps because he felt uncomfortable about some of its possible implications. (The one passage I know where he explicitly contemplated the most extreme implication of *this* degree of open-endedness—the possibility of human populations wholly failing to develop and make history—is one that he himself struck off the manuscript of *German Ideology*. See W 21; 31.) He clearly did think that concrete human activity can realize in varying degree what I have taken to be the characteristics of action; and he in fact considered that revolution-making, which seemed to him action *par excellence*,[23] was necessarily the

[21] See K 573-74; 527: "The development of the contradictions of a historical form of production is the sole historical avenue toward their solution and the emergence of new forms."

[22] Bottomore translates *Wesen* not as "essence" but as "being."

[23] See W 195; 230: "In revolutionary activity the subject's modifying of himself coincides with the modifying of the circumstances."

exception rather than the rule. But perhaps Marx resented one possible implication of this and similar arguments: the view that somehow man can cease to be man, can retrogress to the animal to the extent that he does not actually engage in action as such. In Marx's view conditions may be (and often are) such that within them man is compelled to behave as an animal or is treated as a thing (see F 609; B *169*); but man, to his mind, "is a man for a' that." In capitalist conditions, for example, the worker may actually become the appendage of a machine, but he is a "self-conscious appendage" (K 568; *522*).

Marx certainly resented a related implication of the discontinuity of action, that is, of the intrinsic exceptionality of action *par excellence*. We might label this implication the "only-on-Sunday" conception of history. Instead of being the continuum of man's existence, coextensive with the presence of mankind on earth, history becomes a pulsatory phenomenon, an unpredictable and inexplicable succession of scattered momentous events that dramatically rouse humanity from its animal-like slumber and lift it to another plane. Marx's consistent political rejection of a "putschist" or Blanquist concept of revolution is consistent with his view of history as the totality of man's experience, and with the emphasis he chose to place on the continuing linkage between the renunciation and the realization of action.[24] Some men must always renounce action as others realize it: this linkage is expressed as conflict, which feeds on the unsatisfied needs generated in some men by the fact that their own activity is constrained by the results of other men's actions (W 192; 226-27). Conflict thus presupposes a basic imbalance in the access of different groups to the privilege of action. History is continuous in spite of the discontinuity of action because action, however discontinuous itself, continuously engenders, through the persistence of its results, an asymmetric pressure upon groups.

We shall return to this point later, from a somewhat different perspective. But I must acknowledge here that there are some serious unresolved difficulties in the argument—whether in Marx's own argument or in my reconstruction of it I am not sure. As far as Marx is concerned, at any rate, there is undoubtedly something odd about

[24] On the relationship between the Blanquist and the Marxian concepts of revolution, see Avineri, *Thought of Karl Marx*, Chapter 7.

the fact that he devoted his lifework as a scholar and a politician to revolutionary activity, which he regarded as both expressing and generating human freedom; for at the same time he so emphasized the conditions constraining action that he is often considered an eminently deterministic thinker. Marx, however, probably saw nothing at all odd about this. The very fact that through most of history man is in the grip of necessity, he felt, is the result of past action, and thus of the exercise of freedom. In the same way, he regarded the forcible, conscious expression of freedom through revolutionary action as itself a response to the pressure of necessity: "It is the bad side that produces the movement that makes history, by providing a struggle."[25]

Let us look more closely at the way Marx construed this relationship between freedom and necessity, and in so doing introduce the concept of alienation.[26] Our point of departure will be the fact that action, although it implies a degree of open-endedness in man's activity, can only be determinate: it takes place here and now; it eventuates in certain objects factually endowed with certain properties; it is as it is and not otherwise. In itself, this is a datum that flows directly from the finitude of man and at the same time expresses the peculiar dignity of his condition. Ultimately, concrete individuals, in the pursuit of their individual existence, carry out all human activity; thus this activity can only be "a determinate form, a determinate way of expressing life, a determinate way of life" (W 347; 396).

However, necessity emerges from freedom because the reality men make is not *simply* determinate. Human activity eventuates in something other than a simple tissue of "objectifications" (material objects, ideas, and relations) spontaneously woven by men under the pressure of their needs and shaped by them as a pliable tool for coping with that pressure (G 716). Instead, the results of that activity begin to transcend individuals; they cease to obey the will through which they were originally processed, no longer lend themselves to

[25] Cited by Lewis Coser in *The functions of social conflict* (London: Routledge, 1956), p. 13.
[26] My argument here is highly streamlined and simplified. Among the many sophisticated discussions of alienation that could be cited, I would recommend Peter Berger and Stanley Pullberg, "Reification and the sociological critique of consciousness," *History and theory*, IV (1965), No. 3, pp. 196ff.

the ends for which they were created. The givens of social reality are given only because they were made, yet they have ceased to be accountable to the forces that made them. They can no longer be treated as arbitrary facts possessing no inherent self-justification and no immanent force of resistance. Social reality, in spite of its origins in the action of concrete, goal-seeking individuals, acquires an immanent force of resistance; it emancipates itself from its origins to become self-justifying and self-explanatory.

This process is the essence of the phenomenon of *alienation*. It can best be visualized as a process of inversion (F 716), a "turning of the tables" that takes place in a variety of ways. For example:

1. The subject of the activity may lose control over the object he has created. And the latter may itself become the subject of the continuing process and treat its originator as its own object. "In the capitalist economy things and persons become exchanged for one another; things are personalized and people reified. Will and consciousness are imputed to things, and men become the executors of the movements of things. The will and consciousness of men are then determined by the movement of things."[27]

2. In the same process, the inversion can also involve cause and effect: "For example, here is a man who is only king because other people behave as his subjects. Yet they, for their part, believe themselves to be his subjects because he is king" (K 30-31; 29).

3. The instrument of contact between man and the reality that surrounds him, be it material object, idea, or relation, seems to have force of its own. For instance, a concept or a generalization is an instrumentality of consciousness, a device man works out to deal with reality at a certain level of abstraction removed from the immediacy of raw experience. Nevertheless, "these generalities and concepts acquire significance as mysterious entities" (W 347; 396).

4. Relations that have resulted from a given historical process may be treated, in the face of all evidence that their origins are in the recent past, as timeless embodiments of nature itself. Thus all bourgeois political economy treats its own referents as metahistorical realities (K 50-51; 48).

---

[27] I quote here Kosik, *Dialettica del concreto*, p. 213; this passage paraphrases an argument often formulated in very similar terms by Marx himself.

But why do these and other manifestations of the inversion process, of the phenomenon of alienation, take place at all? This is where Marx's position begins to diverge considerably from that of other sociologists, most of whom have conceptualized the phenomenon similarly but explained its causes differently. The two main answers to the question partly overlap; but they may, somewhat artificially, be characterized as a fatalistic answer and a functionalistic answer. The first treats the phenomenon of alienation as an ultimately inexplicable quality of the human animal that expresses his intrinsic contradictoriness—the "tragedy of culture," as Simmel characterized it.[28] The second answer argues that the process of inversion is a useful, indeed an indispensable, one: only by "deifying" his own artifacts is man kept from tinkering capriciously with them; only by the people viewing their obligation to obey the king as based on his *being* the king will they be motivated to obey him; only thus will order be kept.

There are elements of both these answers in Marx's own, which nonetheless has a very different total orientation. One component of Marx's position resembles the functionalistic answer in that it accounts for the phenomenon of alienation teleologically, by referring to what follows from it and not to what precedes it. But the main consequence of this, to Marx, is not, as in the functionalist answer, the stabilization of the existing order. Rather, Marx emphasizes that the alienation process sets forth the premises of its own subversion. It erects on man's path a series of obstacles, thereby compelling him to advance—if he is to advance at all—by negating those obstacles and clearing them from his path (K 417-18; *386*). As Lukacs phrases it, "history is the history of the uninterrupted subversion of the objectival forms that mold man's existence."[29] The process through which those forms emerge, alienation, is thus the motor of history.

Marx, however, is not entirely comfortable with this kind of interpretation (e.g., K 45; *59*) and insists rather more on a second component of his answer, which is both more original and more fruitful sociologically. He asks not in view of what consequences, but owing to what antecedent conditions does the alienation process develop.

---

[28] See Georg Simmel, "Der Begriff und die Tragödie der Kultur," in *Das individuelle Gesetz* (Frankfurt: Suhrkamp, 1969), pp. 116ff.

[29] Lukacs, *Storia e coscienza di classe*, p. 245.

The question is so formulated, and the basic answer given, in an early text. Marx ponders the notion that under capitalism a worker's activity and the product of that activity no longer belong to him: "If my own activity does not belong to me, if it is alien and coercive activity, to whom does it belong? Who can this being be?" He then discards the notion that it can be the Gods or Nature.

The foreign being to whom labor and the product of labor belong, for whose service and enjoyment the product of labor is destined, can only be man himself. If the product of labor does not belong to the worker, stands apart from him as a foreign object, this can only be possible because it belongs to men other than the worker. If his activity is a torment to him, it must then be enjoyment and vital satisfaction to another man. Not the Gods, not Nature, only man himself can be this foreign power over men. . . . If man relates to the product of his own labor, to his own objectified labor, as to a foreign, hostile, powerful object that does not depend on him, he relates to it thusly because another man, foreign and hostile to him, independent of him, is the master of this object. If he relates to his own activity as unfree, this means that he relates to an activity in the service, under the domination, the coercion, and the yoke, of another man (F 569-70; B *129-30*. See also G 366-67).

Our discussion of alienation has now led us back to a point we encountered in discussing the discontinuity of action: Different men (and different groups) relate in significantly different ways to the same social realities. In particular, different men relate in very different ways to the products of the same labor, some obtaining a control over those products that is denied others. This priority is the core of the notion of property. Through property relations, men arrange themselves in sharply differentiated ways around the products of labor, and this arrangement creates a superindividual power. Man loses control of his own product; his intended instruments cease to "behave" as such and instead begin to control his actions. All these aspects of the alienation process result from a fissure that appears between actors, from a distinctive and forceful relationship obtaining between groups of men. Because of the significance of this fissure, as Marx at one point concluded, there is something false about the usual philosophers' talk of "*the* human being" (W 63; *79*).

But if the alienation process develops from a fissure between contrasting groups of men, we must then ask how the fissure itself develops. Probably one can only answer this question by constructing a fictional model, by stating logical relations between sets of events that are intrinsically unamenable to historical discussion, since they took place on the very threshold of history. Marx's own solution to the problem may be treated as such a model: "The individuals always start off from themselves, always proceed from themselves. Their relations are the relations of their concrete life process. How does it happen that their relations gain a separate existence, that the powers of their life can become more powerful than they? In one word: the division of labor" (W 540; 658).

In fact, the alienation process can be connected with the division of labor either directly or indirectly:

The social power (that is, the magnified productive force resulting from the concurrent operation of different individuals that is brought about by the division of labor) appears to those individuals not as their own power but as a foreign power located outside themselves and no longer under their control. In fact, that force now goes through a succession of phases and stages of development that are of its own making; it does not depend on the will and effort of men but rather directs that will and effort.[30]

With the division of labor ... simultaneously occurs the distribution, and indeed the *unequal* distribution, both qualitative and quantitative, of labor and of its products, and thus of property. ... Moreover, division of labor and division of property are synonymous expressions: in the former the immediate reference is to the activity, in the latter to the products of that activity. ... With the division of labor, there comes into existence a conflict between the interest of the single individual (and his family) and the communal interest of all individuals who enter transactions with one another (W 34; 44).

How does the division of labor accomplish this? Marx's answer is not very satisfactory, partly because, as I have suggested, it is essentially a fictional model and thus requires a great deal of rarefied speculation. Moreover, at the time Marx took up this question he still had only a rough notion of the division of labor, and in particular he had not yet adequately conceptualized the distinction between social and technical division of labor. At any rate, his answer may be summarized in the following terms.[31]

[30] Quoted from Barth, *Wahrheit und Ideologie*, pp. 136-37.
[31] There is a more elaborate discussion of this argument in Barth, pp. 124ff.

The division of labor breaks up the process whereby a primal collective unit—small, tightly knit, and barely differentiated internally—jointly and fully appropriates the results of its own productive activity. Through division of labor this unit is gradually disaggregated into smaller subunits, whose contribution to the productive activity is particularized and acquires significance only by merging with other contributions outside the subunit's immediate control. The merging of the differentiated contributions must of course be regulated, and this regulating function must itself be carried out as one particularized activity (W 229; 267). Regulation emerges mainly as a privileged form of "mental" labor, and acquires a more and more invidious significance compared with all forms of "manual" labor.

As the division of labor progresses, the comparative importance of the various differentiated contributions made by subunits becomes more and more difficult to assess in a manner that is visibly objective and thus uncontentious. The regulating function becomes increasingly removed from the directly productive functions. At the same time, the overall effectiveness of the activity carried out by the subdivided production unit is increased by specialization (K 371-72; 345), and the allocation of the resultant increase in products is intrinsically contentious. Thus there arises, in Marx's words, "conflict between the single [subunit] interest and the collective interest." Eventually, each subunit desires to get more out of the overall productive process than it has put in. Since all subunits cannot simultaneously achieve this goal to their own satisfaction, their interactions can be stabilized only through potentially self-maintaining asymmetric relations in which some subunits are able to lay down the terms of interaction for others. This is where objects become crucial, particularly certain classes of objects.

Since human activity typically eventuates in objects and fixates itself through objects, the divergent interests of subunits are expressed through divergent priorities of access to and control over objects. The end result is necessarily a division of the actors into contrasting groups. Typically, this division is one between a group *in* control and a group *under* control, and not a random scattering of other positions. This is so because the crucial relationship of man to an object involves either possessing it or not possessing it: *tertium non datur*.

Obviously, for such a relationship to be at all significant the objects in question must also be significant. And the outstandingly significant objects are ones that allow their possessors to set the conditions under which nonpossessors can use them to produce other objects—i.e., those objects that within a given society constitute the means of production. It is through these that the ultimate man-object relationship, that between the human subject and nature, is mediated (K 179-81; *170-72*).

The means of production, like all other objects, embody past activity and intervene in present activity. But unlike other objects involved in a productive process, they do not disappear: "They remain in existence apart from the products they aid in making" (K 210; *199*). They are privileged objects because they embody man's striving to shape and control his future. For these reasons, it is critical to find oneself, so to speak, on the right side of the means of production. A man who has no property other than his labor power "must, in all conditions of society and culture, be the slave of other men," those who own the means of production. "He can work only with their permission, hence live only with their permission" (S *87*. See also G *707*).

Thus, if my interpretation is correct, Marx's idea of the causes of alienation is essentially very simple. Alienation does not affect actors at random or uniformly, but is caused by an underlying process through which some actors are dispossessed to the benefit of other actors. The only object that can fail to appear and operate as one's own is that belonging to someone else; what is taken away at one end accrues at the other. Thus the phenomenon of alienation presupposes only two given conditions: the objectness of action, since only objects can be appropriated to oneself or another (K 67; *63*); and the disaggregation of an original collective unit into distinctive subunits that impinge on one another (through their *differentiated* relations to the *same* objects) but do so in the name of at least partly differentiated and contrasting interests, and asymmetrically.

This apparently simple answer may be elaborated in a variety of complex and subtle ways. In the first place, it is merely a fictional construct describing the very beginnings of alienation in human history. Later in the process, the relations postulated in the model—e.g., between the division of labor and property, or between property and the schism of groups—begin to lend themselves to historical and thus empirical discussion, and historical reality reveals an interplay of relations outside the scope of the model. For instance, although the model postulates that alienation arises from an asymmetry between contrasting groups and stresses the power of a controlling group over others, Marx shows that in concrete historical situations *all* parts of the society may be affected by the alienation phenomenon. Typically, the oppressed masses are made to perceive their situation as an unchallengeable fate, an inexorable fact of nature. But the privileged few are no less alienated (consider the wealthy capitalist who behaves as a miser, or the estate owner who is in a sense owned by his estate); and their mode of alienation, though different from that affecting the masses, is somehow complementary to it.

In the second place, what I have formulated as Marx's distinctive view of the causes of the alienation process is not proposed by him as the exclusive answer. As I have suggested, he also advances his own variant of the teleological answer. Furthermore, he accepts to some extent the more common teleological answer I have labeled functionalist.[32] For example, he acknowledges the necessity, within a large-scale productive unit, of having a system of rules to coordinate individual lines of action; and these rules must necessarily be formulated and enforced by a distinctive part of the unit, which to that extent acts on behalf of the whole. But Marx also emphasizes that within the capitalist order this "function" is assigned by a criterion basically opposed to its social purpose, i.e., by private property. The manner in which the function is carried out also makes a significant difference, and within the capitalist order that manner will necessarily be despotic and exploitative.[33] That is, the divergence of interests generated among the participants by the asymmetry of power is at least as significant as the fact that they may actually share certain interests. It is obvious that somebody must manage things; but it makes a great difference who does, according to what criteria, and in view of which specific interests. It is this difference

[32] Recent studies have emphasized this. See, for example, Alfred Stinchcombe, *Constructing social theories* (New York: Harcourt, 1968), Chapter 3, Section II; Augusto De Palma, "L'organizzazione capitalistica del lavoro nel *Capitale* di Marx," *Quaderni di Sociologia*, XV (1966), No. 1, pp. 11-39.

[33] See the excellent discussion of this point in De Palma, "L'organizzazione capitalistica." The most significant Marxian text is probably K 388ff; *359ff*.

that an unqualified functionalist view of alienation usually ignores.

This characteristically Marxian emphasis on the determinate configuration of a given phenomenon (W 21; 32-33. K 247-49; 235-36) is possibly the most important reason why Marx's approach to the alienation phenomenon, however simple in its schematic form, is elaborated by him in a complex and subtle manner. In his view, the question of the "primary origin" (or, for that matter the "essential nature") of alienation is not especially significant. The fact that somehow men are susceptible to alienation interests him less than the specific, determinate kinds of alienation affecting actual men in given historical situations. Social reality, to Marx, displays (perhaps *is*) a severalness of aspects, phases, and modalities of alienation that must be confronted and analyzed as they are. Only by doing so can one understand why and how one configuration of the alienation phenomenon succeeds another, both incorporating and negating it; how at a given time various aspects of the alienation phenomenon condition one another, sustain one another, and conflict with one another.

It is not enough, so far as Marx is concerned, to attribute alienation to the action of a group that appropriates the means of production and excludes another group from them; the specific nature of each group, of the means of production, and of the appropriation-exclusion relationship will vary and must therefore be investigated. One must go beyond Marx's relatively simple statement that he who is denied the means of production will always be the slave of others; one must rather seek out the specific "conditions of society and culture" within which specific forms of slavery are dominant (K 376-79; 349-51).

Marx's work reflects in various ways his commitment to exploring the severalness of alienation. In the first place, Marx distinguishes several basic forms of alienation, particularly the religious, political, and economic forms.[34] At times, he refers to religious alienation as

---

[34] One can also distinguish various aspects of each of these forms. For instance, economic alienation entails for the direct producer an alienation from himself, from his own activity, from his own product, and from other men. For an extensive and sophisticated discussion of Marx's uses of the concept of alienation, see Yves Calvez, *La pensée de Karl Marx* (Paris: Editions du Seuil, 1959), pp. 41-332.

the paradigm of all alienation (e.g., K 47-48, 744; *456, 685*), in view of the peculiarly effective way in which the sanctification of social reality hides from human consciousness the fundamental truth that this reality is man-made. Much oftener, he emphasizes economic alienation; but on the whole, his work reflects a keen awareness of the variety of ways in which man can be dispossessed of himself and of his own works.

Moreover, even to distinguish the various forms is not enough. Within the religious form of alienation, for instance, Marx perceives the distinction of Christianity from, say, a religion that compels man to go down on his knees before the monkey or the cow (S/I *350-51*); again, within Christianity, he perceives the distinction of reformed from Roman Catholic belief, ritual, and morality (e.g., F *585*; B *147*). Each of these configurations, at the appropriate level, appears significant to him not just as a morphological variety, but because it makes a difference to the total nature of the alienation characteristic of a given historical situation.

This sensitivity to the forms and subforms of alienation is accompanied by a strong sensitivity to the historical evolution of each. Thus, to Marx's mind, a state based on the citizenship principle is significantly different from one based on estates (if the latter can be called a state at all); but it also makes a difference how far the principle of citizenship has been carried, say, in widening suffrage.[35] Similarly, capitalism as an economic system is primarily oriented to the production of exchange values and thus inherently different from any system primarily oriented to the production of use values; but it also makes a difference whether the exchange values are produced by hand or by machine, what types of economic units are dominant in a given capitalist system, and so forth.

The Priority of the Economy

We have seen that Marx organizes and explains the severalness of social reality by emphasizing the distinctiveness of the determinate, structured, and historically unique configurations that the process of

[35] On Marx's views concerning the institutional evolution of the modern state, cf. Avineri, *Thought of Karl Marx* and Louis Ansart, *Marx et l'anarchisme* (Paris: P.U.F., 1969).

alienation assumes. This emphasis, however, is countered by Marx's commitment to a comprehensive theory of the relations between various aspects of man's activity, which both engenders and overcomes alienation. I refer, of course, to the notion of a hierarchy of significance among types of human activity (and alienation), a hierarchy best visualized by considering the "relations of production" or the "economic structure of society" as "the real base on which there arises a legal and political superstructure, and to which correspond determinate forms of social consciousness" (W 13; S/I 363). Here, I shall not attempt to confront the many difficult issues, philosophical and otherwise, raised by this thesis, but only to outline my views on its persistent theoretical significance for sociology.

In the first place, we must dispose of a very common interpretation that equates Marx's thesis with "economic determinism." Within the general Marxian conception of social reality, as outlined so far, there is simply no place for determinism, economic or otherwise —if we mean by determinism the view that any kind of action is purely the result of the conditions under which it develops. Action per se, I have argued, is creative and open-ended. The concept of negativity implies the preexistence of a determinate reality, and action must in some fashion "match" that reality if it is to negate it, to shift it about. But this means only that action is determinate *in terms of* the preexistent reality, not that reality determines action.

These general remarks apply to action per se in the Marxian framework, and certainly to noneconomic activity as well, since that activity, in Marx's view, can sometimes be called "action." Action is a making or producing of objects (in the broadest sense); and Marx specifically states that "religion, the family, the state, morality, science, etc., are particular modes of production" (F 594; B156. See also W 26; 37). But even apart from this generic argument for excluding a deterministic interpretation of the relation between economic activity and other activity, Marx offers several indications that there is some open-endedness to noneconomic activity:

1. Moral or factual representations can be well in advance not only of existent reality but also of the developmental tendencies directly built into the structure of existent reality (F 450, 494; E 214, 255).

2. Although there is, as we shall see, a need for compatibility between a society's economic structure and (e.g.) its political constitution, there is no one-to-one correspondence; a given economic structure may be compatible with a range of political constitutions (F 243-95).

3. Superstructural forms have an inertia of their own, and once founded on an economic base they need not vary constantly and consistently with the developments taking place in that base. Indeed, they will not do so in most cases; and one reason for the revolutionary character of major historical advances is the asynchronism of base-superstructure relationships, which necessitates an occasional "clearing of the decks" by revolutionary action. This resistance of the superstructure to the influence of the base confirms, to my mind, that even the building of the former on the latter involves some degree of freedom and puts a purely deterministic interpretation out of the question.

4. Finally, speaking of classical art, Marx remarks that certain superstructural forms do not simply "run ahead" of economic relationships or "lag behind" them, but instead become transtemporal and transcultural, standing as eternal conquests of the human spirit.[36]

Against these reasons for rejecting a deterministic interpretation of economy-superstructure relations one must set a number of statements by Marx (and Engels) that would seem to support such an interpretation. Usually, such statements suggest that the realities of the economic base simply "express themselves" through political, religious, and philosophical ideas or relations that can be treated as "epiphenomena" of those realities. Two points, however, imply that Marx's statements, for all appearances to the contrary, are compatible with a nondeterministic interpretation; or that they should simply be dismissed as sociologically unfruitful, as untrue to what is here viewed as the sociologically viable core of the Marxian conception.

In the first place, many of Marx's statements are not as unequivocally deterministic as they are claimed to be. Take the proposition that in any situation "given economic conditions . . . necessarily obtain a political and legal expression" (W 339; 387). Most commen-

[36] On the problems posed for Marx by such timeless aesthetic achievements, see Barth, *Wahrheit und Ideologie*, pp. 147-48.

tators and critics read the adverb "necessarily" as implying that somehow the economic conditions will mechanically produce certain political and legal structures. But in another sense the same adverb may indicate not a one-way process of causation but rather the indispensability of legal and political forms compatible with the economic givens. But then, if the latter *need* compatible political and legal forms, those forms must *make a difference* to the economic givens—which could otherwise dispense with them—and the determinate configuration of legal and political arrangements must *make a difference* to the determinate configuration of the economic givens (W 181-82; 215).

The necessity, then, does not flow from the economic givens to the legal and political forms; and the adverb refers to a requirement of their co-presence, of the totality that they make up together. This interpretation does not mean that there is no hierarchy of significance among economic forms and other forms, as we shall see; but it does mean that the economic forms cannot simply determine other forms. (And the attribution of some independent significance to non-economic forms need not be a surreptitious, "back-door" sort of operation like that repeatedly attempted by Engels in the 1890's.)[37]

In the second place, many of the deterministic-sounding statements appear to me rather less programmatic and rather more ambiguous than they have seemed to many readers. The most famous statement, a passage from the Foreword to the *Critique of political economy* (1859), may appear to be a forthright enunciation of Marx's general position on the matter. Admittedly, it has strong deterministic overtones, but on close reading it is fraught with ambiguities, abrupt transitions, and strange asymmetries in the argument. The perplexities and difficulties into which Marx was led by his attempt to take a deterministic stand, however, are to my mind nowhere as clearly indicated as in a much less famous text, a footnote in *Capital* referring to the relationship between economic base and religious superstructure: "It is indeed much easier to locate through analysis the worldly core of the nebulous conceptions of religion than to derive from the actual life relations obtaining at a given time their transpositions in

[37] See, for example, Engels's letters to Bloch and to Schmidt (S/II 488ff).

the heavenly realm. The latter is the sole materialistic and thus scientific method" (K 106; 97).

The first sentence here clearly implies that there is at least some degree of freedom in the process whereby a religious superstructure is built on a material base. Otherwise why would the *a priori* "derivation" of the process be any more difficult than its reconstruction *a posteriori*? Once this is acknowledged, the remainder of the statement sounds like an attempt by the "deterministic" Marx to renounce this implication (rather ineffectually, to my mind)—in fact, very much like an exorcistic incantation.

My rejection of a deterministic interpretation of the base-superstructure thesis should not in turn be misunderstood. I am not suggesting that "superstructural activity" always and everywhere avails itself of "degrees of freedom." The point I question is not the notion that such activity *can* be determined but the notion that it *must* be under all circumstances. Action itself, as we have seen, is in a sense exceptional; and a great deal of activity (economic and superstructural) may go on that is not entitled to be called action precisely because it is utterly determined by the persistent results of previous action, particularly of economic action. But determination in this context has to do with the distinction between action as such and mere activity, not with the hierarchy between types of activity or action.

Once we exclude a deterministic interpretation of the relationship between the economic base and its superstructure, we must still make sociological sense of the priority Marx undeniably attributed to the economy, of the stress he consistently placed on the social processes pertaining to the production and distribution of wealth. In the balance of this chapter, I shall propose some interpretations of the Marxian position that in my opinion preserve considerable theoretical significance for contemporary sociology.

First, Marx's "econocentric" conception can be seen as *strictly* related to his overriding preoccupation with working out an analysis and critique of modern society. In the development of this society, the processes pertaining to the production and appropriation of wealth have acquired greater autonomy than ever before; at the same time, they have placed themselves at the very center of the social process, subordinating to themselves all other aspects of that process. In the words of Henri Lefèbvre, "It is capitalism that clearly places economic relations at the center of society."[38] But the interpretation of Marxian thought that Lefèbvre criticizes as "economistic" (much like the one I have rejected as deterministic) errs in maintaining that Marx assumed an *a priori* primacy of the "economic factor"; in fact, the notion was forced on him by the specific features of the historical reality he confronted.

The view that in modern society economic processes have a significance far greater and more apparent than in any other historical situation has been voiced by countless other social scientists and critics, from Durkheim to Weber to Parsons. Karl Polanyi, formulating the idea with specific reference to the social context most directly influencing Marx's mind (particularly in *Capital*), views the totalitarian "marketization" of all social and natural reality by the Industrial Revolution as the essence of what he calls the "great transformation."[39] Marx himself repeatedly stated such views (e.g., W 65-68; 80-84). But he would not have willingly acknowledged that the economy was foremost only in modern times. And in *Capital* he rebukes authors who suggest that the modern economy occupies the position held by warfare and politics in classical antiquity or religion in the Middle Ages.

Truly comical is Mr. Bastiat, who fancies that the ancient Greeks and Romans lived purely from the proceeds of plunder. Surely if someone is to live off plunder for centuries there must always be something to plunder, unless one assumes that the booty simply reproduces itself. It thus appears that the Greeks and Romans must have had a production process—that is, an economy—which constituted the material base of their world just as the bourgeois economy constitutes that of the bourgeois world.... So much is clear: the Middle Ages could not *live* upon Catholicism, nor classical antiquity upon politics. On the contrary, the way in which they respectively sustained life explains why here politics and there Catholicism played the central role (K 60-61; 56-57).

This position strikes me as sound; and it suggests that the Marxian thesis here discussed is more than an extrapolation from modern

---

[38] Henri Lefèbvre, *La sociologie de Karl Marx* (Paris: P.U.F., 1967), p. 11.
[39] Polanyi, *The great transformation* (New York: Holt, 1944).

conditions. Two further statements of its wider significance can be attempted.

Let us assume that what Marx means by "the economy" (and related terms like production process, labor process, and reproduction) is a specific set of human activities related to the production and distribution of material wealth. What kind of priority do these activities possess over other activities, once we have discarded the idea of a generalized causal priority because of its deterministic implications? Two phrases from *The German Ideology* suggest that for one thing the priority is chronological. There are situations where a temporal scheduling of different kinds of activities is necessary, and in these circumstances economic activities are indeed "prior" simply in the sense of having to come first.

One can distinguish men from animals by reference to religion, consciousness, or what have you. Men began to distinguish themselves from the animals as soon as they began to *produce* their means of existence. (W 21; 32).

Men must live in order to "make history." But living involves in the first place eating and drinking, habitation, clothing, and other necessities. The first historical act is the production of the means to satisfy these needs, the production of material life itself; and indeed, this one historical act, a basic condition of all history, must to this day, as for thousands of years previously, be accomplished every day and every hour so as to maintain men in existence (W 28; 39).

This chronological priority of economic activity is not necessarily applicable only to the very beginnings of human development. True, in the "normal" course of history all human activities take place concurrently, and it is difficult to see in what sense chronological priority is reasserted "every day and every hour." But we can still assume that economic activity takes precedence in every situation that demands a drastic rescheduling of activities. Probably, in Marx's view, this assumption applies to all situations of intensive, large-scale social change. And whenever a section of humanity undergoes a sweeping process of development, one can expect that the problem of meeting material needs will again take priority in the whole process. A new epoch is necessarily characterized, before all else, by the ways in which men meet the economic problem.

Examined more closely, chronological priority has important implications that go beyond its literal meaning. By virtue of coming first, economic activities can be said to acquire a distinctive significance as against all others. The ways in which men affect nature and themselves through their productive activities irreversibly modify the circumstances in which all other activity must take place. Those activities, indeed, generate and shape the resources that will be employed in all other tasks; discrepancies of interests and asymmetries of power emerge that unavoidably limit the freedom with which all other tasks can be confronted.

Marx phrased this point in a variety of ways, some questionable. For example, of the following two sentences from *The German Ideology*, the first has deterministic connotations that make it, to my mind, quite unacceptable; the second, however starkly formulated, strikes me as so plausible as to be very nearly a truism. "The class which has at its disposal the means of material production has by the same token at its disposal the means of mental production. . . . The ideas of the dominant class are in every epoch the dominant ideas" (W 46; 60).[40] Here, Marx recognizes implicitly that mental production cannot be construed as simply a prolongation or a projection of material production, since ideas can in fact be produced by individuals and groups that do not control the means of material production. What this control decides is the relative power of different ideas—that is, the probability that particular ideas will be officially promulgated, systematically acted on, and forcibly sanctioned as guides to social behavior.[41]

It would seem from my argument so far that the priority of economic activity is not an ontological priority but simply a result of the factual necessity for carrying out economic activity before all other activities when certain circumstances apply. And once carried out, economic activity leaves products that unavoidably affect the whole context of later activities. By phrasing the argument differently, one could also say that it is not so much economic *action* that

[40] The order in which these phrases follow one another in Marx's text is the reverse of that in which I quote them.

[41] On the necessary connection between the power structure and the social enforceability of alternative sets of ideas see Ralf Dahrendorf, "On the origin of social inequality," in Peter Laslett and W. G. Runciman, eds., *Philosophy, politics, and society*, second series (Oxford: Blackwell, 1962), pp. 88ff.

has priority over other kinds of action as it is economic *alienation* that has priority over other kinds of alienation.[42] I am aware that neither of these formulations is very satisfactory, and that the sociological implications of each are difficult to spell out and even more difficult to test. But it does seem to me that by approaching the problem in this way one can accord an order of priority to economic activities without allowing them a generalized causal priority.

We need not assume, in discussing the priority of economic action, that Marx singles out this action as a specific set of activities differentiated by their content from all other activities, or that he accords it preferential treatment because of that content. His emphasis on the economy may in fact reflect a certain approach to *all* kinds of activity: the notion that all of social reality is continuously produced by activity, is the result of praxis, is *made*. By this interpretation, Marx "goes to the economy" essentially because the concrete economic processes seem to him the best paradigm for the larger process of the making and unmaking of social reality by man.

Indeed most of the texts in which we have so far sought a characterization of *action* as such refer expressly only to *labor*. And Marx clearly felt that labor is (as Hans Barth phrases it) "the epitome of all the strivings, both practical and theoretical, that men must undertake in order to maintain their own existence."[43] It is chiefly in labor that we find the characteristics of creativity, consciousness, objectness, and all the others that Marx attributes to action. It is primarily through his more or less direct struggle with nature, through labor, that man modifies both the world and himself. The sociological significance of all this lies in the insight that the labor process and its actors provide into the making of *all* social reality.

In the draft version of *Capital*, Marx clarified the reasons for his lifelong concern with the production and distribution of wealth:

Leaving aside its narrow bourgeois form, what is wealth, if not the universality of needs, potentialities, enjoyments, productive powers, etc. that individuals produce and exchange? What is it, if not the full development

---

[42] This is perhaps implicit in Marx's suggestions that the whole alienation phenomenon is ultimately based on the fact of scarcity, which is also the major stimulus for economic activity as such. This point has been much developed by J.-P. Sartre in *Critique de la raison dialectique* (Paris: Gallimard, 1962).

[43] Barth, *Wahrheit und Ideologie*, p. 124. This point is also made by Avineri and Kosik in the works already referred to.

of man's control over the powers of nature—those of his own nature as well as those of so-called "Nature"? What, if not the limitless expansion of his creative capacities, without any preconditions other than previous historical evolution, so that the totality of that evolution—the evolution of all human powers as such, with no *previously* established standard—becomes an end in itself? What is this, if not a situation in which man . . . does not seek to remain something molded by the past, but is in the absolute process of becoming? (G 387; 85. *See* also G 440.)

In this view, what Marx sought to establish through his insistence on the priority of the economy was a materialistic understanding of man's uniqueness as an *acting* being. As he notes even in his early writing, this conception of human activity had been developed, up to his own time, mainly in an idealistic form that emphasized contemplative, aesthetic, and institution-making activities.[44] With this emphasis there was typically associated a pronounced distaste for, an unwillingness to consider, the activities that express man's sensuousness, his desire to satisfy material needs by engaging in a struggle with nature and shaping concrete reality.[45]

Marx emphasized economic activity in an attempt to reverse this emphasis—to attack the idealistic habit of treating as independent entities the human powers that originate from man's total confrontation with reality and should not be abstracted from this confrontation. The economy appealed to him (particularly in a capitalist-industrial context) as a means by which the objectness, negativity, and sociality of action, as well as the emergence of alienation, could best be studied. The making of social reality by man is particularly apparent in the production and distribution of wealth. Above all, the industrial form of that process reveals man's intrinsically practical orientation to reality, his disposition to tinker with existing arrangements, and his ability to produce a surplus by purposefully deploying effort.

The history of industry, its objectified existence, is the open book of man's essential forces, the human psychology perceptibly displayed, although so far it has not been perceived in its connection with man's essence but only

---

[44] This is explicitly stated by Marx in his first "Thesis on Feuerbach." See W 533; 645.

[45] This is one of the main points of Marx's rather repetitive and overstated critique of Max Stirner's ideas in *The German ideology*; see W 183; 218.

in an external relationship of utility. . . . In ordinary material industry we are confronted with man's essential forces, objectified as tangible, separate, and useful objects. A psychology that leaves this book shut, and thus ignores the most tangible and accessible part of history, cannot become a real science dealing with authentic fact (F 602; B 162-63).

But the fact that the study of economic phenomena provides access to "man's essence" does not imply that it provides *easy* access. Economic relations throw up their own peculiar smokescreen of appearances:[46] especially in modern, capitalist conditions, they seem to be relations between *things*, not between *men*. "Political economy" contents itself with these appearances; but the critique of political economy goes beyond them and examines the emergence of things from human labor. Finally, the *verification* (in the literal sense of the term, that is, true-making) of this critique is intrinsically a practical, social, and revolutionary task.

Thus, whatever the theoretical and practical obstacles to verification, the essential truth to be learned from the economy is, once again, the making of social reality by man. In this view, one value of the Marxian emphasis on the economy lies in its reminder that "in the beginning was the act," that in the human world whatever exists should be treated as the result of a forceful, conflict-ridden process of *making*. By contrast with Durkheim's contention that social facts should be treated as *things*, the point of Marx's emphasis lies in the imperative that social facts should be treated as facts—that is, in the root-meaning of the term "fact," as things *made*.

[46] See on this crucial point Vittorio Rieser, "L' 'apparenza' del capitalismo nell'analisi di Marx," *Quaderni di sociologia*, XV (1966), No. 1, pp. 57ff.

5. *The Theory of Modern Society*

In reconstructing Marx's conception of modern society (that is, Western society in the middle and late nineteenth century) I shall emphasize a series of points each of which both complements and supersedes the previous ones. This way of organizing the argument bears some resemblance to the way Marx's own thought on this question developed. For instance, my "first approximation" was worked out by Marx in the first half of the 1840's, and the later approximations are based on developments in his thought from the second part of that decade on. However, in most of Marx's mature writings, and particularly in *Capital*, the insights into the nature of modern society that I have arranged sequentially in fact merge, or are kept distinct at most for the sake of exposition. Thus my arrangement is not a recapitulation of "stages" in Marx's thought but simply a workable outline for my own discussion and a way of emphasizing the distinctiveness and forcefulness of Marx's view of modern society.

First Approximation: Social Relations in the Civil Society

In keeping with the Hegelian tradition, Marx conceptualizes modern society in the first place as a "civil society." The German term, *bürgerliche Gesellschaft*, can also be translated as "bourgeois society." Marx is fully aware of this dual meaning, and to his mind it involves a crucial insight. Modern society is not just one in which the "social" has gained a measure of independence from the "political"; it is also deeply shaped by the interests and activities of the first modern social class, the bourgeoisie (W 76; 93). The bourgeoisie's economic superiority allows it to progressively dominate social affairs at large, to become the *collective maker* of modern social reality.

If one adopts an analysis (and a critique) of social reality that con-

siders all the differentiated spheres of existence and relatively autonomous lines of activity that characterize modern society, one can
detect several general characteristics of modern social relations and
can identify the historically unique ways in which the alienation process realized itself in nineteenth-century Western society. Unavoidably these characteristics overlap, but in Marx's writings the following seem particularly significant and distinctive.

Egoism. This is what Marx had to say of Bruno Bauer's statement
that the units of modern society were "isolated, self-seeking atoms":

> If we are to speak exactly and prosaically, the members of the civil society
> are no atoms. The characteristic property of an atom is the very fact that
> it has no property and therefore no relationship to other beings outside
> itself that results from the necessity of its own nature. The atom has no
> needs, is self-sufficient. The world outside it is an absolute vacuum—empty,
> meaningless, and silent—exactly because the atom contains in itself all
> fullness. The egoistic individual in a civil society may well, in his foolish
> imagination and lifeless abstraction, fancy himself an atom, an absolutely
> full being of a spiritual kind, having no relationship and no need, self-
> sufficient. But nonspiritual physical reality pays no attention to this fancy;
> each of the individual's own senses compels him to believe in the signifi-
> cance of the world and of the individuals outside him, and his profane
> belly reminds him every day that the world outside him is not empty but
> can instead fill him up. Each of his essential activities and properties, each
> of his life impulses, becomes a need, a longing that renders his own self-
> seeking a seeking for other things and men outside him. However, the need
> of one individual has no obvious significance to the other egoistic indi-
> vidual who may have the means to satisfy that need. Thus the latter has
> no immediate connection with that satisfaction; and thus each individual
> must create such a connection, relating somebody else's need to the object
> of his own need. It is thus ... interest that holds together the members of
> the civil society ... who are atoms only in their fantasies, but are in reality
> beings quite different from atoms (F 813-14).

The atomistic imagery, then, may be misleading when taken literally; but this same passage shows that it is not far from the truth
in some senses. Indeed, it is a general methodological principle for
Marx that representations of social reality, however inadequate, always spring from some actual feature or tendency of that reality,
although they may convey it in a distorted fashion (see W 184; 218.
K 637; 589). Furthermore, these representations often have significant

consequences if men choose to act on them. No man is an atom, in that no man lives in a vacuum, indifferent to the reality outside himself. But a man who views himself as an atom, though contradicting that view every time he relates to something or somebody outside himself, will at the same time *verify* that view owing to the peculiar nature of the relations he establishes with the outside. His external relations will tend to disprove that he is an atom because they will be entered under the pressure of needs, and no atom has needs; but precisely because they are oriented to the satisfaction (that is, the negation) of needs, they will at the same time imply, however misleadingly, that he *is* an atom after all.

In Marx's view, the members of a modern society typically behave in a way that we can label "egoistic," a way that both proves and disproves their atomism. They establish ties meant to insure their *independence* from others, but the ties are those of *dependence*. Men are activated by interest, that is, by a personal concern with the configuration of the reality around them, although as atoms they assume that reality to be indifferent to them. Indeed, they *act as if* it were, in that they approach reality—and particularly other beings like themselves—purely as a collection of objective resources without intrinsic significance, with no relevance other than an application to their own needs. But this perception of reality in turn reacts on those who hold it. As atoms, they have no intrinsic significance of their own, no stable property, no hard core of identity; they differ from other bits of objective reality only in the particular configurations of resources they represent.

In this sense, all members of the civil society are essentially like one another: bundles of resources and needs. Each acknowledges another only when that other's resources can satisfy his own need; and vice versa, he is acknowledged by the other only when the reverse is true (F 623; B *181*. See also G 156). To this extent each man possesses the certainy of his *own* unique reality and perceives himself as essentially different from all other bits of reality, nevertheless recognizing that he and those others are essentially equal. He can only preserve his feeling of uniqueness by standing guard on his own resources, looking after his own needs. In this situation, security becomes "the highest social concept of the civil society"; but at the same time, "Security is ... the assurance of one's egoism" (F 474; B 25-26). Rights are acquired by individuals acting as social equals; and yet those rights allow the individual actually enjoying them to keep all others at arm's length, to preserve the sense of apartness and personal worth that alone can support his feeling of selfhood (F 472; B 24).

Abstraction. The foregoing implies that the egoistic members of civil society relate to one another abstractly. Each individual sees his abilities and resources, or for that matter his needs, as essentially abstractable, that is, separable from himself: they lend themselves to manipulation, by himself or other individuals, as disembodied entities. Individuals are expected to exhibit certain qualities in the marketplace and various others in public life, family life, and sociable intercourse. The need for showing a given quality is determined by the nature of a particular situation, which can draw the qualities appropriate to itself out of the individual, abstracting them from his concrete identity, combining them with other qualities, and objectively assessing them. "It is basic to alienation that each sphere [of social life in the civil society] imposes on men a different criterion; morality has one, political economy another. Each is a determinate alienation of man, and each forms around one specific sector of the alienated activity of man and relates in an alienated manner to all other alienations" (F 614; B *173*).

Accidentality. There is an inescapable fluidity in the social life of a civil society. Relations are continually formed and terminated by individuals who feel new needs and act on the opportunities presented by new resources and situations (F 186; B *148*). This motion has a blind, mechanical logic of its own; the individual may try to protect himself from it or exploit it for his own benefit, but he will never recognize it as something of his own making.

Affected by this motion and unable to appropriate or control it, the individual perceives social reality, and his own position within it, as dominated by randomness. As we have seen, the abstracted aspects of reality to which he commits his own egoistic interests at different times are unrelated to one another. The various aspects of his total position within society seem to vary at random with respect to one another, and they offer no support for a feeling of identity or individ-

uality (W 623-24; 482). The firm sense of belonging that characterized the estate system of stratification in older societies has been
dissolved by the advent of the class system.

The distinction of rank is no longer a distinction between autonomous
groups with distinctive needs and activities. . . . Now it produces mobile,
unstable circles in which membership is arbitrary and has money and training as its main criteria. . . . The status group typical of modern society . . .
is a grouping of masses that forms fleetingly; its very formation is arbitrary and does not amount to an organization. [Such a grouping] is not
something shared, a community that encloses the individual . . . but merely
an external determination of the individual. It is not inherent in his activity
and does not relate to him as would a community organized according to
stable laws and affording him social relations (F 361).

For example, in modern society workers enter employment singly,
with an arbitrarily chosen master and without entering at the same
time into relations with other workers (K 376-77; 349). They compete
with both their employers and their co-workers; they operate within
relations that every day throw them back into isolation (W 61; 77).

Freedom and equality. The contrast of modern society with the
estate system is critical. The individual, instead of being part of a
corporate body that simultaneously binds him and sustains him, confronts all other individuals as equals who share with him a situation
of freedom. The individual can direct his actions according to his
own will. The typical relations he forms with others are freely entered; they are bridges that the individual, availing himself exclusively of his own resources as a human being, arbitrarily throws over
an infinite and undifferentiated social space toward a point he freely
chooses to connect with. By contrast, the estate system "separates
man from his general essence, makes him an animal who is immediately coterminous with his own determinateness." The Middle Ages
are the "animal history," the "zoology" of mankind (F 263-64);
Marx also calls them "the democracy of unfreedom" (F 295).

Secularism. The social relations typical of medieval society were
embroidered with a variety of myths, moral assumptions, and values
that made those relations meaningful to the participants but at the
same time obscured what was actually involved in concrete terms. A
thoroughgoing process of disenchantment, carried out by the bourgeoisie, has irreparably destroyed this "political, patriarchal, reli-

gious, and sentimental embroidery" (W 396; 450). The relations typical of modern society have a matter-of-factness and fluidity that preclude any mystification of the old kind.

The bourgeoisie ... has pitilessly torn up the diverse feudal ties that connected a man to his natural betters, and has left between man and man no other tie than naked interest. ... It has drowned the holy awe of religious fervor, of chivalrous enthusiasm, of philistine sentimentality, in the icy water of egoistic calculation. ... It has divested of their holy appearance all activities previously considered honorable and viewed with pious awe. ... All that is holy is profaned, and men are finally compelled to view with sober eyes their life conditions and their relations with one another.[1]

Reification and its subjective manifestations. This process of disenchantment does not mean that man has finally come into his own in modern civil society, that he has reclaimed all his human abilities. The romantic and religious mystification that the bourgeoisie overthrew is only one way in which man can hide the essential truth about himself: his authorship of social reality. That truth is as hidden in modern society as it was in medieval society, although in a vastly different way. As Marx suggested in a trenchant passage from *Capital*: "At the time they stopped burning witches in England, they started hanging banknote forgers" (K 917; 837).

In modern society, man surrenders his authorship of social reality not to a transcendental entity or to a few men endowed by blood with a "natural" superiority, but to social reality itself, to the objects that make up his world. The world having been profaned, man sees himself as surrounded only by things, views himself as a thing, and attributes the fluidity of social reality to a movement inherent in the things themselves. Things are not treated as man's own products and tools; instead, men behave as the products and tools of things. Things move about and combine with other things as if of their own will, although that will may be expressed through the conscious activity of men.

This specific, historically unique configuration of the alienation process, which we may call reification, appears in many social attitudes and patterns of behavior. Clearly, in a world perceived as con-

---

[1] Marx, *Frühschriften*, edited by Siegfried Landshut (Stuttgart: Kröner, 1964), 528-29. This quote is, of course, from the *Communist Manifesto*.

sisting of things the relation between the subject and such things is crucial. Since, as we have posited, things cannot be acknowledged as of the subject's own *making*, the subject can relate to them only by possessing them, accumulating them, or consuming them. In modern man, "all passions, all activity, must end in greed" (W 612-13; B 172).

One can perhaps distinguish two aspects of this relationship. The first, which Marx emphasizes (particularly in his juvenile writings on "the Jewish question"), is referred to as "huckstering" (*Schachern*) (F 481; B 34). Things are perceived as having their own innate laws of motion, which are not a product of man's reason; however, an individual can acknowledge these laws and try to exploit them for his own benefit. He speculates on the immanent motions of things, on their aptitude to satisfy other people's wants, in order to enter with those people into relations advantageous to himself:

Each man speculates on the possibility of creating a *new* need in another, so as to compel him to make new sacrifices, to subject him to a new dependency, to lead him to a new kind of enjoyment and thus of economic ruin. . . . Each product is a bait with which to hook another man's money, which is regarded as his essence; each actual or potential need is a weakness that will lead the flies onto the flypaper. . . . Every necessity is an opportunity to approach one's neighbor with the most amiable look on one's face, and say to him: My dear friend, I give you what you need; but you know the necessary condition; you know with what ink you must commit yourself to me. I cheat you when I procure you an enjoyment (F 608-9; B 168-69).

Marx is less explicit about the other typical aspect of greed, to which he often refers by coupling the terms *Haben* or *Besitzen* (possession) with *Genuss* (enjoyment) (e.g., F 598; B 159).[2] This attitude is complementary to the first (as is shown by the last quote); but here the posture of the subject toward a thing is not manipulative but purely receptive, consummatory, dominated by his needs as he perceives them. The greed of both rich and poor, Marx emphasizes, has a certain quality of abstractness and unauthenticity (F 619-20; B 178). Since the subject does not recognize that the things he needs are of his own making, consuming and/or accumulating them does not convince him that he is reappropriating himself through them, growing

---

[2] See the discussion of "daily cares" in Kosik, *Dialettica del concreto*, pp. 75ff.

subjectively by making them his own. His relation to them is purely dependent.

Another subjective attitude typical of the civil society would seem to contrast with the previous ones, since it finds expression not in a subject/thing relation but in a carefully cultivated relation of the subject to himself, or to other subjects perceived *as such.* In fact, the subject purposefully rejects too close an involvement with things and turns to his own resources, seeks within himself (or within a small circle of friends and family) values and meanings that a trafficking with external objects would preclude. To the social system's tendency to treat man as a pure object, the individual opposes a commitment to lofty intellectual and aesthetic concerns: the "absolute values" of morality, the "eternal truths" of religion, or the disinterested cultivation of an authentic sense of the dignity and tragedy of human existence (W 423; 482).

The contemporary Marxian philosopher Kosik has criticized what he considers the chief expression of this attitude in our time, existentialism. He argues that existentialism, with its yearning for "authenticity," is so individualistic and subjectivistic that it fails to pose an effective challenge to reification:

Man must *realize* authenticity if he is to *live* authentically. The individual alone cannot alter existing conditions and uproot evil. . . . Can one lead an authentic existence in a nonauthentic world? In existential modification, the individual subject awakens to *his own* potentialities and chooses them. Existential modification is not a revolutionary transformation of the world but the *isolated drama of an individual in the world.*[3]

A subjective orientation of this kind not only fails to negate the givens of the situation but at times complements them. Availing himself of the degree of freedom left open by the differentiation of intrinsically uncoordinated spheres of existence, the individual simply repairs in one sphere (e.g., in his family life) the damages inflicted on him by the strains present in other spheres. The same man who coldly exploits another's needs in the marketplace can cultivate intimacy and exercise altruism with his relations and friends; and because of this he can go back to his "huckstering" with restored self-confidence and self-respect.

[3] Kosik, *Dialettica del concreto,* p. 97.

Second Approximation: The Market Economy as the
Anatomy of the Civil Society

In following this reconstruction of Marx's analysis of the civil society, the reader has probably been bothered by a persistent feeling of *déjà vu*. Indeed, the foregoing bears a close resemblance to many other sociological accounts of modern society. Had I systematically brought into the argument the many learned references to pre-modern society that Marx introduces by way of contrast, the resemblance in particular to Tocqueville's comparison of aristocratic and democratic society would be even more apparent.

But there are differences. I have pointed out those characteristics of modern social relations that in Marx's view *cut across the distinction between the various spheres of social activity*. However, since Marx postulates and endeavors to establish a hierarchy of significance among those spheres, this account can only be a first approximation of his analysis. Such "cross-cutting characteristics," to Marx, imply that modern society is a totality; and this totality, in turn, is grounded on the prior significance of *one* sphere of activity, the economy. The determinate way in which economic activity is carried out in modern society affects all other analytically relevant aspects of that society: "The anatomy of the civil society is to be sought in political economy" (S/I 362).

To my mind, no exactly comparable argument can be found in Tocqueville. As we have seen, Tocqueville also identifies some organizing principles whose significance affects all of democratic society. But he stops at these principles—or rather, he elaborates their consequences more purposefully than he does their causes. When he does seek for causes, he produces such notions as the "passion" or "irresistible inclination" of democratic peoples for equality and well-being. That is, his explanation is largely a process of abstracting from a variety of *explananda* a smaller number of more general and abstract characteristics, comprehensive of the former and made up essentially of representations (beliefs, values), which are then treated as the *explanans*.

No such procedure will satisfy Marx, for it is tainted with idealism, with the vice of "treating shadows as solid things." One cannot account for the characteristics of a society by postulating ideal principles that somehow float over history and then "embody themselves"; one must look for the determinate ways in which actual men, constrained in their action by the results of the past (which do include representations), have gone about meeting the problems of their existence. To Marx's mind, there is an order of priority among these problems, and among the spheres of activity directly connected with them. As we have seen, the exact nature of that priority is a difficult and controversial issue.[4] But there is no doubt about the Marxian approach to explaining the typical relations of modern society: "Go to the economy."

What is to be learnt by going to the economy is best discussed in two distinct approximations: the one developed in this section corresponds roughly to the argument in the first four chapters of *Capital*; the other, which will be developed as our fourth approximation, applies mainly to the rest of Volume I of *Capital*.

I have suggested, when speaking of reification, that the members of civil society, though deeply involved with things, have completely forgotten their authorship of those same things, which seem endowed with a will of their own. The opening sentence of *Capital* reveals that the surrender of the authorship of social reality by the members of the civil society is not just an aberration or a widely shared misapprehension of the facts; the objective nature of wealth in modern society accounts for much of man's surrender to things. "The wealth of societies in which the capitalistic mode of production is dominant appears as an 'immense collection of commodities,' and the single commodity is the *elementary* form of that wealth" (K 3; 3).

Now, commodities are indeed products of labor and thus "authored" by man; but in the modern economy they behave as if their condition as the material receptacle of value were a property wholly their own (K 23; 22). This happens because their value appears not as a constant but as something capable of expansion (K 63; 59-60). As if forgetting his earlier rejection of an atomistic view of civil society (but we have seen that he was in fact ambivalent about that

---

[4] My own discussion implicitly points up this difficulty. In Chapter 4 I opposed a deterministic interpretation of the relationship between the economy and other spheres of social existence; however, the argument in the following pages probably has some deterministic undertones.

view), Marx speaks in *Capital* of the "merely atomistic behavior" of actors as resulting from the configuration of their economic relations, a configuration "independent of [their] control and of their conscious individual operations—that is, reified" (K 74; 69). The social relations built around commodities are viewed as relations between things and not between people because in a sense they *are* so in fact.

This circumstance (which obviously clarifies many of my earlier remarks about civil society) stems from the specific nature of commodities. Marx analyzes that nature in the first place within the context of *circulation* of wealth, since a commodity is in fact something produced for others with a view to exchange (K 10; 9-10). From the producer's viewpoint, the commodity is significant not because of its ability to satisfy wants but because in return for it he will get someone else's product (K 51; 48). This will happen whenever the commodity appears not as possessor of intrinsically useful qualities but rather as the embodiment of productive labor; it will happen, in fact, *to the extent that* the labor embodied in the commodity approximates the quantity of labor "socially necessary" for producing that kind of commodity at that given time (K 8; 7). Thus each producer necessarily depends on other producers (in the extreme case on *all* other producers). The satisfaction of his own wants depends on his ability to satisfy their wants (in most cases indirectly), and that ability is measured against the average labor expended to produce a given commodity. Each producer tends to specialize in producing a single commodity, and thus comes to depend on others for practically all the commodities he needs.

For all these reasons, a developed commodity economy is, more obviously than any other economic system, a *social* economy: its processes involve a multitude of criss-crossing relations of mutual dependence between all individuals. At the same time, the basic units of the process—the commodities, each with its own "guardian"— are discrete entities, each bent on improving its own terms of exchange with all others, each helping (but in an uncoordinated, random manner) to determine the overall structure of the network of relations. Ultimately, all commodities, and through them all their "guardians," affect one another, but they do so each on its own behalf. All commodities presuppose a single, homogeneous constituent:

human labor, or more precisely, "socially necessary" abstract labor power. And yet each commodity confronts the others as standing for a separate, intrinsically competitive self-interest.

The parallels between this aspect of the capitalistic economic process and the "nonatomistic atomism" (or "egoism") of civil society are apparent. As we have seen, in a capitalistic economy the producers produce for one another through exchange. But exchange, as opposed to the surrender of one's product to others within the context of a relationship of personal subordination, presupposes that producers are legally independent of one another, that they come to terms freely and as equals, through contractual relations. At the same time, there is a compulsion behind the multiple acts through which such relations are entered and dissolved; not a moral or political compulsion, but rather the compulsion of a generalized search for advantage, the compulsion for each individual to realize to the utmost the value objectively embodied in the commodity of which he is the "guardian": "To the producers ... therefore, the social relations connecting their respective labors appear as what they are, that is, not as immediately social relations of the individuals at work but rather as thing-like relations between people and social relations between things" (K 49; 46).

If we explore the institutional requirements of this type of economic system, we may throw further light on the characteristics of civil society. The contradiction between the social nature of the economic process as a whole and the private nature of its constituent units makes two things indispensable: first, an institutionalized, relatively stable arena where commodities can test themselves against one another and verify, as it were, the homogeneous nature of their ultimate constituent, human labor; second, an institutionalized and stable medium through which the transactions between units can be carried out. The arena in which commodities are thrown together is the market, and the medium through which they affect one another is money. In turn, the nature of market relations and the nature of money offer the best clues to a number of points made in my first approximation.

Market relations. The competitiveness of the market lies behind the fluidity and accidentality of social relations in civil society. The product acquires its objective social value, its most important characteristic for the producer (K 49; 46), only on the market, where a multitude of determinants outside the producer's control fix that value (G 433, 564). So far as the producer is concerned, the process is arbitrary, motivated by no concern for his own destiny or for the limitations of his understanding (K 89-90; 84-85). In the capitalist system (by definition, as we have seen) commodity production becomes dominant; hence the market grows to include more and more relations, gradually becoming coextensive with the whole of society.[5] Most particularly, the market encompasses labor, treating it as just another commodity subject to the multiple, unstable, unpredictable market relations that link *all* commodities (K 163-65; 153-54). Through labor power, the crucial facility of man's distinctively human actions, the human subject himself is "marketized," the significance of his very self is blurred.

Other insights into the marketization of civil society can be obtained by examining the conditions that must be present if labor is indeed to be treated as a commodity. Marx states several requirements: (1) Labor power must be placed on the market by the laborer acting as its owner. (2) Given the fact that labor power inheres directly in the laborer's person, the laborer must be the owner of his own person. (3) He must meet the buyer of labor power as a legal equal. (4) He must sell his labor power for a definite time. (5) He must be unable to sell other commodities, be without everything that is required for the realization of his labor power; that is, he must be dispossessed of the means of production (K 154-56; 145-47).

The historical processes leading to the realization of these conditions coincide, in Marx's view, with the progressive dissolution of the older society:

the dissolution of the servile relation that binds the laborer to the soil and to the lord of the soil . . . the dissolution of the property relations that make him a yeoman, a free, working petty landowner, a tenant (*colonus*), or a free peasant . . . the dissolution of the client relationship in its different forms, in which *non-owners* appear in the retinue of the lord as co-consumers of the surplus produce and in return wear his livery, take part in his feuds, offer real or imaginary personal services, etc. (G 402-3; 104-5).

---

[5] On this process, see Polanyi, *The great transformation.*

What Marx is here describing is the dissolution of the "other side" (indeed, the *under*side) of the aristocratic society discussed by Tocqueville. Marx looks not at the high and mighty but at the direct producers, at the populace. Tocqueville, as I have argued, to the extent that he attempted to explain rather than describe the passing of aristocratic society, spoke mainly of the emergence and triumph of new "passions" and "principles," aided and abetted by the centralizing drive of the monarchs. Marx was aware of the contribution made to the process by monarchical absolutism, and of the role played in it by forcible, political acts (S/I *248, 332-33, 338.* Also K *895;* 912; *817, 833*). But he establishes the *causes* of the transition as economic, and locates them in the greater productivity of economic relations established on the market (e.g., K *924-25; 844-45*). Once freed from the constrictions of particularistic relations of subordination (and from the legal and technical restrictions of the guilds), human labor power, operating in the market economy, realizes its potential, drives out products other than commodities, and destroys the texture of premodern society.

Money. The money medium impinges on modern social relations in ways that Marx began to locate early in his writings (F *631*ff; B *189ff*). The abstractness and randomness of most social relations in the civil society are directly connected with the inherent properties of money. Money itself is abstract and impersonal: it vests in its owner powers wholly unrelated to his own "individuality"; it evokes a limitless greed, it operates as the universal "divider and unifier," and it deprives all objects of intrinsic significance and worth (see F *608-9*; B *168-69*).

Marx's later writings particularly investigate the role of money as the primary manifestation of capital. Money is seen as a specific commodity that society has made into the universal equivalent, the general medium through which all other commodities enter relations with one another (K *193*ff; *181ff*). It is both the point of departure and the point of arrival for the prototypical exchange sequence of the capitalist economy, "money-commodity-money." In this sequence, there is typically *more* money at the point of arrival than at the point of departure; thus money uniquely reflects the process of value expansion characteristic of the commodity economy as a whole (K *200*;

189). Naturally, under these conditions, "The end of each exchange act . . . comes to represent the beginning of a new one. . . . If one sells for the sake of buying, there is a final goal external to the circulation process, the satisfaction of needs. But here the circulation of money as capital becomes its own final goal, since value expansion only takes place by the process beginning over anew. Thus the movement of capital is inherently endless" (K 146; *137*). This fluidity extends to the social relations in a civil society, transforming the individual into "a being perpetually in a state of tension" (F 586; B *148*. See also G 311-12, *415*).

To summarize, the determinate conditions under which men produce and distribute wealth in modern society (although we have so far analyzed this process only in the sphere of commodity circulation) bias all aspects of human existence. The atomism of men's conduct, the abstractness and instability of their relations, the randomness of the ways they affect one another—all these characteristics reflect the historical uniqueness of a situation in which wealth is created and distributed as if by and for the sake of objects. The assumption is that objects in themselves are productive once they are brought together on the market and related through the money medium (G 240).

Kosik has brilliantly conceptualized this Marxian position as a rejection of the view that *homo economicus* in bourgeois thought is no more than a useful heuristic construct:

Homo economicus is man as part of the [capitalist] system, as a working component of the system; and as such he must possess the fundamental characteristics required for the system's functioning. . . . If *homo economicus* is an abstraction . . . his abstractness is determined by the system, and only outside the latter does he become an empty abstraction. The system [the economy as a system] and *homo economicus* are two inseparable entities. . . . It is not theory that reduces man to abstraction, but reality itself. The economy is a system and a pattern of relations within which man is continuously transformed into *homo economicus*. . . . It draws him into an objective mechanism that subsumes him and shapes him into its own semblance. . . . The economy makes of man a determinate abstraction: it absolutizes, exaggerates, and emphasizes some determinate qualities of man, whereas it deemphasizes others because they are casual and pointless within in the economic system. . . . As an element of the system *homo economicus* is [not a fiction but] a reality.[6]

---

[6] Kosik, *Dialettica del concreto*, pp. 101-4.

Of the many Marxian texts one could quote to substantiate this interpretation of Marx's thought (as most concisely expressed in W 393-95; 448-51), I shall use one that comes at the end of *Capital*, I, Chapter 4. Here Marx both states the position that I have adopted as a "second approximation" and prepares a formidable critique of it, thus leading up to the following two approximations.

The sphere of the circulation or exchange of commodities, within which the buying and selling of labor power occurs, is in fact a true Garden of Eden of the innate rights of man. The uncontested rulers here are Freedom, Equality, Property, and Bentham. Freedom! Indeed, the buyer and seller of a commodity, e.g. of labor power, are determined only by their own free will. They enter a contract as two individuals who are free and juridically possess the same worth. The contract is the result, whereby their wills find a common legal expression. Equality! Indeed, they relate to one another exclusively as commodity owners and exchange equivalent against equivalent. Property! Indeed, each disposes only of what is his own. Bentham! Indeed, each of them is solely concerned with himself. The only force that brings them together into a relation is their own utility, their own individual advantage, their own private interest (K 176; *164*).

"Going to the economy," then, has revealed the basis for the specific institutional principles that govern the civil society. Or has it?

Third Approximation: The Problem of Social Order

To approach the wholly different conceptualization of social and economic relations that Marx is about to undertake at this point in *Capital* (mainly on economic grounds), we must raise questions to which he pays little *explicit* attention: Can the civil society persist *as a society?* Can principles ultimately originating from the market interrelations of commodity owners (or those of the commodities themselves) effectively regulate, make peaceable and predictable the social intercourse of individuals? Can any solidarity, any sense of belonging together, any binding limitation on the ways in which individuals relate to one another, be maintained through the sole medium of money and market transactions, with no constraints on means and ends of action other than those flowing from the calculation of private advantage?

The same early texts that I have used as my main sources for the first approximation clearly suggest that Marx recognized the problem of social order in these terms, whatever his reasons for not emphasizing it. In particular, the view of society as a Hobbesian "war of all against all" presents itself repeatedly (e.g., F *463*; B *15*). In the civil society, Marx writes, individuals are sets of needs, and they are perceived by each other only to the extent that they become useful to each other (F *623*; B *181*). "If you want to be *ökonomisch* you must spare yourself any concern with the common interest, any compassion and trust" (F *613*; B *172*). *Marx's* later conceptualization of the capitalist economy emphasizes the contradiction between the sociality of the labor process and the private nature of the actors in that process;[7] and it also emphasizes the "anarchy of production." These ideas point to a conclusion that Shlomo Avineri has recently stated, unequivocally raising the problem of order: "[In Marx's view] the only possible contacts between individuals behaving according to [the *homo economicus* model] are antagonistic. No human action aimed at solidarity can ultimately be immanently derived from it. Even if relations deriving from this model will not be explicitly antagonistic, man will still regard other men as means."[8]

Such a view lends itself to two different arguments. One may argue that modern society, being in a condition of actual anarchy, will soon end as a society; that what the observer is watching are merely its death throes. Or one may argue that there must be some hidden force acting to place nonutilitarian and nonegoistic restraints on interindividual behavior, thus keeping a potential state of anarchy from becoming actual and tearing society apart. The second approach is the beginning of all sociological wisdom. Tocqueville had already articulated it in criticizing the many reactionary-apocalyptic interpretations of the French Revolution.[9] And Durkheim, as we shall see, was to make it the main theme of his polemic against individualistic social philosophies. In this approach one must logically ask what the hidden binding force is. What keeps modern society from actually degenerating into the war of all against all? As we shall see, Marx's treatment of this problem is distinctive and forceful. Before developing it as my fourth approximation I will look briefly at other important sociological answers to the same problem and attempt to reconstruct the way Marx might have criticized them.

[7] This conceptualization, greatly expanded in *Capital*, was already foreshadowed in F *630*; B *187*.
[8] Avineri, *Thought of Karl Marx*, pp. 17-18.
[9] Tocqueville: A *17-18*.

Again, we can start with Tocqueville, who, like Marx, poses the problem of order with explicit reference not to any society but exclusively to modern society—in his own terms, to democratic society. Tocqueville's two models of despotic and republican democracy embody the two main sociological solutions (other than Marx's own) to the problem of order. Both solutions conceptualize modern society as "civil society," and proceed from this conceptualization to locate order-sustaining processes either (as it were) *above* or *below* that society. Tocqueville's despotic democracy, the first solution, can be considered a pessimistic elaboration of Hobbes's solution to the problem of order. Here the centrifugal, anarchical tendencies inherent in the civil society are countered from above, by the concentration of enormous, unchallengeable power in a central government that ensures order by imposing on all citizens a uniform, oppressive subjection.

Raymond Aron, with implicit reference to the problem of order, has stated as follows the second alternative, that embodied in Tocqueville's model of republican democracy: "In an equalitarian society that would be self-governing, a moral discipline [must be] established, as it were, in the individual conscience. The citizens must be subject, within themselves, to a discipline which is not imposed merely by fear of punishment."[10] Here the problem of order is solved ultimately by forces (moral attachments, shared cognitive presuppositions) operating "below" the civil society, binding the interactions characteristic of that society to a set of hidden ideals.

Marx's critique of the modern state, although it does not explicitly refer to the problem of order, seems to me to contain a persuasive rejection of the first answer. However, Marx does not deal directly with the Leviathan as imagined and feared by Tocqueville, but mainly with an idea that for our present purposes can be considered an optimistic variant of the Hobbesian solution: the Hegelian theory of the state. Hegel sees the state as the great "mediator" of the contrasts inherent in civil society. The society itself he envisages as a realm in which isolated individuals, driven by their needfulness, enter fleeting, acquisitive, and competitive relationships. Above this stands the state, a sovereign realm where public activity is carried out and political existence is enacted. In their capacity as citizens the members of the

10 Aron, *Main currents in sociological thought* (New York: Basic Books, 1965), I, 200.

civil society become variously active in that realm. And as they abide by its rules, acknowledging to this extent the sovereignty of the public interest, citizens transcend their own individual needs; instead, they exhibit a shared interest in the greatness of the state, in the achievement of a superior design of justice that is able to moderate the conflicts characteristic of civil society.

Marx devoted a great deal of critical attention to this view of the state, and I will here outline at least the main results of his critique.[11] In doing so, one must first dispose of a widely shared view that Aron has expressed thus: "Tocqueville's historical diagnosis [of modern society] differs from that of . . . Marx. Instead of giving priority to . . . capitalist society, as Marx did, he gave priority to the democratic reality."[12] In this bare, unqualified formulation, such a view of the Tocqueville-Marx contrast is nonsense, since it ignores Marx's strong awareness of the *political* dimensions of modern social reality.

Essentially, the conceptualization of modern society as capitalistic and that of modern society as democratic are not at the same level. Marx, so to speak, works *within* the latter conceptualization, which he discusses repeatedly and effectively, implicitly assuming its relevance even when he does not discuss it.[13] That is, he assumes that the society he analyzes is democratic in a sense close to that most often adopted by Tocqueville: it entails the separation of the public and the private sphere, the citizenship principle, the withdrawal of juridical recognition and political significance from status differentials, the development of differentiated organs for the conduct of public affairs, the "reduction of the law to the enacted law," and so on.[14] Marx is not trying to override one descriptive characterization of modern society with another, but rather to develop an explanatory analysis; and in doing so he characterizes modern society as capitalistic.

Some aspects of Marx's critique of the Hegelian state echo Tocqueville's rejection of the view that purely constitutional arrangements

---

[11] The most important sources are probably Marx's manuscript notes and commentaries on Hegel's philosophy of law, some of which are now available in E *passim.* For a good secondary treatment see Avineri, *Thought of Karl Marx,* Chapter 1.

[12] Aron, *Main Currents,* I, 183.

[13] This is shown, among other things, by Marx's stress on the significance of the French Revolution. See Avineri, *Thought of Karl Marx,* Chapter 7.

[14] These and other characterizations were advanced for the first time in Marx's writings on Hegel (F *passim*).

can maintain freedom and order in democratic society. The two men agree, in particular, in doubting the common man's ability to actually divest himself of his particularity and egoistic interests when he enters the public sphere to carry out an occasional public act. Marx remarks that the Hegelian conception of political participation is an "ecstatic" one: it presupposes the citizen's willingness and ability to step out of his worldly concerns, to soar above himself into the heavenly realm of the state (F 405; E *192*). This criticism strikes me as clearly compatible with those advanced by Tocqueville. More generally, although Tocqueville appears much more willing to recognize the autonomy of the political sphere, his appeal to normative controls as the ultimate binding force in republican democracy seems to me to qualify that recognition so heavily that his overall position may not differ widely from Marx's allegedly reductionistic view of politics as an "epiphenomenon of the class struggle."

But let us look more closely at Marx's critique of the state's alleged role as the mediator of contrasts in the civil society. This critique (and, for that matter, Marx's view of modern political phenomena in general[15]) is rather more discriminating and sophisticated than his notorious characterization of the state as the executive committee of the bourgeoisie. The general burden of the critique is, of course, that the state cannot effectively mediate the civil society's contrasts; but Marx develops this point through a variety of related arguments:

1. The state's mediating activity is marginal and relatively inconsequential. A legislature where serious public debates take place between informed, well-meaning lawmakers may indeed enact legislation that curbs the exploitation of labor, for instance by shortening the length of the working day (K 336; *311*); and a dedicated body of public servants may gather the information required for such legislation, as well as supervising its actual enforcement.[16] But the total significance of such political operations is necessarily small: the bourgeoisie will not allow any serious encroachment on its prerogatives and will rapidly adjust its strategy to whatever political action has been taken.

---

[15] See Avineri, *Thought of Karl Marx*, Chapters 7-8.
[16] The intensive use Marx himself made of official documentation on work conditions in Britain, especially in *Capital*, show his high regard for this aspect of the activities of government.

2. The state's purported mediation is essentially illusory. The public sphere is not really a realm where individuals cease to be abstract commodity owners, as they are in the market economy, and begin to interact *effectively* as free and equal agents. What appears on the political scene is merely another abstraction from the real individual, in this case the "citizen." The two abstractions are equally alienating, and the two alienations complement one another. The political, "heavenly" abstraction presupposes the economic, "terrestrial" abstraction; it cannot effectively negate the latter, or abolish the factual conditions of inequality and constraint that the civil society imposes on the great majority of people.

The political state relates to the civil society in the same spiritual manner as heaven to earth. It stands in the same contrast to that society, transcends it in the same way that religion contrasts with and transcends the finitude of the profane world (F 461; B 13). The limit of political emancipation lies in the fact that the state can be a free state, without man becoming a free man. . . . The state, after its own fashion, abolishes the differences of birth, rank, education, and occupation by denying political significance to those differences . . . by treating all the components of the people's concrete life situation purely from its own standpoint as a state. Nonetheless, the state allows private property, education, and occupation to develop their own effects, after their fashion, and to express their own particularity (F 458, 460; B 10-11, 12).

3. The state is not just an ineffectual umpire that cannot regulate the contrasts of the civil society in a truly impartial manner, actually on behalf of the common interest. Its purported mediating activity may in fact turn out to be a barely disguised partisanship. Through the action of the state, individual men or groups more powerful than their fellows can bypass the competition of civil society, can advance their power at the expense of weaker parties and under cover of pursuing the common interest. "The state is no longer anything but the organizational form that the bourgeoisie gives itself as a guarantee of its own property and interests—a guarantee both against the non-bourgeois and for one bourgeois as against another. . . . Although politics ideally stands above the power of money, it has in fact become money's bondsman" (W 62; 78. F 483; B 36). This is, of course, the most commonly acknowledged Marxian view of the state and of political action. Much less noted are the last two arguments.

4. No effective mediation can be exercised by the state because the organs through which the state must operate are themselves a distinctive *part* of society; and as such they cannot effectively act on behalf of the whole society, as they claim to do. This restriction applies in particular to the bureaucracy, which constitutes the only "estate" (in the traditional sense of a corporate, privileged group) of modern society. The bureaucrat, himself a private person like all members of the civil society, is immediately endowed with public powers, which he constantly uses and abuses to advance himself and his estate (F 313ff; E *182ff*).[17]

5. Finally, Marx advances an elaboration of this last point. The main text in question is somewhat obscure, but may suggest an interpretation that Tocqueville developed independently. " 'Police,' 'courts,' and 'administration' are not deputies through which the civil society administers its own general interest; rather, they are deputies of the state and act for the state against the civil society" (F 320; E *189*). Note that this statement implies an evaluation of the civil society wholly different from the one expressed so far. The civil society is here treated as possessing shared interests, as involved in a unified struggle against the state. This notion of a state that "makes war on society" is an intriguing one, and finds some echo in other Marxian writings (e.g., S/I *269, 284, 332-33*). But Marx does not elaborate it, and perhaps could not have seriously entertained it.

For all these reasons, Marx rejects the Hegelian conception of the state as mediator of the civil society, and thus implicitly rejects what I have indicated as the first main solution to the problem of social order. The second solution depends on beliefs and values shared across the society, which counteract and temper the disruptive effects of individual commitments to self-advantage. Marx's attitude toward this solution is, again, a complex one, although it lends itself easily to oversimplification. In the following early text, he states the basic materialistic position on the general significance of ideational elements in society, referring not so much to the specific problem of order as to the general historical effectiveness of those elements.

---

[17] For some useful comments on the significance of these Marxian explorations of "the bureaucratic phenomenon" see: Avineri, *Thought of Karl Marx*, pp. 48ff; Lefèbvre, *Sociologie de Marx*, pp. 119ff.

Men are indeed the producers of representations, ideals, etc.—that is, real, effective men, conditioned as they are by the determinate development of their productive forces and of the social intercourse associated with that development. . . . Quite to the contrary of what is practiced in German philosophy, which descends from heaven to earth, we must ascend from earth to heaven. That is, we do not start from what men say, imagine, and represent to themselves . . . in order to arrive at the living man. We start off from operating, active men, and, taking their actual life processes as the point of departure, we also treat the development of the ideological reflexes and echoes of that process. . . . Morals, religion, metaphysics, and the rest of ideology, with the corresponding forms of consciousness, do not preserve, to our eyes, the appearance of autonomy. They possess no history, no development of their own; it is men, in the process of developing their material production and their material intercourse, who also modify . . . their own thought and the products of that thought. It is not consciousness that determines life, but life that determines consciousness (W 26; 37-38).

The deterministic overtones in this statement might at first suggest a crudely "debunking" approach to ideational elements, a view that denies ideas any real significance. But this interpretation is untenable. As I have suggested previously, the notion that ideological forms must "correspond" to material relations does *not* imply that these ideological forms are of no consequence. Otherwise, why would they be produced in the first place, and why produced "correspondingly"? There must be a distinctive benefit from the production of ideology, or else no time or resources would be wasted on it. And in spite of Marx's commitment to "debunking" norms and other ideational elements, he indicates at least two kinds of payoff they can be expected to produce:

1. Normative elements may *directly* perform a manipulative function for a group by upholding its superiority over another group and stressing the latter's duty of submission. For example: "In the course of capitalist production there develops a working class that owing to education, tradition, and habit regards the requirements of that mode of production as self-explanatory natural laws" (K 895; 817).

2. Normative elements may *indirectly* perform a manipulative function by diverting the attention of one group from certain concerns that would lead it into conflict with another group. This is

probably the key contention of the famous characterization of religion as "the opiate of the people," and of the following less known and less general statement: "The mortgage that the peasant has on heavenly possession guarantees the mortgage that the bourgeoisie has on the peasant's possessions" (S/I *187*).

But a manipulative significance, however argued, is not the only property of normative and ideational elements. In the first place, one should not infer that these elements are consciously fashioned and spread through society with an eye to the above payoffs. The correspondence of norms with determinate relations may be purely objective and may remain unperceived, particularly by individuals. Moreover, ideas such as the constitutional programs of liberalism, which fundamentally express the interests of the bourgeoisie, may be taken so seriously and evoke such an intense commitment that they sometimes motivate *dis*interested action by the bourgeoisie itself (e.g., W *174; 209-10.* K *355; 329-30*).

Quite apart from their significance as supporters or controls of group interest, normative elements perform functions not just for one group but also for the total society in which groups interact. Marx acknowledges, for instance, that only through shared definitions of the situation are the levels of aspiration of the members of a society set (S/I 94) or given commodities selected as money (K 66; 61). The institutionalization of a commodity economy presupposes that "the concept of human equality has acquired the fixity of a popular prejudice" (K 33; 31); and there is a special affinity between this kind of economic system and Christianity, "with its cult of the abstract human being" (K 56; 53). Marx implies, as I have suggested above, that social relations are perceptual, and therefore, in a sense, exist in the consciousness of the individuals who are bound by them (although he also insists that relations are not primarily facts of consciousness, but rather parts of objective reality as encountered by the individual's consciousness). Finally, Marx holds quite clearly that there is an inescapable "consciousness component" in the emergence and the development of alienation, and that a similar but opposite component is needed if alienation is to be overcome (see F 561; B 122. K 47-48, 573; 45, 526-27).

Despite these indications that Marx recognized the "integrative functions of ideology," the "cohering effect of commonly held values and ideas,"[18] it seems to me that on the whole he rejected the idea of explaining the maintenance of order in civil society by reference to normative elements (to the extent that he discussed this idea even by implication). There are three main reasons why he could not accept such a view:

1. It is patently inapplicable to modern society, whose most distinctive and universal values reflect, in Marx's judgment, a specifically antisocial orientation. The normative elements characterizing modern society, if anything, engender the problem of order and cannot be expected to solve it.

2. Normativistic interpretations of the social order most often view normative elements not just as supports of the existing order, but as the causal factors that produced it and shaped it from its inception. Marx denies any such primacy to representational elements in general, and thus to normative ones (G 82). Indeed, this denial is essential to his lifelong materialistic polemic against the idealistic heritage, to his critique of those who would equate reality with ideas (W 63; 79) and the movement of reality with the movement of ideas rather than with the struggle of human groups (armed also with ideas) against nature and one another.

To better deal with the problem of order, this Marxian position could be phrased as follows. The normative elements, like all of social reality, are man-made. Their determinate configuration indeed affects the total situation within which they are evolved, and they do help maintain it. But for exactly this reason the determinate configuration of normative elements cannot be left to chance: it originates from the existence of power relationships that allow one group, as against all others, to shape the *dominant* normative elements. Whatever integrative or other effects can be rightfully attributed to the normative elements (and these effects are certainly considerable), the form and continued operation of these elements must ultimately

---

[18] For discussion of a modern opinion on these functions, see Anthony Giddens, "Power in the recent writings of Talcott Parsons," *Sociology*, II (1968), No. 4, p. 269.

depend on asymmetric relations of power that are independent of norms.[19]

3. A third Marxian argument against the normativistic solution to the problem of order is crucial for the transition to our next approximation, and it also involves a criticism of the Hobbesian-Hegelian solution. This argument can be summarized as follows:

The normativistic solution is wrong not because of its inherent flaws but because it solves a misperceived problem. The civil society model is at bottom a partial, superficial, and inadequate conceptualization of modern society; it catches only appearance and ignores hidden nature. The imagery of egoistic individuals, each a commodity producer/owner/seller, entering with one another into free, equal, fleeting, and calculative market relations and thereby generating an inherently unstable social context, is inherently deceptive. The problem of order as normally posed in the sociological tradition —i.e., the problem of locating the more or less hidden sources of stability of *that* context, assuming *those* relations—is thus a pseudo-problem, or at any rate an ill-posed problem. It takes for granted what should be challenged: that the basic social relations of modern society do take place among free, equal, and egoistic "guardians of commodities."

One may concede, in the abstract, that *if* the civil society were an adequate conceptualization of modern society, then order within it would have to be guaranteed "from below" by shared normative elements, or "from above" by a state as conceived by Hobbes and Hegel. But surely one must first determine whether there is not something more to modern society than the features and problems outlined in my first two approximations.

The problem of order as generally posed and discussed assumes the *truth* of those two approximations; but the solution to the problem may well lie in pointing out their *untruth*. The solutions outlined so far both complement (again from above or from below) the civil society taken as a given; both are "taken in" by the notion of

---

[19] This general argument has been extensively articulated, as a critique of Parsons, in Johann Bergmann, *Die Theorie des sozialen Systems von Talcott Parsons* (Frankfurt am Main: Europäische, 1967).

the civil society. For his part, Marx (notably in the chapters of *Capital* after the fourth) criticizes those solutions not so much by challenging the *explanans* of each as by challenging the *explanandum* of both.

What is ultimately in question is the nature of the units to be ordered. From Hobbes on, these units are taken to be individuals; and order is a problem because of the inherent tendency for social intercourse to degenerate into a war of all against all. This view is inherently equalitarian. Just as Descartes (in *Discours de la méthode*) addresses himself to ratiocinating units endowed with roughly the same capacities for forming clear and distinct ideas, so Hobbes contemplates warring units with roughly the same ability to exercise fraud and coercion. As Hobbes poses it, the problem of order arises from the fact that no one of the units to be ordered is much stronger than any other. Such a condition, given Hobbes's assumptions about man's lust for power and wealth, would indeed engender a war of all against all—a random conflict going on all the time and everywhere, presupposing or bringing about no stable alignments and no pooling of resources. No unit could ever overpower the others and impose even a temporary order.

However, even if we assume that no Hobbesian individual unit is significantly stronger than another, no such equalitarian assumption is warranted once the problem is reformulated as the ordering of relations between *collective* units. In this case, the ordering can rest directly (or at any rate ultimately) on imbalances obtaining among the units' respective resources for ratiocination, coercion, fraud, or what have you; and no sources of order need be construed either below or above the field of interaction generated by the units themselves and their relations. No fiction of a *pactum societatis et subjectionis* need be advanced; no mysterious, self-originating moral entities need be postulated, except where they perform ancillary, intervening functions. In this scheme of things, normative ideas become instrumentalities, embellishments, or "lubricants" of the real ordering process.

Furthermore, among collective units to be ordered conflict need not (perhaps cannot) be conceptualized as it is by Hobbes, that is as a random, ceaselessly repetitive, utterly pervasive affair occurring all over an unstructured, undifferentiated, infinite social space. The conflict between collective units can fashion, and be affected by, distinctive social contexts. Each event in this struggle builds upon (and negates) the results of previous conflict. The very idea of collective bodies presupposes alignments; and any shift in these alignments changes the nature of the contending parties and thus the nature of the conflicts themselves. In the same way, the object of contention can significantly change over time. This, too, affects the very nature of conflict, since certain resources become irrelevant and others crucial. Above all, conflict between groups can, and normally will, impose a social order. It stabilizes interaction and makes it predictable. The results of group conflict are allocated in systematically biased ways, structuring the expectations and opportunities for action of different groups and assigning each group to a distinctive location in a differentiated, structured social space.

This solution to the problem of order, when applied by Marx to modern society, becomes our fourth approximation to the nature of that society. But first, let me present a passage that contains the clue to the whole argument. It comes immediately after the passage on "freedom, equality, property, and Bentham" already quoted, and ends Chapter 4 of *Capital*:

As we move from this sphere of simple circulation or exchange of commodities, which provides the common variety of free trader with the images, concepts, and criteria needed for his evaluation of a society composed of capital and wage labor, we seem to note a change in the characters of our drama. The man who started as the owner of money strides forward as a capitalist. The owner of labor power now follows him as his laborer; the one is full of importance, complacent, and enthusiastic about his business; the other defeated-looking and reluctant, like one who has taken his own skin to the market and can expect to gain nothing but a tanning" (K 176; 164-65).

Fourth Approximation: Surplus Value and the Class Society

Since the approximation just presented is essentially a transition, let us be clear about the relation between this fourth approximation and the first two I outlined. The view of the civil society and its "anatomy" offered in those approximations is not to be discarded as untrue or considered a delusion that Marx has foisted on his readers. Indeed,

this last model both confirms and disproves the earlier ones. It *is* true
that the owner of money and the owner of labor relate to one another as commodity owners, and as such their relation is in fact an
embodiment of "freedom, equality, property, and Bentham." The
model of "civil society" is a *true* representation of modern social
relations, and theories of political economy accurately describe the
structure of those relations. Finally, *homo economicus* sums up the
actual requirements of an individual's functioning within civil society.

But from our present viewpoint, all these truths relate to a situation that is itself deceptive, a system that maintains itself by continuously positing untruths as the truth about itself. Modern society, in
other words, is thoroughly alienated, and is unable to recognize the
truth about itself; but this very inability is an intrinsic aspect of the
way in which modern society actually works (G 716).

It may be ultimately untrue that commodities are the center of the
modern economic process; for that process, like all social processes,
necessarily goes on among people, who produce all commodities.
But *effectively* the process does go on as if it took place among things,
involving people only in their abstract capacity as "guardians of commodities." And the market actually does treat labor power as a commodity, as though it were not the very essence of man, something
that lies, as it were, upstream of all other commodities. As we shall
see, the crucial processes of the capitalist system (and of all economic
systems) take place in the sphere of production; but value, around
which the system revolves, is realized and can only be realized on the
market, in the sphere of circulation. In sum, the civil society appears
to be something it is not; but that appearance is not haphazard in its
configuration or irrelevant in its consequences. It is not unrelated to
the ultimate truth about man and his works, but both veils it and
reveals it (e.g., K 47-48; 45).

As I have already pointed out, the capitalist economic system, by
ranking exchange value over use value and abstract labor over concrete labor, displays the essential truth about man: his absolute po-
tentiality, his ability to transcend through praxis all determinate configurations of his existence. But capitalist theory imputes that ability
not to man, but in the sphere of distribution to the self-propelling

motion of commodities and in the sphere of production to the power of self-expansion inherent in capital.

To treat labor (i.e., the very medium through which man makes and remakes his own world and himself) as just another commodity is particularly misleading. Labor alone is basic to the productive process as a whole; but in the capitalist system it is treated as just one component of it, bought and sold on the market through the free exchange of equivalents, and is thereby combined with the other two alleged components, capital and land. Labor is the only source of the yearly surplus yielded by the productive system, but that surplus is commonly seen as having three independent sources: capital (compensated through profit), land (compensated through rent), and labor (compensated through wages).[20] Wages appear to remunerate all labor, whereas they actually account for no more than the worker's subsistence and the training costs of him and his replacement; they do not pay for the surplus value that abstract labor generates over and above *its own* value; instead, this surplus becomes the foundation of profit (K 198-99; *188*).

These are all aspects of the crucial truth about the capitalist economic system: the fact that it maintains itself and expands through asymmetric, exploitative social relations. The institutions through which the system operates force the essential actors of the production process, the owners and sellers of labor power, to conduct their activity while surrendering all its fruits except those necessary to maintain them in existence so that the system can continue. The owners of the means of production (which are only the results of previous labor) appropriate the fruits of the labor power they have purchased, benefiting from the production process without contributing to it—or at any rate benefiting to an extent disproportionate to their contribution (if any) as managers.

The sociological significance of this thesis, which Marx expresses mainly in economic terms, lies in its drastic rephrasing of the problem of order. As I have already suggested, the characteristics of the civil society normally postulated as posing the problem now appear largely illusory. There is no true equality in the employment relation, the most crucial relation of civil society, since one party exploits the

---

[20] Marx, *Capital* (Moscow: Foreign Language Publishing, 1962), III, 794ff.

activity of the other. There is no true freedom in that relation, since the party who has only his own labor power is forced to sell it on terms set by the employer. The worker is inevitably inferior to the employer, if not to him as an individual then to him as a member of the employing class. The contractual nature of the employment relationship is itself illusory, being demanded exclusively by the fact that in the capitalist model both parties must ideally appear to be free (G 368).

The Benthamian notion of a convergence of individual interests in the unplanned advancement of superindividual interests is also a fiction, since the owner of labor power is not moved to enter the employment relation by his own interest (unless the term is defined in such broad terms as to make it meaningless), but is rather coerced to enter it because he lacks control of the means of production. And the surplus he generates is not the object of a superindividual interest, since it is appropriated by the employer (G 409, 566). It makes no more sense to say that employer and employee share interests, or work toward a common interest, than it does to say the same of the relationship between an animal and the leech that sucks its blood. Employer and employee indeed belong together, but only because of the coercive pressure the former can exercise on the latter (not a matter of explicit, legally recognized, politically enacted coercion, but of implicit, factual, economic coercion).

The Marxian challenge to the accepted image of the civil society and its attendant conceptualization of the problem of order firmly denies that the units to be ordered are individual units. As the capitalist system of production gradually displaces other systems to which it is intrinsically superior, the capitalist production relation encompasses more and more of the population, and thus affects an increasing share of the activities carried out in the society. Moreover, that relation (owing to its primary dependence on *abstract* labor) tends to affect all the people brought under its sway in roughly the same ways; it shapes the opportunities, beliefs, and goals of laborers in a basically consistent manner. To an even greater extent, men relate to one another, visualize one another, and affect one another as *either* sellers *or* buyers of labor power. On the surface this homogeneity of outlook appears to be related to the fact that both parties to the employment relation are essentially guardians of commodities. But this kind of alienation, reification, is only the superficial aspect of a far more basic alienation, which results from the asymmetry between exploiters and exploited, and which engenders fundamentally opposed interests on the two sides.

For Marx, the *true* units of modern society are classes: that is, increasingly massive, homogeneous, and contentious alignments formed by the divergence of interests arising from the employment relation. And he contends that the progressive socialization of the production process during industrialization will produce increasingly large production units, with an increasingly large employment of capital, an increasingly advanced division of labor, and increasingly despotic and exploitative relationships between employers and employees. From this standpoint, the notion of an "atomistic" civil society appears even more deceptive. Not only are the apparent fluidity, impermanence, and equalitarianism of social relations in the civil society illusory, but the employment bond becomes increasingly persistent and coercive as it is embodied in large-scale production units.

In this context, Marx develops a critical version of the functionalistic interpretation of managerial roles, to which I have already referred in Chapter 4. The subjection of the worker to the capitalist is determined not only by the objective requirements of coordinating operations in the production unit, but also by the fact that the worker works *for* the capitalist, in the capitalist's interest. As a specific function of capital (and not just of the production unit's operating as a unit) managerial authority is characterized by its immanent dedication to the production of profit for capital. This circumstance gives to management distinctive and otherwise unaccountable characteristics of exploitativeness and despotism; and these characteristics, in turn, both arise from and sustain the antagonistic interunit relations of the capitalist economic system (K 373ff; *346ff*). Furthermore, since the objectively necessary coordinating functions of management are carried out over the worker's head and not in his own interest, the individual worker tends to perceive the whole production process as being carried out not by himself and his fellows but by the capital that has brought them under its sway (G 111). In the same way, Marx shows that the alienation embodied in production relations underlies the alienation "projected" by the political economy (i.e., the alienation that regards things as manipulating men and not vice versa).

Let us summarize the ways in which Marx criticizes and transcends the Hobbesian conceptualization of the problem of social order without denying its validity as a first-order approximation. First, the units to be ordered are not individual but collective. This applies to two types of units: (1) *production units*, which are inherently collective, being based on cooperation, and which tend to increase in size as industrialization advances, forcibly coordinating the labor of increasingly large masses of people; (2) *classes*, which progressively unify on one side all workers as such, irrespective of their production units, and on the other all capitalists as such, irrespective of the production units they control.

The relationships between production units are typically competitive, and they engender an ordering based on the extent to which each unit succeeds or fails in organizing production according to the situationally appropriate "mix" of the so-called factors of production ("appropriate" almost always means an organization that will achieve the greatest possible exploitation of the workers). The relationships between classes are intrinsically antagonistic, both within each production unit and throughout society as a whole.

Both types of relationship engender order, in the sense that they standardize relations and stabilize interaction. But this ordering process cannot be interpreted in Hobbesian-Hegelian terms (as imposed by a transcendent political entity), Durkheimian terms (as based on an underlying value consensus), or Benthamian terms (as resulting from the unplanned convergence of independently pursued interests). According to Marx, order results from power imbalances, from the ability of some units to have their own way against the resistance and at the expense of other units. To this extent, Marx's is a Hobbesian view. But he does not feel that power imbalances result from the conscious actions of a sovereign entity endowed with absolute and abstract powers of command. Instead, they are caused by differing degrees in access to and control over objective, historically variable, sets of objects: the means of production. Control, in turn, can be established and maintained only because the units to be ordered are collective entities organized around the means of production from the beginning. They are not, as in the Hobbesian vision, individuals characterized only by a set of compelling natural urges and by intrinsically equal natural faculties for satisfying those urges.

The Prospects of Modern Society

It is sometimes argued that because Marx solves the problem of order in coercive terms, with reference to power imbalances, he solves the problem of social change in the same way; power, it could be said, stabilizes but is itself inherently unstable. This fundamentally correct view, if formulated so simply, short-circuits Marx's own argument, which is rather more complex. In fact, what Marx emphasizes about power imbalances is not their intrinsic instability but rather their intrinsic tendency to build up (e.g., K 676-77, 751; 627, 689-90). In principle, those with power will tend to gain more, whereas the "have-nots" gradually lose what little power they may possess. In Marx's view, power is not inherently unstable; it is undermined not by some mysterious nemesis, but by objective, identifiable conditions resulting from the interaction between power's own dynamic qualities and the context in which they operate.

The attempt to locate the specific conditions that effect the subversion of power relations characteristic of modern society is an integral part of Marx's theory of that society. Again, it is a complex attempt; and it does not easily lend itself to sociological interpretation and assessment, since Marx conducted it largely in economic rather than sociological terms. Some of the economic arguments that carry the main burden of Marx's analysis are the following, which I shall not discuss further:

1. The apparent anarchy of relations between economic units is, up to a point, counteracted by the objective requirements of the allocation of social labor, which favors capital concentration and rationalization of production, and thus limits the seemingly erratic development of market relations. But beyond that point, the ordering is subverted by a kind of higher-level anarchy, which finds expression through repeated and increasingly disruptive economic crises.

2. The inescapable trend toward larger and larger production

units progressively destroys the sole basis on which their power relations can be established, that is, competition.

3. The capitalist strategy of profit maximization can only be pursued through strategies (particularly those pertaining to the ratio of
variable capital to fixed capital) that engender a fall in the *rate* of
profit and thus undermine the ultimate point of reference for the
whole process of exploitation.

Most of Marx's *sociological* arguments for the inevitability of a
revolutionary subversion of the capitalist system are actually descriptions of the sociological consequences (or sociological components)
of trends projected through his economic arguments. In particular,
his notorious generalizations about the "polarization" of class relations and the "increasing impoverishment" (absolute or relative) of
the exploited class actually state the expected impact on the stratification system of *economic* tendencies—increasing capital concentration, the progressive encroachment of the capitalist mode of production on nonindustrial sectors of the economy, increasing exploitation,
and so on.

Marx also offers a recurrent argument, perhaps amenable to sociological formulation, for the increasing contradiction between the self-
sustaining growth of production *forces* (that is, the social and material technology of advanced industrialism), with their inherent emphasis on the social nature of the production process, and capitalist
production *relations*, which are directed toward private profits. This
contradiction, in Marx's view, could be terminated only if the logic
of forces asserted itself over the logic of relations and "socialized"
those relations by abolishing wage labor, private ownership of the
means of production, and other capitalist institutions. Unfortunately,
I find Marx's distinction between production forces and production
relations rather opaque, and for this reason I have not employed it
so far and will not use it here, in spite of its frequent recurrence in
Marx's writing.[21] But his sociological argument for the expected
breakdown of the capitalist system can perhaps be phrased by using
as its presuppositions a few points about the general nature of social
action that I developed earlier (Chapter 4).

---

[21] As a sophisticated example of the use to which such a distinction can be put,
see De Palma, "L'organizzazione capitalistica," *passim.*

The first presupposition concerns what may be called the "reaction of action upon the subject—the idea that in the course of coming to terms with a given situation men change the situation and thereby change themselves, acquiring needs and faculties incompatible with the persistence of the situation. If such a speculative notion can be taken as grounds for any kind of prediction, one may predict that the ultimate protagonists of the capitalist production process, the wage workers (not as individuals but as a class; this follows from a second presupposition, which concerns the *social* nature of the subject) are necessarily modified by their own operations, which reshape the reality around them, and undergo a subjective development that is intrinsically incompatible with their supinely carrying on their role as exploited toilers. (This argument, incidentally, is an extremely simplified, and correspondingly impoverished, paraphrase of the involved and sophisticated paradigm of historical development that Hegel worked out in his "dialectic of the master and the slave.")

Another presupposition derived from the general notion of action concerns the role of consciousness. The revolutionary subversion of the capitalist system requires that a subjective modification occur in the ultimate actors of the production process. In turn, this subjective modification involves the development of forms of consciousness (definitions of self and of reality on the part of the actor, conceptualizations of one's own and of the opponents' resources, awareness of the respective interests and acknowledgement of their contrast, etc.) that allow the collective actor in question to stand apart from the givens of the situation in order to exercise leverage on them, to negate them. This coming to awareness cannot, in Marx's thought, be interpreted simply as an adjunct of the laboring class, as something accruing to it from the outside. Only through it does the proletariat come into being as a "class for itself." But as long as *other* forms of consciousness, compatible with the alienated self-image of the civil society or at any rate not amounting to a revolutionary critique of it, are also prevalent among the proletariat, proletarians cannot form a class as an acting unit; they will continue to be objects rather than subjects of the historical process and the production system.

Aware of the significance of class consciousness, Marx holds that the concurrence of three circumstances will eventually allow the praxis of the proletariat to produce a revolutionary class consciousness. First, there must be an elaborate body of intrinsically valid, inherently revolutionary ideas (and these were precisely what Marx and others were trying to develop). Second, there must be an international labor movement, an organizational medium through whose revolutionary activity the exploited masses can acquire revolutionary ideas and verify these through action. Finally, there must be objective situational conditions—polarization, impoverishment, etc.— that will make greater and greater masses receptive to the new ideas and force them to become involved in the revolutionary action of the labor movement.

As it happens these three circumstances have never occurred together, at least in the industrially advanced countries where Marx expected to see the first signs of revolution. Thus the envisaged consciousness change failed to materialize, and the revolution did not take place. And Marx's whole argument, including its sociological aspects, was falsified by the course of events. But it is important to locate the exact point at which the argument came to grief. Marx recognized the consciousness change as a *distinctive* and *indispensable* moment in the development of the revolutionary situation he was predicting; but he failed to recognize it as a *contingent* moment, one that did not have to occur. He tried to impart to an inherently open-minded argument a degree of "empirical closure" that proved fatal. We may well wonder why Marx felt the need for this closure. There were two reasons, which are more closely related than they at first appear to be.

In the first place, Marx's thought had some deterministic content, which in its later phases found expression mainly in economic arguments concerning the immanent, inescapable tendencies of the capitalist economic system to break down irreparably. As we have seen, arguments of this kind were used not only as predictors of the economic collapse of capitalism but also as statements of the conditions under which revolutionary class consciousness would develop as an independent component of the revolutionary situation. That so much analytical weight was carried, at various points of Marx's total discourse, by essentially the same argument is certainly a symptom of the empirical closure of that discourse, and thus of its inherent precariousness.

In the second place, the pressure toward empirical closure came from Marx's unshakable belief in the coming of the revolution. All too often, in discussing the consciousness change of the proletariat, Marx appears to reason that *because* the development of appropriate forms of consciousness is essential to the revolution, that development will inevitably take place. This is of course a correct line of reasoning if one assumes the inescapable necessity of revolution (which Marx did mainly on economic grounds); but it involves denying any independent causal significance to the consciousness change as a distinctive and indispensable component of the revolutionary situation.

In my opinion, these two pressures toward empirical closure—the *deterministic* pressure of assumptions about inescapable economic developments and the *prophetic* pressure of a belief in inevitable revolution—are both caused by Marx's failure to think through and accept certain implications of his own views on man and history. Let us go back to the 1835 passing-out essay from which we started our discussion on Marx, and to the question there posed concerning the modifications that Marx later applied to his juvenile statement of man's peculiarity.

I said previously that the most crucial modification was probably Marx's expelling the deity from his argument, which he did quite explicitly. But however consistent he was about negating the deity in his later writings, he may not have followed up all the implications of this negation. In the 1835 formulation, the deity performed two essential and related functions: it assigned man's "general goal," and it guaranteed, at least to the human species as a whole, the final achievement of that goal through the agency of man himself. Once the idea of a deity is abandoned, one might perhaps say that either nature or man himself becomes responsible for assigning man's goal; but, in my view, neither entity can be said to guarantee the *achievement* of that goal. That is, the expulsion of the deity logically means that *all* of mankind's actions acquire the same inherent perilousness the 1835 essay recognizes in the individual's choice of a calling ("a great privilege . . . but at the same time an act through which he may ruin his whole life, thwart all his plans, cause himself misery").

This implication Marx finds thoroughly unacceptable, indeed unthinkable. He never comes to terms with the notion that there is no ultimate guarantee of the success of mankind's pilgrimage, with the *absolute* riskiness of that pilgrimage. And yet this uncertainty is but the extreme expression of the open-endedness that he recognizes as inherent in human action. His unshakable belief that mankind cannot ultimately fail, that indeed it must certainly triumph, contradicts his view of how it goes about its task. Such a belief, I feel, has little to do with the fact that Marx is a dialectical thinker; in dialectical terms, after all, it is legitimate to assume (as Marx does) that "mankind only sets itself such problems as it *can* solve," but illegitimate to assume that mankind *will* solve them. And this unproven assumption, to the extent that it shapes the development of Marx's thought, is bound to create discontinuities, obscurities, and difficulties.

Marx's assurance about the accomplishment of mankind's goal leads directly to the "prophetic" component of his thought: the tendency to argue from the assumed certainty of revolution in order to prove the noncontingent character of certain aspects of the revolutionary situation. Indirectly, the same assurance generates the deterministic component of that argument. To the extent that Marx feels uneasy about deriving explicit expectations for the present and the immediate future from his certainties about the distant future, he *has* to formulate the relationship between past, present, and future in deterministic terms. If the future cannot guarantee the development of the present in the expected direction, then the past must do the job; it must be construed as a sequence of utterly determined events, obeying an infallible logic. In fact, Marx uses *both* the future and the past to give developments in the present and the immediate future a predictability that is both incompatible with the open-endedness of human action and spurious when examined in the light of actual events.

But if this is a correct interpretation of how and why Marx came to grief, then regarding his sociological argument as *entirely* falsified, as made utterly untenable by the failure of his predictions, may mean throwing out the baby with the bath water. It is true that once the prophetic-deterministic components of Marx's theories concerning social reality and modern society are correctly located and "neutralized," his thought loses its appeal as an infallible guide to action. But at the same time, much of it is still sociologically viable and uniquely enlightening.

EMILE DURKHEIM

SOURCES

As far as possible the research for this section has been conducted on original-language editions of Durkheim's writings. The most important among these are referred to throughout the section in abbreviated form, as indicated below.

D. *De la division du travail social*, 8th ed. (Paris: P.U.F., 1967). After each page reference to this edition the italic numbers following the semi-colon refer to the corresponding paging in *The division of labor in society*, translated by George Simpson (New York: Free Press, 1964). Some passages that I will cite were omitted by Durkheim from the second and later editions of the book, although they appear in Simpson's translation.

R. *Les règles de la méthode sociologique*, 6th ed. (Paris: P.U.F., 1967). Here the italic numbers refer to *The rules of sociological method*, translated by Sarah Solovay and J. H. Mueller (Glencoe, Ill.: Free Press, 1950).

S. *Le suicide: Etude de sociologie*, 2d ed. (Paris: P.U.F., 1967). Here the italic numbers refer to *Suicide: A study in sociology*, translated by J. Spaulding and George Simpson (Glencoe, Ill.: Free Press, 1951).

F. *Les formes élémentaires de la vie religieuse: Le système totémique en Australie*, 5th ed. (Paris: P.U.F., 1968). Here the italic numbers refer to *The elementary forms of religious life*, translated by J. W. Swain (New York: Collier, 1961).

All translations from these writings, unless otherwise indicated, are my own. I have, however, been unable to use original-language editions of two other books, for which I have used the following English translations (the references to these books therefore give only the italic paging).

P. *Professional ethics and civic morals*, translated by Cornelia Brookfield (London: Routledge, 1957). The English edition of "Physique des moeurs et du droit."

SP. *Sociology and philosophy*, translated by D. F. Pocock (Glencoe, Ill.: Free Press, 1953).

6. A Typology of Societies

In discussing Karl Marx, I at one point (Chapter 5) raised the problem of order. As I noted, this problem was not one of Marx's major concerns; but it was to loom larger and larger in the development of sociology as a distinctive discipline. This was particularly true in France, where the term *sociologie* originated, and where the new discipline of that name found rather early (although not without difficulty) a firm academic footing. The problem of order is central in the work of Émile Durkheim (1858-1917), the greatest French sociologist and the man who contributed most to establishing the discipline's academic credentials.[1] Indeed, it is largely due to the tremendous influence of Durkheim's thought that contemporary sociological theory still assigns a very high priority to that problem.

At the end of the nineteenth century the problem of order did not present the same burning urgency, the same charge of "metaphysical pathos" that it had had for Hobbes in the seventeenth century and for the French Restoration thinkers around the beginning of the nineteenth. To those writers the problem of order arose through a personal trauma, through the immediate experience of the large-scale, shattering social *dis*order resulting from the English Civil Wars and the French Revolution.[2] A century after the Revolution, however, one

[1] See Terry Clark, "Emile Durkheim and the institutionalization of sociology in the French university system," *European Journal of Sociology*, I (1968), No. 1, pp. 37-71. For a biographical sketch, see Henri Peyre, "Durkheim: The man, his time, and his intellectual background," in Durkheim et al., *Essays on sociology and philosophy* (New York: Harper, 1964), pp. 3-31.

[2] A German commentator, Kurt Schilling, has written: "Hobbes's social ideas spring immediately from the experience of the Civil War." Quoted by Luciano Cavalli, *Il mutamento sociale* (Bologna: Mulino, 1970), p. 127. The influence of the "twin revolution" has been emphasized by Robert Nisbet; see, for instance, *The sociological tradition* (New York: Basic Books, 1966), Chapter 2.

could see that Restoration writers in particular had rather overstated their alternatives: either a return to the pre-Revolutionary order, *or* a final breakdown of human society in utter chaos.[3] The project of turning the clock back had proved unworkable, yet society had not ceased to exist.

Instead, the irreversible changes wrought by the French and the Industrial Revolutions had brought forth a new society, whose nature the practitioners of the new discipline of sociology were busy analyzing. In the middle and later nineteenth century the dominant sociological orientation, based on English utilitarianism and chiefly propounded by the social philosopher Herbert Spencer (1820-1903), praised the "civil society" issuing from the "twin revolution." It was not just a viable social arrangement brought about in spite of all prophecies of doom by triumphant political and economic liberalism; it was the very embodiment of reason, the standard by which all previous societies had to be judged, the finally attained end of a grandiose, irresistible process of evolution.

Within this perspective, which we can label utilitarian, the problem of order was not so much solved as discounted.[4] In retrospect, concern with it seemed only a short-sighted emotive reaction to the stresses unavoidably resulting from society's triumphant progress toward a liberal, commercialized, industrial society. It seemed somehow perverse that so much pathos should have been engendered and so much effort expended over the wrong questions. Earlier thinkers had asked how to prevent the individual from freely deploying his own resources to his sole advantage, how to commit him to means and ends originating outside himself, and how to superimpose the control of public authorities, with its coercive connotations, on the spontaneity and rationality exclusive to individual action. To the utilitarians, social order, if the term was to mean anything at all, could only be the automatic outcome of the myriad choices that the liberal system continuously led individuals to make—in the market-

---

[3] The overstatement had already been noted by Tocqueville. See Tocqueville, A 17-18.

[4] On utilitarianism, see: C. B. MacPherson, *The political theory of possessive individualism* (Oxford: Oxford University Press, 1962); Talcott Parsons, *The structure of social action* (Glencoe, Ill.: Free Press, 1949). Chapter 2.

place, in the polity, and in all other areas of social intercourse.[5] It was natural and proper that these choices have no other end in view than the increase of one's own well-being, and no other restraint than the consideration that each individual owed the freedom of every other individual. The liberal state, indeed, existed solely to guarantee these things.

Anybody who felt that this was not enough, that for society as such to survive and prosper there had to be a logic transcending the individual's sole responsibility for his own welfare, had only to consider the increasingly humane laws, the progress of science and enlightenment, and the spectacular increase in wealth of the European nation-states during the nineteenth century. He would quickly realize that no such transcendent logic was required. The utilitarian perspective, in fact, could clarify not only contemporary social conditions but also the whole course of past social evolution. The individual, who had so triumphantly come into his own in modern times, had been responsible, however obscurely and unknowingly, for the totality of that evolution. Self-interest had motivated that evolution from the very beginning, and all social systems had expressed but one fundamental social process: the joining and parting of individuals acting in cooperation, competition, or conflict.

Only an ignorance of these facts had led earlier analysts of society to postulate a superindividual level of social reality, with distinctive resources and needs of its own. An inadequate analysis of social reality into its ultimate components—namely, the concurrent choices of self-seeking, calculating individuals—had left an opaque residue, which was then treated as the transcendent source of morality and order, the realm where social equilibrium was ordained and preserved. Of course, such misleading notions could be explained by the ignorance of past ages; and they had once had a sort of crude plausibility. But it was now the business of social science to show how at bottom the individual's search for advantage had actually been the mainspring of the social process throughout history; and how the so-called social order, far from being a precondition of that

[5] On the central significance of choice for the liberal order, see C. B. MacPherson, *The real world of democracy* (Oxford: Clarendon Press, 1966), especially pp. 6-7.

process, was a result of it, a more or less stable equilibrium automatically produced by individuals through their own free choices and interactions.

A favorite empirical field for the elaboration of this basic thesis was the historical development of the division of labor, which was treated as the process whereby individuals, in pursuing their own welfare, had progressively differentiated and specialized their activities, to the great benefit of themselves and of society. This same theme, the division of labor, was the ground on which Durkheim launched his sustained attack on the utilitarian tradition and its understanding of the problem of order. His argument was embodied in a book first published in 1893, *De la division du travail social*. This book will be the principal source of discussion throughout this chapter. However, my own treatment of it will be highly selective, and will in fact pay little attention to the specific theme that provides its title. Moreover, I will occasionally refer to another work, *Leçons de sociologie* (published posthumously in 1950), which gives the text of a lecture course, "Physique des moeurs et du droit," repeatedly taught by Durkheim around the turn of the century.

The Flaws of Individualistic Theory

In the utilitarian analysis, society is no more than a set of individuals who maintain relations with one another, relations that arise through acts of will and are governed exclusively by considerations of individual advantage. If these relations are to be formed and continued efficiently, each individual must be free to make his own choices, to deploy and risk his resources according to his best judgment. The paradigm of all utilitarian relations is that of exchange, which presupposes a certain differentiation in the resources available to different parties; and an extensive network of exchange relations is likely to encompass a great variety of men and resources. Relations persist in a stable form essentially to the extent that the parties have an interest in maintaining them. Given this fact, actors other than the specific individuals related need do nothing but stand off; even agencies with authoritative functions are only expected to restrain each of the parties from perpetrating fraud or violence on the other and thus altering the normal interplay of interests. The essential authoritative function, then, is the application of preestablished sanctions, so that individuals will be able to assess the consequences of their own actions. If this is done, the "enlightened self-interest" of individuals will be the only subjective ingredient necessary to construct stable networks of relations between individuals—that is, to maintain social order.

Durkheim challenges this theoretical construction on all its points, arguing in the first place that it is scientifically unsound and misleading, and in the second place that its pragmatic implications are dangerous. The first argument is of course the one he develops at greater length, and it entails the following basic points:

1. It is essential to the whole utilitarian imagery that the individual be a *prius* and the society a *posterius*: the individual is presupposed, and society is merely the result of his self-interested cooperation with others. But, says Durkheim, if the individual is defined in utilitarian terms this "deduction of society from the individual" amounts to a "creation *ex nihilo*" (D 263; 279). It is true that individuals act as *échangistes* (D 402; 406), and that as they do so they form cooperative relations, continuously expanding the existing network of associations. But individuals who act this way must be generated by a previous social process in which association is not born of cooperation but instead precedes it.

Durkheim states the utilitarian position, as advanced by Spencer, quite simply:

Given that the individual is not alone in this world but is surrounded by rivals who dispute the means of his existence, it is in his own interest to establish with his fellows relations that are a help rather than a hindrance to him. Thus society is born; and the whole social process amounts to an improvement of these relations so that they will more fully produce the effects for which they were intended (D 334; 342).

But the individual here postulated, one able to visualize his interests and seek out the best means to them, is himself a product of social evolution, and a late product at that. The very concept that a single human being is conscious of having continuing interests and exchangeable resources of his own, set apart from the group to which he belongs, is a relatively recent idea; and only at the risk of grave misunderstandings did the utilitarians read it back into early social conditions to which it was wholly foreign. Both philogenetically and ontogenetically, the process of individualization can only develop as a progressive differentiation and autonomization of entities that were originally submerged within a comprehensive group identity.

2. In fact, even the utilitarian understanding of the relations between individuals under modern conditions—an understanding summarized in the thesis that all basic social relations are of a contractual nature—is seriously inadequate. In the first place, modern social life involves a complex and steadily growing body of authoritative regulations that do not owe their validity to contractual agreements or relate merely to the supervision of contractual relations (D 184-97; 206-20). In the second place, "Not everything within a contract is contractual" (D 189; 211). Authoritative norms, again, establish the conditions under which the encounter of the parties' spontaneous wills leads to enforceable mutual obligations, regulate these obligations in ways that the parties did not contemplate or might have arranged otherwise, and protect interests that the spontaneous interplay of individual wills might jeopardize (P xvii-xviii). "In sum, the contract does not suffice itself but is possible only through a regulation . . . that is of social origin" (D 193; 215).

3. Both the considerations advanced under Point 2 imply that utilitarianism underestimates the significance of public, authoritative action in modern society and wrongly sees it as concerned solely with the enforcement of contractual obligations—or as Durkheim puts it, the maintenance of a "negative solidarity" in which the citizens' only duty is not to interfere with each other's rights (e.g., D 88, 98; 119, 129). In reality, owing to this vast and growing public regulation, individuals find themselves under a series of obligations: "Society is not dissolved into a dust of juxtaposed atoms. . . . We are enmeshed in a network of obligations" (D 207; 227).

4. But the existence of general obligations means that the subjective elements governing the conduct of the individual cannot, as in the utilitarian framework, be reduced to those of an egoistic, calculating nature; they do not exclusively encourage (or even allow) him to consider only his own interest in choosing his conduct. The norms produced by public regulatory activity, or for that matter those of morality, "compel the individual to act toward ends that are not his

own, to make concessions, to consent to compromises, to take into account interests that transcend his own" (D 206-7; 227).

This is particularly apparent in pre-modern societies, where individual considerations never figure as prominently as in modern ones; but it also applies to later societies. In general, if the utilitarian appeal to spontaneity of choice requires that egoism be the only subjective impulse to action, only disruptive consequences may be expected from it. The attempt to consecrate egoism as a *moral* principle, if taken seriously, involves a failure to recognize "the essential element of moral life, the moderating influence that society exercises upon its members, which curbs and neutralizes the brutal impact of the struggle for existence" (D 174; *197*).

But if morality involves the limiting of the individual will, it necessarily requires the operation of a principle or agency transcending the individual and capable, by virtue of this position, of exerting pressure on him. As Durkheim put it:

There are no morals without discipline and authority. . . . Morals do not look like obligations to us, that is, do not seem like morals to us—and therefore we can have no sense of duty—unless there exists about us and above us a power which gives them sanction. . . . The material sanction . . . is the outward sign . . . that there is something above us to which we are subordinate (P 73).

On this basis the problem of order is met squarely and solved, rather than sidestepped as in the utilitarian approach. The latter, we have seen, considered order as merely the mechanical outcome of the mutual impacts of in principle uncoordinated individuals; no preoccupation with order is required on the part of these units, order being only an ex post facto construct of the scientific observer:

Spencer at one point claims that the activity of sociologists resembles the calculus of a mathematician who, given a certain number of spheres, deduces the manner in which they must be combined in order to achieve an equilibrium between them. But this is an inappropriate comparison that has no application to social facts (D 342; *350*). . . . A state of order . . . among men cannot follow of itself from any entirely material causes, from any blind mechanism. . . . It is a moral task (P *12*).

In other words, order depends on the existence and operation of subjective components of individual action that are irreducible to self-advantage—"representations, sentiments, and tendencies" that can exert outside pressure on the individual actor. These supports of order are not products of wholly individual considerations but must be postulated as preexistent to individual conduct, as supplying the individual with at least some of the basic criteria for his action. Order, in other terms, is not a resultant of individual action, but a presupposition of it; it lies upstream, not downstream.

I have outlined Durkheim's major reasons for regarding the utilitarian approach as scientifically inadequate. His argument really amounts to saying that the problem of order is a serious one and has as much significance for modern, "civil" society as for other, less advanced societies. If modern society were in truth nothing more than a set of freely entered, willfully designed exchange relations between self-seeking individuals, it would disintegrate into utter chaos. It persists and functions in fact because of a hidden framework of order, which finds visible expression in the norms that guide and restrain individual action. This framework, however, cannot be taken wholly for granted, since it must continuously overcome the disruptive tendencies of human egoism, which are strengthened under modern conditions. Order does exist, since society could not exist without it, but it is fragile.

In fact, Durkheim's arguments concerning the nature of order, when properly read, appear not just as de facto statements, but as clarifying the conditions that *must* be met if society (and thus mankind) is to survive (D xl, 147; *34-35, 173*); they are prescriptive as well as descriptive. If the norms fail to restrain individual wills, social life will become impossible. But the possibility that norms will fail is built into their very nature as subjective entities that have an extrasubjective source. Norms can only restrain to the extent that they are responded to, acted upon; but since they are not an intrinsic part of the individual, he may refuse to act on them and let other, wholly egoistic factors guide him.

In accordance with this understanding of order, Durkheim's critique of utilitarianism (and of other individualistic theories) is not exclusively scientific, but is to some extent a moral critique of utilitarianism's potential threats to society. The utilitarian misconstruction of social existence, especially that of modern social conditions, can itself exercise an influence on individuals; it can encourage their disruptive tendencies and corrode the very special framework whose existence utilitarians deny.

The notion that where the individual has come into his own (as in the liberal system) the action of public authorities can be reduced to purely policing functions is demonstrably incorrect; but it may, for all that, be acted on, impeding the necessary expansion of public functions. Worse, it may lead to the dismantling of the existing normative structure, engendering a state of "anomie," or normlessness (D 357-63; 353-60). The demonstrable necessity for the law of contract to restrain the blind action of pure market forces in the interest of justice (P, Chapter 16) may be disregarded if the liberal faith in automatically achieved equilibria continues to orient legislation (or to discourage it). All these dangers are implicit in the hold of the utilitarian approach on the public imagination, and Durkheim feels, in turn, morally obligated to denounce them.

These moral concerns were not as urgent in Durkheim's early writing as they later came to be, and at the time he wrote *Division* his outlook was largely optimistic. He assumed that the ordering forces at work in modern society were too powerful to be seriously impeded by the utilitarian conceptions then held by many social scientists, who deserved criticism more for failing to detect those forces (D 394; 398) than for holding them back through false teachings. Even the current state of partial anomie and public unconcern for justice and equality of opportunity were serious but not fatal shortcomings, and they stood a good chance of being remedied in due course.

Durkheim's thought at this point (1893) had a noticeably deterministic cast, and he assumed that certain spontaneous developments in the social process, the manner of social intercourse, the division of labor, and the dimensions of society always involved a concurrent increase in the solidarity of the society—that is, in "the bonds that attach us to one another and to society, which join a mass of individuals in a cohesive whole" (D 393-94; 398). This did not mean, however, that social development involved no serious qualitative change, that solidarity was always of the same nature, or that society itself was always the same. It was only one of the tasks of sociology to put forth generalizations obtaining for all societies and human groupings. For example: "Men cannot live together without understanding one another [*sans s'entendre*], and thus without making sacrifices for one another and binding one another in a strong and durable manner" (D 207; 228).

Another task was to show how the vital bonds of mutual understanding and obligation varied from one social situation to another. Much of *Division* confronts this task by the device (which Tocqueville also used) of working out two contrasting ideal types, which set the boundaries for all significant social configurations. It is to this typology that we now turn.

Types of Society

Although Tocqueville's typology (aristocracy versus democracy) is parallel to Durkheim's, the two have rather different scopes. Tocqueville contrasts the social conditions obtaining within the same set of large-scale sociopolitical units (the Western nations) before and after the "twin revolution" that began in the late eighteenth century. His typology cannot be directly used to survey a longer period of social evolution, nor can it be applied to a different set of units. Durkheim, by contrast, deals with all past and present societies, of whatever scale. He describes a transition much more basic than the twin revolution, one undergone by Western societies many centuries before the latter; indeed, his examples are only partially useful in discussing the later developments.

Obviously, Durkheim's argument has a much higher order of generality than Tocqueville's, and bespeaks a sustained concern with wider sociological questions than the one to which Tocqueville addresses himself ("What is the nature of modern society?"). In the same way, the focal theme of Durkheim's typology—the nature of solidarity, or the problem of order—is more analytical than Tocqueville's explicitly *moral* concern for the fate of individual freedom under democratic conditions. And at least some of the moral implications of Durkheim's theme are at variance with that concern of Tocqueville's.

I have just said that Durkheim's theme is the nature of solidarity. However, he elaborates two ideal types of society, and each type involves characteristics that are analytically quite distinct from solidarity. The whole point of this exercise lay in showing that the nature of the solidarity found in societies varies systematically with several other characteristics. Solidarity was the center of Durkheim's analytical concerns in *Division*, but no generalized priority attached to it on this account. In fact, to the extent that Durkheim orders the various aspects of his typology in terms of dynamic significance, solidarity appears to possess the status of a dependent rather than independent variable.

Thus those discussions of *Division* that focus on the question of the nature of solidarity to the exclusion of the other aspects of Durkheim's typology, or too narrowly subordinate the latter to the former, are potentially misleading—all the more so if my later contention that the dichotomy of mechanical and organic solidarity is the weakest of those in the typology proves true. Therefore, I have tried to display *all* aspects of Durkheim's typology of societies. I have grouped them into three clusters of variables, and within each cluster I shall compare the two ideal-typical societies elaborated by Durkheim, which I have designated simply as "type *A* society" and "type *B* society." Naturally, the operation of grouping the variables into clusters entails some difficulties, since several pairs of variables overlap conceptually. And for any given variable one cannot be sure of the exact division between *A*-type and *B*-type values. But such difficulties are unavoidable in working with broad typologies.

First Cluster: Morphological Variables

In many of his writings (e.g., R 112ff; *113ff*), though possibly nowhere as clearly as in *Division*, Durkheim assigns the greatest importance to "morphological" variables; the dimensions and physical configuration of a society's territory, the size and settlement of the population, the differentiation of patterns of activity in the society, and so on. His two ideal-typical societies are characterized in the first place by their differences on these variables.

Type A society. This society has small dimensions, both territorial (D 272; 287) and demographic, and the density of its population is low (D 238; 257). The subunits of the population are "juxtaposed" to one another—that is, there is little differentiation or interaction between them—and the society as a whole can be characterized, from this standpoint, as "segmental" (D 150; *175*). Moreover, there is little differentiation or interdependence within subunits, or segments (D 152; *176-77*). In such a "system of segments that are homogeneous and similar to one another" (D 157; *181*), individual parts can be added to the whole or taken away from it without disturbing its overall equilibrium, which is minimally dependent on specific, differentiated contributions from the various parts.

Type B society. The opposite characteristics are present here. The space over which the society's components regularly interact is large; but so is the number of individuals, so that population density is relatively high. The subunits to which individuals belong are numerous, internally heterogeneous, and differentiated from one another in their activities (D 157; *181*). These subunits entertain frequent and regular relations with one another over considerable distances (D 361; *369*); and they affect one another significantly and as interdependent parts of an advanced organism, not marginally and as juxtaposed segments in a primitive organism. Accordingly, parts cannot be added to the whole or taken away from it without risking serious disruption.

Second Cluster: Institutional Variables

The extent to which social activities are differentiated also bears on the central question pertaining to this second cluster: How many identifiable, distinctive, patterned sets of sustained activities are carried out in the society, and how are they related to one another?

Type A society. Since there is little division of labor within and between an *A* society's subunits (D 158; *182*), there is also little differentiation of institutions—that is, of sets of norms regulating distinct areas of social activity.[6] Within the total flow of activity going on in the society, the distinguishable streams are few, and these are carried out within a very few basic frameworks of regulation, the most important of which are kinship, religion, and locality (e.g., D 143, 152-54; *169, 176-78*). There is considerable overlap even between these frameworks, and between the groups operating within each one. Thus religion is often a property of the larger kinship unit, and kinship ties typically exist among all the inhabitants of a locality. Even where some kind of occupational differentiation takes place, as in

---

[6] On the concept of institution, see Chapter 8.

the larger and somewhat more advanced societies of this type, the occupational units (castes) also operate as kinship and religious units (D 306-8; *317-19*).

Generally speaking, the dominant institutional patterns in this society emphasize ascriptive criteria (D 152-55; *177-80*), and are highly tradition-bound (D 109; *138*). Social control is close and demanding (D 287-88; *300-301*), and the individual's compliance with social regulation is monitored and sanctioned by the community at large, or by agents (typically elders) who occupy a generalized position of higher social significance. Law is not a distinctive body of rules differentiated from those of morality and religion. Its commands are generally addressed to everybody, very widely known, and invested with sacredness. Accordingly, the sanctions attached to them are typically "repressive" in nature: that is, they are punishments inflicted on the offender by the society as a whole or on its behalf, and they express widely shared, sharply defined, and deeply held feelings about what is legitimate and proper (D 38ff; *72ff*). Under this kind of law, particularly in societies most closely approximating the *A* type, property is generally held by groups rather than individuals; its objects are almost exclusively land, dwellings and their appurtenances, and are *extra commercium* because of the close connection of these objects with kinship and religious institutions (D 154-55; *179*).

The universal hold of kinship, religion, and locality means that in these societies it is often impossible to speak of government, of political authority as a distinguishable institution (D 170-71; *193-94*). Even where sets of practices and bodies of personnel do perform governmental functions, they have, like everything else in the society, strong religious connotations (D 173; *196*), and operates as though they embodied the society as a whole; they relate to other parts of the society as a master relates to his possessions, not as one differentiated, functionally specialized agency to others (D 155-56; *180*).

Type B society. Here, again, the type can be described simply by positing characteristics opposite to those listed for the type *A* society. The division of labor (as we might suppose from what was said about morphological variables) is advanced (D 169; *192*) both within and between subunits of the society. A great number of activities have become differentiated and are specifically regulated, and the continued existence of individuals and of society requires the regular, inter-dependent concurrence of many of them. Accordingly, the significance of religion is less, and it no longer assigns meanings or lays down rules for all fields of existence (D 143; *169*). The religious beliefs themselves (as in the case of Christianity) have become more abstract, and religious and moral norms are less narrow (D 137, 144; *163, 169*). Kinship and locality, too, have retained only part of the significance they possess in type A societies (S 428-34; *373-78*). The membership that now provides the individual with criteria for action bearing on his most cogent and persistent concerns is his role in an occupational group; recruitment to these groups is on the basis of achievement, and the general pattern of recruitment has a great influence on the society as a whole (D 208; *228-29*).

As I have said, the norms regulating behavior are mostly differentiated, and are aggregated into distinct groups affecting different sets of activities and different memberships. Norms addressed to all members of the society, sustained by widely and deeply held feelings, sharply formulated, and highly resistant to change are a small proportion of the total body of norms (D 137; *163*). Most norms are instead secular (D 208; *228*), changeable, often generically formulated, and concern relatively small constituencies within the society and relatively restricted aspects of its total activity. The policing of norms is largely entrusted to specialized institutions. Legal norms—here quite distinguishable from those of a religious or moral nature—are mainly backed by "restitutive" sanctions, whose enforcement is intended simply to restore the specific relationships that were altered by a violation (D 83; *115*) and does not express a wrathful outburst of offended feelings. Under this type of law property is generally held by individuals, concerns mainly movable objects, and is freely exchangeable on the market. But the most characteristic legal institution is contract, a transaction creating and transferring rights between individuals according to a freely entered agreement (D 93; *123*).

In a society of this type, which rests so totally on the interdependence of differentiated activities and the combined effect of distinguishable agencies, there is particular need for a special agency to regulate the way in which the various activities and agencies bear on one another. Thus type B society necessarily possesses distinct governmental activities and bodies, agencies whose characteristic feature is that "they alone are entitled to think and act on behalf of the society as a whole."[7] The state is strictly a decision-making agency, specialized to produce guidelines for action on problems that affect the society at large but surpass the competence of all other subunits of society; however, once the decisions are made those other subunits are typically the most involved in carrying them out (P *81*).

Probably Durkheim means by this that in a type *B* society the government must respect a line of demarcation between the state and society. It must not, however, compromise its ability to perceive and decide the many complex social problems that require authoritative solution. In Durkheim's view the "form of state" best suited to meeting these two potentially contradictory requirements (and thus the form appropriate to societies most closely approximating Type *B*) is democracy. Not unlike some contemporary political theorists of the "general systems" persuasion,[8] Durkheim characterizes democracy by the multiplicity, regularity, and reliable operation of the arrangements whereby continuous and extensive two-way communication exists between the state and society without jeopardizing the boundary between the two. Thus both the authority of the state and the autonomy of society are preserved.

We must . . . not say that democracy is the political form of a society governing itself, in which the government is spread throughout the *milieu* of the nation. Such a definition is a contradiction in itself. . . . The State is nothing if it is not an organ distinct from the rest of society. . . . Nevertheless communications between this especial organ and the other social organs may be either close or less close, either continuous or intermittent. . . . Certain institutions . . . enable the people to follow the working of government (national assembly, parliament, official journals, education intended to equip the citizen to one day carry out his duties, and so on) . . . and also to communicate the results of their reflections (organs for rights of franchise or electoral machinery) to the organs of government (P *82-83*).

Other passages of this text (one of the *Leçons*) emphasize that the communication must be two-way; and that with the appropriate institutional engineering such communication gives democratic gov-

---

[7] P *48*. The translation is partly erroneous here, and I have taken account of the original in modifying it.

[8] I am thinking of such works as David Easton, *A systems analysis of political life* (New York: Wiley, 1965).

ernments a particular authoritativeness (P *95ff*). As a result, "democratic societies . . . are more malleable and more flexible" (P *84*),
and "democracy . . . is the form that societies are assuming to an
increasing degree" (P *89*).

Third Cluster: Solidarity Variables

Extracting the key morphological and institutional characteristics of
Durkheim's two ideal-typical societies from scattered passages has
been a fairly straightforward matter. Serious difficulties begin, however, when one attempts to systematize the arguments Durkheim advanced about the nature of the solidarity typical for each society.
This is somewhat surprising, since the distinction between "mechanical" and "organic" solidarity is the avowed central theme of *Division*; indeed, some secondary literature treats it as the sole significant
contribution this book made to sociological theory.

There are, to begin with, two terminological difficulties. Durkheim
discusses at length the meanings of "mechanical" and "organic"
solidarity, but nowhere does he define solidarity itself. Moreover, he
employs a number of other terms—integration, cohesion, harmony,
order, *discipline, unité*—that are obviously related to one another
and to solidarity, but he does not say how they are related.

More serious difficulties stem from the inherent inadequacies of
Durkheim's contrast between the mechanical solidarity associated
with type *A* societies and the organic solidarity associated with type
B societies. Some formulations of this contrast (e.g., D 205; 226) simply suggest that mechanical solidarity stems from a "similarity of
consciousness" among the individual members of a type *A* society,
and organic solidarity from the division of labor characteristic of
type *B* societies. However, there is in my judgment an unacknowledged asymmetry between the two terms of the comparison. Although there is a direct, logical relationship between "similarity of
consciousness" and solidarity, the relationship of solidarity to division of labor is indirect and contingent; otherwise Durkheim would
not need to devote a whole section of his work to "anomalous forms
of the division of labor," i.e., forms that somehow *fail* to engender
solidarity.

That the link between division of labor and solidarity is indirect is also shown by Durkheim's alternative definitions of the two kinds of solidarity (e.g., D 99; *129*), which suggests, again, that mechanical solidarity rests on similarity of consciousness, whereas organic solidarity rests on the correspondence and interdependence of the differentiated activities carried out by collective and individual components of a type *B* society. But this formulation, whatever its intrinsic merits,[9] contradicts Durkheim's own criticism of utilitarianism (as reconstructed above), which states that social solidarity is in all cases solely grounded on moral bonds, feelings of obligation, and "altruism" (D 207; *228*), so that it cannot derive from such a purely objective fact as the correspondence between one's own needs and somebody else's activity (D 260-61; *276-77*). Since this criticism must be considered an integral part of Durkheim's argument on solidarity (D 181, 208, 392-93; *203-4, 228, 397-98*), his distinction between the two types of solidarity must be conceptualized compatibly with that criticism. The trouble is that no wholly convincing conceptualization can be worked out, as the following attempt will prove.

We might begin by concentrating on the fact that in a few passages (e.g., D 147, 393; *173, 398*) Durkheim links mechanical solidarity to similarity alone, with no mention of consciousness. Correspondingly, in other passages (D 147-48, 351, 396; *173, 360, 401*) references to consciousness are linked with solidarity as such, or with organic solidarity. This suggests one constraint on our conceptualization of mechanical and organic solidarity: namely, that solidarity is, at bottom, *always* expressed through consciousness, through the subjective elements that permeate society and impinge on the actions of individuals. A second basic constraint is implicit in Durkheim's rejection of utilitarianism: among all these subjective elements, only those restraining the individual's search for his own advantage, those that exert a moral pressure on him, can be expected to contribute to solidarity. Within these two constraints let us see if, under the heading of "solidarity variables," we can make some useful additions to our outline of the ideal-typical societies.

Type A society. As I have just said, all solidarity is a matter of consciousness. According to Durkheim, all the manifestations of con-

---

[9] See the emphasis on this distinction in Alvin Gouldner's introduction to a translation of Durkheim's *Socialism* (New York: Collier, 1962).

sciousness (sentiments, beliefs, mental representations, etc.) must occur within the biological frameworks constituted by individual human organisms. Distinctively *human* forms of consciousness, however, originate within but not from the individual; they are produced by the coexistence and association of a plurality of interacting humans. Human consciousness, that is, is wholly and exclusively a social product, of which the organism, inescapably particular and individual (D 175; *198*), is only a receptacle.

Within the consciousness residing in a given individual one can distinguish two components, two complexes of "mental furniture." These are both social in origin, but differ in that one is shared with all other members of society, whereas the other is not. It is characteristic of a type *A* society that the elements of consciousness shared by all members of the society far outnumber the elements we might call idiosyncratic. In other words, practically all the mental life of type *A* individuals revolves around ideas and sentiments that they hold in common; consciousness here is not just social in origin (for all consciousness is), but is collective in nature. The individual's consciousness merges almost completely with that of his fellows.

The problem of establishing and maintaining solidarity under these conditions is solved easily—and one may well say "mechanically." Solidarity exists to the extent that individual actions are not guided primarily by private, idiosyncratic criteria. And in a type *A* society the individual is effectively dominated by collective, shared criteria. True, these societies, with their rudimentary division of labor, necessarily have a low technological and economic attainment, so that the inherently "egoistic" pressure of purely physical demands must be considerable. However, "For everything beyond the circle of such physical necessities, the consciousness . . . lies wholly outside oneself" (D 175; *198*).

Thus the crucial ingredient of the type *A* solidarity is the predominance of the shared over the idiosyncratic components of consciousness. Closely related to this characteristic are several others that deserve mention:

1. Collective mental states are "numerous": that is, they encompass most of the objects associated with one's existence. This is indicated, according to Durkheim, by the vast and diverse body of proverbs and folk knowledge present in type *A* societies. This charac-

teristic is logically implied by the very prevalence of collective consciousness, which could hardly dominate the mental life of the
individual if it did not address itself to most of the objects of his
interest.

2. Collective mental states are sharply and narrowly defined (D 45,
72; *79, 104*). Norms prescribe accepted behavior in great detail; and
conceptualizations of reality are rather specific, allowing little flexi-
bility in their interpretation. Again, Durkheim feels that this characteristic of the collective consciousness is reflected in the rich prover-
bial lore of type *A* societies.

3. Collective mental states are extremely durable. Given the last-
mentioned characteristic, close definition, there does not exist a set
of accepted alternatives from which marked changes in the collective
consciousness may evolve. This also follows from the next characteristic.

4. Collective mental states are strongly held. The images they hold
up to the individual consciousness are vivid and evoke an intense
emotional commitment, which typically finds expression in the "repressive," punitive nature of the sanctions applied when an individual challenges or violates those images (D 67, 78; *99-100, 109-10*).

In sum, the consciousness of individuals in type *A* societies is almost exclusively made up of sentiments and ideas that each man
shares with all his fellows. These sentiments and ideas encompass and
sharply define all aspects of his existence, are uniform not only over
space but over time, and are adhered to with a single-minded, almost
passionate intensity. From the utilitarian perspective, this situation
brutally suppresses the autonomy of the individual. But Durkheim
feels differently: "If in [these collectivities] such little place is made
for the individual personality, it is not that it was artificially repressed
or held back, but quite simply that at this point in history it *did not
exist*" (D 171; *194*). Another formulation of the same point maintains
that the individual is here more "acted on" (*agi*) than he is "a source
of spontaneous activity" (D 144; *169*).

As I have suggested, it makes sense in such a society to speak of
solidarity as "mechanical," in the sense that order here is not problematical. The individual is directly attached to the society (D 74;
106). And the society can easily "move as a whole" (*avec ensemble*),
for within it "the social molecules . . . do not possess movements of

their own" (D 100; *130*). In his last book, *Elementary forms of religious life* (to be discussed in Chapter 8), Durkheim returned to this characterization of "primitive" societies:

The group realizes ... an intellectual and moral uniformity of which more advanced societies offer only very rare examples. Everything is common to all. Movements are stereotyped; everybody carries out the same movements in the same circumstances, and this conformism of conduct merely reflects that of thought. All consciousnesses being caught in the same currents, the individual type is nearly confounded with the generic type. Everything is uniform, and by the same token simple (F 7-8; *18*).

Type B society. To begin with, we may characterize the solidarity present in this type of society by contrasting it with the solidarity I have attributed to type *A* societies. In a type *B* society the facts of consciousness that are collective—that is, universally shared, sharply defined, strongly entertained, and persistent over time—make up a much smaller portion of the total consciousness than they do in a type *A* society. In type *A*, "The only kind of mental life that is really developed is that which is common to all members of the group." In type *B*,

A new kind of mental life appears. Individual differences, which previously were lost and confounded within the mass of social similarities, disengage themselves, acquire saliency, and multiply. A great many things that found no place in the consciousness now become the objects of representations. ... Each individual becomes a source of spontaneous activity. Distinctive personalities take shape, become aware of themselves.... The mental life of the society ... has ... no other substratum than the consciousness of individuals, which becomes more extensive, more complex, and more flexible (D 339; *347-48*).

But if the idiosyncratic components of the social consciousness now overshadow the shared components, the problem of solidarity can no longer be solved "mechanically" by merging the individual consciousness with the collective one. The individual is no longer directly attached to the society; this attachment, the essence of solidarity, must now be established through the medium of individualized and differentiated consciousnesses, through the attachments obtaining between individuals.

How can this happen? At one point Durkheim suggests that in type *B* societies the individual consciousnesses come together not through their similarity but through their very dissimilarity (D 17; *54*). But he promptly acknowledges that this is too simplistic a solution: "Difference, as well as similarity, *may* be the cause of mutual attraction. Yet such an effect cannot be produced by just *any* difference" (D 18; *55*. My italics).

On the face of it, the only differences that may be expected to sustain "mutual attraction" are those that complement one another: the needs and resources of one differentiated actor, to the extent that they coincide with the resources and needs of another, may well bring and hold these two entities together. But this is obviously a utilitarian line of reasoning, and it appeals essentially to egoistic interest—that is, in Durkheim's view, to the antithesis of morality and solidarity. In fact, at least one passage in *Division* seems to suggest that all differences, as such, reflect individual interests and necessarily motivate egoistic behavior: "Scientifically speaking, one's conduct is egoistic to the extent that it is determined by sentiments and representations exclusively personal to oneself" (D 175; *197*).

But if we accept this, we must reject the idea of a solidarity based on differences, abandoning the attempt to conceptualize a kind of solidarity characteristic of type *B* societies; for typically, in these societies, the idiosyncratic components of consciousness are dominant. On such assumptions type *B* interindividual relations can be reduced to the utilitarian contractual model; they will at most link one individual to another, and this only in a superficial, unstable, conflict-ridden manner. They will not, even indirectly, link individuals with the society as a whole, or make society "a cohesive whole" (*un agrégat et un cohérent*. D 394; *398*). Type *B* society, that is, cannot possess solidarity, which can be established only to the extent that the society is not "true" to type *B*, to the extent that individual dissimilarities are bounded by underlying similarities.[10]

Societal Change

Side by side with the "static" treatment of the two ideal-typical societies outlined above, *Division* contains a "dynamic" theory of devel-

[10] I am by no means the first to point out the difficulties raised by Durkheim's distinction between mechanical and organic solidarity. Parsons and Nisbet, in particular, have argued against its tenability.

opment in which the analytical priority of morphological variables and the deterministic orientation that I have previously attributed to Durkheim become apparent (D Book II, Chapters 2-3). Morphological characteristics are the independent variables, institutional variables are dependent, and solidarity variables may appear as intervening variables. Wherever and whenever a society's morphological characteristics change from the configuration associated with type *A* societies to that associated with type *B* societies (this I shall call *A/B* change), *this* change, both directly and through the intervening effect of a similar change in the solidarity variables, brings about *A/B* changes in the institutional variables.

Naturally, this is a rather rigid formulation, and it does not reflect the fact that there is a considerable conceptual overlap between the dependent and independent variables. In particular, the variable extent of the division of labor directly bridges the gap between the morphological and the institutional. Nor does this formulation reflect the extent to which Durkheim's argument implies the possibility of *A/B* morphological changes occurring in a society but failing to produce analogous changes in the other two clusters of variables—with the presumable result that the society in question ceases to exist as a society, or possibly reverts to type *A* morphological characteristics. In spite of its rigidity, however, the formulation seems to me to convey the main lines of Durkheim's argument, and it can be somewhat expanded.

Morphological changes. Morphologically, a type *A* society is one with a small territory, a small population, and a low demographic density; its subunits are similar, homogeneous, and self-sufficient, only infrequently impinging on one another. The crucial *A/B* change here involves a reshuffling of the constituent subunits, so that the "walls" separating them become more and more permeable and the "social matter" is allowed to enter "wholly new combinations" (D 159; *183*). Each subunit impinges on a greater number of other subunits more frequently and in more varied ways than before. The same development also takes place within subunits, at the level of the individuals. Both within subunits and between subunits more and more people form frequent, diverse, repetitive relations with one another.

This crucial morphological change—an increase in the "moral density" of the society, as Durkheim calls it—must be preceded by more concrete morphological developments: an increase in the territorial and demographic dimensions of the society, and most critically an increase in the population/territory ratio ("material density").[11] And depending on moral density is the decisive morphological/institutional development: an increase in the differentiation of social matter, again at both the group and individual levels, through an accelerating process of division of labor. Thus even within the morphological sphere one can spell out (with some reservations, since Durkheim is not entirely clear about the terms involved and their interrelations) a sequence of *A/B* changes resulting in the wider morphological change: (1) an increase in material density; (2) an increase in moral density; (3) an increase in social differentiation and division of labor.

There is some contingency in the transition from (2) to (3), and for this reason Durkheim's argument may be less rigidly deterministic than the sequence appears to be. The increase in division of labor is predicated upon the assumption that the society will survive as a society without reverting to a type *A* material and moral density. Since an increase in density intensifies the struggle for existence between individuals and other subunits, the society must become more differentiated *if* it is not to destroy itself.[12] Thus in principle the destruction of the society can be visualized as an alternative step 2, and to this extent the latter involves some degree of contingency.

As I have stated, the division of labor bridges the conceptual distinction between morphological and institutional variables. For this reason, some of the institutional changes will flow directly from morphological changes; but most of them require intervening changes in the variables pertaining to solidarity.

Solidarity changes. The critical *A/B* change in the sphere of consciousness consists of an inversion in the ratio between shared and idiosyncratic components of individual consciousnesses. The increased size and the increased material and moral density of the society multiply both the subjects and the objects of consciousness; as a result, the number of shared beliefs, feelings, and representations

[11] Note that Durkheim had some reservations on the extent to which these or any other variables should really be regarded as "ultimate." See D 330; *339*, and R 80; *80*.

[12] In R 92-93; *92-93*, Durkheim advances some afterthoughts on this point.

diminishes—if not absolutely, at any rate relative to the totality of consciousness in the society. More and more, consciousness is made up of elements that are less permanent, less sharply defined, and less strongly held.

These characteristics need not be postulated purely on the basis of my previous typological treatment of the solidarity variables, but may be otherwise explained. For instance, the majority of the facts of consciousness *must* lose sharpness of definition and allow a certain latitude in their interpretation; otherwise they would lose all significance in the face of the multitude of diversified objects produced by the ongoing morphological changes. But if there is a certain variety in the ways certain objects are interpreted at a given time, this variety becomes a "pool" from which successive modes of interpretation can emerge to become dominant at other times. Not only this variability over time, but also another critical characteristic of the new social consciousness—its increasingly marked intellectualism, matter-of-factness, and "universalism"—can be related back to the morphological changes. As Durkheim says, "The more the *milieu* is subject to change, the greater the part that intelligence comes to play in existence" (D 256; 272-3). Finally, the normative power of the facts of consciousness that are still shared is undercut by the breakdown of traditionalism in an increasingly changeable social landscape, and by the consequent discrediting of the ascriptive authorities (kinship and local "betters") who, in the type A society, bore the main responsibility for transmitting and sanctioning the norms (D 276ff; 291ff).

This treatment of A/B change in the solidarity variables is not entirely in keeping with Durkheim's own, since he later advanced, side by side with the notion earlier emphasized as a "shrinkage" of the collective consciousness, the notion of its "weakening" (e.g., D 144; 169-70). In this view, not only does the collective consciousness come to occupy a smaller section of the total consciousness, but its own content becomes less intense and less sharply defined. But if one regards the high intensity and sharp definition of a fact of consciousness as two corollaries of its collective nature, this second conceptualization is unacceptable; and it is perhaps another expression of Durkheim's trouble in distinguishing mechanical and organic solidarity. In any case, the main line of the argument as sketched above seems to me clear and convincing: together with the morphological differentiation that an increasingly large and dense society must undergo if it is not to perish through disorder, which is caused by that morphological process, there takes place an enlargement and diversification of the society's consciousness. The enlargement, indeed, takes place mainly *through* diversification, i.e., at the idiosyncratic pole of the typical individual consciousness. Corollaries of this basic development are the increasing mutability, diminishing intensity, and lesser normative force of the facts of consciousness. All these phenomena join with the increased division of labor that is directly associated with the morphological transition, and together determine the institutional aspect of the overall *A/B* change.

Institutional changes. Although the developments discussed under the previous two headings are diffusely treated in two chapters of *Division*, this work contains little discussion of the transition from the institutional configuration associated with type *A* societies to that associated with type *B* societies.[18] In fact, the only detailed and rewarding analysis of institutional change it contains deals with the transition from primarily repressive to primarily restitutive law (D 119ff; 147ff). This lack of sustained discussion probably reflects Durkheim's view that the institutional variables are mainly dependent ones in the overall process of change. Here, I shall follow Durkheim in avoiding detailed examination of *A/B* changes in the institutional realm. The main line of development, at any rate, is fairly clear: a steady differentiation and secularization of institutions whose end result, in Durkheim's view, is an increasing autonomy of the individual. In modern times, however, this process tends, in various spheres of social life, to lag behind what is required by the increasing division of labor; hence the autonomy of individuals in those spheres appears much too absolute and unrestrained.

[18] The best discussion is in P, *passim.*

7. The Primacy of Norms

In *Division,* Durkheim attacked the utilitarian tradition on two related but distinguishable grounds: for being *individualistic,* that is, for reducing the social process to the transient relationships of individuals; and for being *utilitarian,* that is, for narrowly construing all individual action as intrinsically self-seeking and calculated. There is, of course, a significant connection between these two aspects, as Durkheim pointed out in *The rules of sociological method* (1895), his first book after *Division:*

If society in fact is only a system of means instituted by men in view of certain ends, these ends can only be individual ones, since only individuals can be in existence previous to society. It is . . . from the individual that the ideas and needs leading to the formation of societies originate; and if everything comes from him, everything is necessarily explained [exclusively] by reference to him. . . . Accordingly, sociological laws need not be anything but corollaries of the more general laws of psychology (R 97; 97).

But if any utilitarian social theory is necessarily individualistic, the converse need not be the case. Accordingly, having dealt with utilitarian individualism to his own satisfaction in *Division,* Durkheim attacked, in *Rules* and in *Suicide: A study in sociology* (1897) a non-utilitarian variant of individualism that was then being propounded by Gabriel Tarde (1843-1904).

Tarde's position was consistently individualistic. Like the utilitarians, he viewed the entire social process as the outcome of activities engaged in by individuals, whom he regarded as discrete centers of initiative, each inseparably associated with an organism and each spontaneously controlled from within. But he did not view the market transaction as a viable model of the relations between individuals, and his reduction of sociology to psychology did not presuppose a rationalistic understanding of the individual psyche's operation. Instead, he explicitly emphasized the "ideal" components of action (beliefs, feelings, and evaluations) that Durkheim had condemned the utilitarian tradition for slighting.

Tarde placed an individualistic construction on the genesis and operation of these ideal elements. They might *seem* to operate from outside the individual, to be properties of the collectivity that validated and sanctioned them. But, Tarde argued, this only happened if and to the extent that ideal elements, originating within the psyche of an individual, became generalized over a number of associated individuals through being spontaneously echoed and adopted by each. The ideal ways of acting and thinking characteristic of a collectivity became characteristic and acquired normative significance only because of the individual's basic propensity to "imitate" his fellows—a propensity as basic to Tarde's model as the propensity to enter contractual relations had been to the utilitarian model. Like the contractual relation, Tarde's imitative act could initiate relations between individuals who at first felt no solidarity with one another, shared no belonging. And even imitated feeling could sustain further interaction between the same individuals facilitating further imitation and even engendering obligations and other constraints on spontaneity. But in all this, the individual psyche was the starting point. As Durkheim noted:

Imitation is a purely psychological process, as is shown by the fact that it can take place among individuals connected by no social bond. A man can imitate another without their being solidary with one another or with a group on which both depend, and in itself the propagation [of a manner of acting] through imitation cannot make them solidary. . . . [For imitation to occur] it is not necessary that there exist any intellectual or moral community between them, nor that they exchange services, nor even that they speak the same language; and they are no more bound to one another after its occurrence than before (S 107; 123).

As far as Durkheim was concerned, this would not do. Tarde did conceive the crucial act of imitation in nonutilitarian terms, he did devote great attention to the "ideal" elements of action, and he recognized the difference they made to the social process once they had emerged. But for all this, he was attempting to build a sociological theory on individualistic premises, and Durkheim thought such an attempt doomed from the start. It was doomed on epistemological grounds, since Tarde failed to locate a realm of reality *sui generis*, distinguishable from the operations of the individual psyche, that sociology could elect as its own subject, thus asserting its scientific autonomy, its scholarly dignity, and its pragmatic relevance. And on substantive grounds, Tarde's formulation failed because it did not acknowledge that once the ultimate components of action were placed exclusively within the individual's psyche (be he conceived as *un échangiste* or as an imitative animal) no coherent solution could be given to what Durkheim considered the crucial sociological and social problem: the binding and guiding of individual lines of action from a collective center, through collective constraints and in the name of collective interests. "There can be no sociology unless societies exist, and . . . societies cannot exist if there are only individuals" (S 38).[1]

The rules of sociological method, as its title indicates, develops Durkheim's epistemological critique of Tarde's psychological-individualistic approach to sociology. *Suicide*, on the other hand, presents a substantive critique of individualism per se: Tarde is the main object, but not the only one; there are also repeated refutations of what could be called the "utilitarian" interpretation of suicide (e.g., S 154-55, 236, 250ff, 265ff; *156-57, 219, 331ff, 242ff*), in the form of a sustained, distinctively *sociological* analysis of this major social phenomenon. Throughout, Durkheim aims at conclusions transcending a description of suicide alone, but he attains them from the ground up, that is, inductively.

Suicide is, above all, a book about suicide; and it remains to this day a model sociological monograph, preserving much of its significance as an empirical study.[2] I use it as the principal source for this chapter. My treatment, however, will focus primarily on its wider theoretical argument, referring to the phenomenon of suicide only

---

[1] This quote is from the Preface to the first edition of *Suicide* and does not appear in the current French edition I have used.

[2] For a contemporary methodological assessment of *Suicide*, see Hanan Selvin, "Durkheim's *Suicide* and problems of empirical research," in S. M. Lipset and Neil Smelser, eds., *Sociology: The progress of a decade* (Englewood Cliffs, N.J.: Prentice-Hall, 1960), pp. 132ff.

occasionally. Essentially, I will conduct a back-to-front reading of the text such that its inductive *démarche* is inverted. As a consequence, I will concentrate on the later and more general parts of the book rather than the earlier and more topical parts.

Society as a Distinctive Realm of Reality

Durkheim had argued in *Division* that society cannot be treated purely as the resultant of individual actions, and that human collectivities are something more than clusters of individuals—that indeed, only on this account can human collectivities be said to exist. Arguments at the same level of generality are advanced in *Rules*, and to a lesser extent in *Suicide*. But in the latter work these arguments are proposed on strictly empirical grounds, through a close examination of differing suicide rates drawn from an impressive array of statistical data.

Durkheim establishes one major conclusion: distinctive and relatively stable suicide rates are associated with social circumstances. For example, if we calculate the suicide rate (number of suicides in a given year over total population) for a number of different countries and years, we find that it varies from country to country, and that both the country rates and the relative differences between country rates remain very much the same from one year to another. The same result turns up in the examination of suicide rates for different religious, occupational, age, and marital-status groupings within national populations. Furthermore the differentials in the rates among the above (and other) groupings vary systematically as between one country and another. In most countries, for instance, the rate for the liberal professions is higher than that for other occupational groupings to roughly the same degree.

These uniformities suggest that suicide rates are properties of the populations or subpopulations in question as wholes and not as collections of discrete individuals. "Every society is predisposed to yielding a determinate proportion of voluntary deaths. . . . Every nation, collectively, possesses its own inclination to suicide" (S 343; 305). Hence Durkheim's analysis of suicide rates is inherently sociological, since it is concerned with collective units: "It is the social [suicide] rates we must take as the immediate object of analysis. . . . Leaving aside the individual *qua* individual, his motivations and ideas, we shall inquire . . . into those characteristics [*états*] of the different social *milieux* that determine the variations in the suicide rate" (S 143, 148; *148, 151*). Through a complex argument that I will not consider here (S Book I), Durkheim concludes that these very characteristics, which must be postulated to account for the distinctive, stable suicide rates of the different social *milieux*, are themselves social (rather than natural or psychological); they are not simply in operation *in* the society, but are properties *of* the society.

The necessity of postulating such characteristics definitely establishes, to Durkheim's mind, the existence of society as a distinctive realm of reality that cannot be considered a plurality of interacting individuals:

> It is true indeed that society has no other acting forces than those of individuals. . . . [But individuals] in coming together [*en s'unissant*] form a psychical entity of a new kind, which . . . possesses ways of thinking and feeling of its own. . . . The group formed by the associated individuals is a reality of a different order from each individual taken singly. . . . The collective states are grounded in the nature of the group and are in existence before they can affect the individual as such and bring about in him, by achieving a new form of organization, a purely self-contained existence (S 362; *320*).

The Components of Society

Durkheim also phrases the point just developed by stating that society is a whole greater than the sum of its parts (R 102; *102*). Strictly speaking, as he implicitly acknowledges (S 361-62; *320*), this is a contradictory statement. Whatever is in the whole other than the sum of its parts must itself be a part, by definition. And in fact, one uses the statement to mean: there is more to the whole that what somebody says are its only parts; somebody is committing a fallacy by his incomplete enumeration of parts.[3]

According to Durkheim, those who recognize only individuals as the components of society commit such a fallacy. True, individuals are indeed society's only *acting* components, and all human doing and thinking must take place through them. But the *what* and *how*, as against the *who*, of doing and thinking always reveal nonindi-

---

[3] This point is *relatively* explicit in P 73.

vidual components of the society, and the identification of these components eliminates the fallacy. Ultimately, in Durkheim's view, what is exclusively a property of individuals is the ability to deploy or not deploy conscious effort in response to ways of doing and thinking that are in themselves the properties not of individuals but of society. Society, in fact, can be said to exist exactly if and to the extent that individuals are confronted with ways of doing and thinking that they can (by deploying effort) make their own, but which are not intrinsically of their own making. Conversely, no social reality can emerge purely from ways of acting that originate entirely within the individuals, that is, from purely private facts.

This formulation of the Durkheimian position is misleading if it seems to present the actual alternatives of either the individual *cum* society or the individual doing and thinking in ways entirely of his own making. In fact, there can be no such things as individuals without a society. Take away the latter and the individual himself disappears as a concept, since he is ultimately the cumulative, patterned resultant of his own positive or negative responses to ways of doing and thinking originating outside himself. The irony of an individualistic social theory is that it negates not only society but also the individual.

Thus, if I have traced his argument correctly, Durkheim sees two kinds of components that make up society: on the one hand individuals, and on the other *collective* ways of *individual* doing and thinking. But this position summarizes a rather more involved one, which can be reconstructed from *Suicide* and includes the following components:

1. Individuals.

2. A vast and varied body of artifacts. For example: "houses and buildings of all sorts . . . avenues of communication and transport . . . instruments and machines in use in industry and in private life . . . the written language . . . [and] those definite formulas in which are summarized the dogmas of faith or the rules of law, when they become externally fixated in a consecrated form" (S 354; 313-14). These are all significant components of society in that all of them, after their own fashion, "become autonomous realities, independent of individuals" (S 354; 314). However, their impact on social life is

derivative, since each of them comes into existence purely as the embodiment of particular elements already present in the social consciousness. Houses and buildings embody "a given type of architecture"; instruments and machines embody "the state of technology"; and so on.

3. It thus seems appropriate to designate as a distinctive (and much more significant) component of society the "actual and living" representations, sentiments, and conceptions that lie behind artifacts and are "signified" by them.

4. We must also classify as a separate component those aspects of social consciousness that are not embodied in artifacts—currents of feeling of a more diffuse or transitory nature, which may have a momentous impact on collective life without altering or removing the objectified signs of the more persistent feelings and notions referred to as Component 3.

5. The first four components are those I have culled from a few pages in *Suicide* where Durkheim, without explicitly asking what society is made of, deals with the question in a fairly sustained manner. Toward the end of the book he introduces what might perhaps be considered a further component:

The manner in which the social elements are assembled and organized....
Given a population formed by a certain number of individuals distributed [over a territory] in a certain fashion, there results a determinate set of collective ideas and practices.... According to how numerous the component parts are and to what plan they are arranged by, the nature of the collective entity necessarily varies, and consequently its ways of thinking and doing vary (S 446; 387).

It seems to me that the last component is not at the same level of analysis as the others. It lies, as it were, upstream from them, and it appears to answer the question "What makes the components of society take the shape they do?" rather than the question "What are the components of society?" The passage just quoted, of course, also reasserts the priority of the morphological elements already posited in *Division*; but this priority bears on a concern (developmental rather than functional) that is foreign to the main argument in *Suicide*. Within that main argument, Durkheim subjects his set of components to a process of elimination, eventually concluding, as we shall see, that Component 3 is by far the most crucial one.

The Strategic Priority of Norms

In *Rules*, Durkheim had already sketched a less elaborate typology of social components while attempting a broad classification of "social facts" (R *5ff*; *3ff*). Leaving aside individuals and morphological elements, he presented two contrasting categories: (1) "ways of acting" (*manières de faire*), or "physiological" social facts (this corresponds to our Components 3 and 4); (2) "ways of being" (*manières d'être*), or "anatomical" social facts (much like Component 2).

Durkheim then argued (as he was to do again in *Suicide*), that the anatomical social facts were really less significant, since "ways of being are nothing but consolidated ways of acting" and are thus merely derivative. Of course, once the objectified components of society are discounted "ways of thinking and doing" emerge as the social facts *par excellence* (R xvii; *xlix*). But these are purely "things that people carry around in their heads," mental facts, representations. Both *Rules* and *Suicide* clearly proclaim: "Social life consists entirely of representations. . . . Essentially, the social *milieu* is made up of collective ideas, beliefs, habits, and tendencies (R xi; *xli*. S *339*; *302*).

This is the conclusion we have anticipated. The distinctive reality of society revolves around the *what* and *how* of human affairs. Society is made up of patterned ways of doing and thinking that are external to the individual, although they can only be acted upon and thought out (or fail to be) through the agency of the individual himself. The adjective "patterned," incidentally, implies that transitory and diffuse tendencies (Component 4) cannot claim much significance. Society, for Durkheim, is the totality of the relatively stable and well-defined representations that direct the behavior of individuals (both what the individual does and what he thinks) by establishing a standard for this behavior and exerting pressure on the individual such that he will conform to the standard.

For the moment, we may refer to all such representations as norms. We shall see in the next chapter how a norm operates, how it exercises its pressure on the individual and concretely affects his behavior. Here I shall examine the related problem of the norm's structure, mostly following one of Durkheim's numerous discussions of the theme, a set of "theses on the determination of social facts" that he submitted to a French learned society in 1906.

Not all representations that set a standard for individual conduct actually qualify as norms proper, as moral rules; in addition, there are technical, or "mechanical," rules. Both kinds of rules prescribe a line of individual conduct; and both kinds, being standards *for* conduct and not descriptions *of* conduct, are open to the possibility that conduct may in fact depart from the standard, although this failure to conform is typically punished by some sort of "unpleasant consequence." However, only in the case of technical rules do the consequences occur mechanically, that is, through the operation of an objective necessity. When somebody fails to observe, say, a legal rule (which is a distinctive and important type of moral rule), the negative consequences flowing from the violation do not obey the same intrinsic, matter-of-fact necessity.

Two examples from my own childhood in Fascist Italy may clarify the difference. When I was learning to read and picking readable signs out of my surroundings, I frequently noticed two very similar notices. One, hanging from high-tension electric towers, said, "Chi tocca i fili muore" (whoever touches the wires dies); the other, painted in block letters on the walls of many houses and public buildings, stated "Chi tocca la Milizia avrà del piombo" (whoever touches the Militia, i.e., the paramilitary organization of the Fascist Party, will catch lead). In the first case, death would follow automatically without any voluntary human intervention, and could be predicted purely from an analysis of the operation of touching a high-voltage wire. In the second case, death would come from a voluntary human act, and could not be predicted by analyzing the operation of "touching" the Militia. As Durkheim would say, the link between the violation of the rules and its unpleasant consequence was in this case purely a synthetic one; and he reserved the term "sanction" for such consequences: "A sanction is a consequence of an act that does not result from the content of that act but from the violation by that act of a preestablished rule" (SP 43).

From the structural standpoint, the relation between a norm and behavior is intrinsically open-ended; that is, the norm's effect on behavior is always contingent on the effort voluntarily expended in response to it. One can perhaps distinguish (although Durkheim does not) two areas of contingency: performance contingency and sanction contingency. The first separates the norm's command from compliance with it, and rests on the fact that norms, being external to the individual, bring about the congruent behavior not automatically but through the mediation of consciousness (S 113, 115; *127, 129*) and must overcome subjective resistance (S 361; *319*). The second similarly separates compliance or noncompliance from the sanction (respectively positive or negative) and rests, as we have seen, on the synthetic nature of the link between the rule and the consequences of its observance or violation.

Durkheim pays no sustained attention to sanction contingency, probably because the application of a sanction relating to a given norm becomes itself the object of a second-level norm addressed to another individual, so that what is sanction contingency from the standpoint of the first-level norm appears as performance contingency from the standpoint of the second-level norm. Another reason why Durkheim does not explicitly discuss the sanction contingency is his concern lest an individual be overly concerned with calculating the magnitude and probability of the positive sanction for conformity or the negative sanction for violation. In this case, the specifically *moral* nature of the pressure (*contrainte*) that the norm is supposed to exercise upon conduct may be progressively obscured in the individual's own mind. This phenomenon, if widespread, would have a profound and dangerous destabilizing effect on society in general; thus Durkheim considers it both analytically and morally imperative to deemphasize the sanction contingency and concentrate on the direction of individual responses to the first-order norm. It is consistent with this preoccupation that Durkheim should systematically discount the role of force in maintaining individual conformity with norms (e.g., S 279; *251-53*). His resulting construction of the impact of norms on behavior, as I have said, will be discussed in Chapter 8.

In this section I have presented a reduction of the social order to the norm that I consider essential to Durkheim's whole argument, in

Suicide and elsewhere.[4] A close reader of *Suicide*, however, might consider this reduction invalid, pointing out Durkheim's repeated suggestions (S 264, 288, 311; *241, 258, 179*) that society should be seen not only as the fount of normative regulation but also as the object of individual attachments, and that the cohesion of society and the regulation issuing from society are two distinctive dimensions of the social order. Given this, should we not define the components of society in a more differentiated way than I have done so far in this chapter?

But the distinction between cohesion and regulation, like that between mechanical and organic solidarity, may be one on which Durkheim places more weight than its analytical tenability warrants. In particular, his interpretation of the differential suicide rates of various religious groups implicitly suggests that in his own view a society's cohesion depends on the extent to which individuals are made the subjects of norms, and is thus a product of regulation. The fact that in one passage (to be discussed presently) his distinction between "egoistic" and "anomic" suicide is linked to that between cohesion and regulation (or rather between lack of the former and lack of the latter) is not decisive, for two reasons. In the first place, the distinction between egoistic and anomic suicide can be alternatively construed in terms of different types of norm. In the second place, Durkheim's own attempt to base the distinction on that between cohesion and regulation is intrinsically faulty. This can best be seen from a longish footnote (S 311; *279*) in which Durkheim insists that cohesion and regulation *should* be treated as mutually independent variables but fails to establish his case.

In this footnote, Durkheim suggests that besides the three types of suicide he postulates—egoistic, altruistic, and anomic, resulting respectively from defective cohesion, excessive cohesion, and defective regulation—one could recognize a fourth type, fatalistic suicide, that results from excessive regulation. Now, sociologists who are dealing with two mutually independent two-valued variables (here, values of

---

[4] See Rene Koenig, "Gesellschaft," in Rene Koenig, ed., *Soziologie* (Frankfurt am Main: Fischer, 1958), p. 128: "Damit wird die soziale *Norm* sichtbar, die für Durkheim den Begriff Gesellschaft als den Inbegriff des geregelten Verhaltens erscheinen lässt." For some critical remarks on this point, see Chapter 9.

defect or excess, minus or plus) that affect the same phenomenon are accustomed to comparing them by generating a simple fourfold table. This is obtained by "crossing" the two variables to make four cells. For example, with variables *A* and *B*, and values of plus or minus, one obtains

		Variable *A*	
		$+$	$-$
Variable *B*	$+$	$+A, +B$	$-A, +B$
	$-$	$+A, -B$	$-A, -B$

But there is no way of constructing such a table with Durkheim's pretended independent variables as its two coordinates and his four types of suicide as its cells; that is, no "property space"[5] comprising the four types will result from actually treating his two variables as independent and crossing them. Durkheim's argument would yield the following tabular arrangement:

		Variable *A*	
		$-$	$+$
Variable *B*	Cohesion	$-C$ egoistic suicide	$+C$ altruistic suicide
	Regulation	$-R$ anomic suicide	$+R$ fatalistic suicide

But this is obviously not a real fourfold table. "Variable *A*" is not a variable; and "Variable *B*" is not one but two variables. Cohesion and regulation are juxtaposed, but they cannot be "crossed," either because they are not independent of one another or because they belong to two different levels of conceptualization. I have already suggested that Durkheim's own treatment assumes the dependence of cohesion on regulation in spite of his claims to the contrary. At any rate, Durkheim's repeated discussions of the nature of society,

[5] On this concept see Allen Barton, "The concept of property space in social research," in Paul Lazarsfeld and Morris Rosenberg, eds., *The Language of social research* (Glencoe, Ill.: Free Press, 1955), pp. 40-53.

the concept of social fact, and morals unequivocally indicate that in his thought normative regulation has no rival as the central and critical component of society.

Some Key Norms

So far I have spoken of norms in quite general terms; but Durkheim, in *Suicide* and elsewhere, pays considerable attention to the variety of norms that characterize a society (indeed, if the argument so far has any validity, *make up* a society). Much of his attention goes to norms associated with specific societal subunits and specific social institutions (P *passim*). Book III of *Suicide*, however, at two points (S 363ff, 416ff; *321ff, 363ff*) discusses three norms that he considers universal in that they are to be found in the "moral constitution" of *any* society (and perhaps of any group). Since he arrives at these norms inductively, arguing from his previous classification of the "suicidogenic currents" (egoism, altruism, anomie), it would be rash to assume that in his view the types exhaust the class of universal norms; after all, the study of phenomena other than suicide might have led him to construct a different set of such norms. However, the three he does locate are certainly among the most important universal norms, and they certainly possess a high level of generality. In fact, each is not so much a single norm as a "metanorm," a broad normative principle that any given society might embody in a variety of single norms, each with specific sanctions attached to it.

On the basis of his analysis of suicide rates, Durkheim suggests that all societies *must* harbor the following moral ideas:

Metanorm A. The individual ought to acknowledge, and advance through self-denial or if necessary self-sacrifice, the interest of the society to which he belongs, as well as that society's superiority over himself as an individual.

Metanorm B. The individual ought to attach some significance to his own personality, feel responsible for himself and toward himself. His conduct ought to be to some extent guided from inside himself, by his own conscience. In sum, he ought to develop his individuality.

Metanorm C. The individual ought to extend by his action the boundaries of his own existence and the existence of his fellow human beings. He should not be bound by slavish, indiscriminate loyalty to whatever norms are in existence.

These three norms, which Durkheim insists are to be found in every society, are at the same time complementary and incompatible: they both support and limit one another in a delicate equilibrium. As Durkheim said in *Division*, without reference to any specific norms: "Moral life, not unlike that of the body and the mind, must meet different and even contradictory requirements. Thus it is naturally made up in part of contradictory elements that limit and control one another" (D 7; 44).

In *Suicide*, however, Durkheim argues that in the "moral constitution" of each society one of these metanorms will tend to overshadow the other two. For this reason the norms, though universal, assume a variety of configurations. In particular, one may expect that different "mixes" of metanorms will characterize one society as against another, one phase in the development of a society against another phase, and one subunit of society against another subunit. For instance, comparing the moral constitutions of "primitive" and "advanced" societies, we would find that in the former metanorm *A* prevails over metanorms *B* and *C*, whereas in the latter metanorms *B* and *C* are more pervasive and cogent than metanorm *A*.

The Normality of Deviant Behavior

The social realm is made up of norms, and no society can survive without establishing and maintaining Durkheim's three metanorms, as well as many others. But this does not mean that only positive effects will come from the presence and operation of norms. Aside from the fact that any norm, as such, is inherently subject to being violated (the "performance contingency" we have identified), the very observance of any given norm may develop effects that contradict the assumptions and demands of other norms—and as we have said, this is especially true of the broader metanorms. Moreover, in a relatively differentiated society one must also expect that a given norm will not apply uniformly; there will be social areas where it is weak and ineffective, and other areas where it is propounded and upheld with such intensity that individuals "overcomply" with it.

For all these reasons, the basic metanorms, indispensable as they are to each society, may be expected to produce unintended negative effects, since each of them creates and strengthens some tendencies of behavior that are directly opposed to the others. In particular, their currency may engender the specific deviation that is suicide. The *explanandum* mentioned earlier—the distinctive and stable suicide rates that characterize given populations—can thus find its *explanans* in the extent to which the "moral constitution" of a given society or its subunits reflects this or that relationship between the three metanorms. "The social rate of suicide can only be explained sociologically. It is the moral constitution of a society that determines its proportion of voluntary deaths at any given moment" (S 336; 299).

Let us see how Durkheim articulates this generalization. Take, to begin with, a society (or social subunit) whose rules and institutions tend to emphasize metanorm *A*, the necessity of self-denial for the common good. Here, the individual is continuously reminded of the superiority of society over himself, of the sanctity of his own obligations to the group; he has little or no sense of himself as an independent center of initiative, as an irreplaceable, morally unique reality, as the beneficiary of his own efforts and the source of his own sense of personal worth. In some cases, a society with this normative emphasis may actually command or expect a man to commit suicide under certain circumstances, so that suicide cannot even be considered a form of deviant behavior. But even in a society that does not permit suicide under any circumstance there may be a high suicide rate due *indirectly* to metanorm *A*, which diminishes the individual's sense of dignity, the significance and uniqueness that a society gives to its single members.

Similarly, we might find a subunit of society whose characteristic norms overemphasize the value of abnegation and self-denial, stressing the individual's obligation to sacrifice his own idiosyncratic needs and tendencies to the demands of the group (a professional army, for example). It is understandable that an individual in this subunit, even when not expressly commanded, expected, or morally permitted to commit suicide, would nonetheless dispose of himself on very slight provocation. Again, the supremacy of metanorm *A* does not permit him to feel that his individual life is worth living when he is confronted by a momentary setback or some other source of irritation and dismay.

In sum, societies or groups that overstress metanorm *A* while inadequately observing metanorms *B* and *C* may be expected to yield a relatively high "contingent of voluntary deaths," mostly owing to the excessive hold the group has on the individual and the little space he has for feelings of personal dignity and significance. This is the type of suicide that Durkheim calls "altruistic."

By contrast, in societies where the mix of metanorms strongly favors metanorm *B*, the individual is encouraged to think of himself as an autonomous source of initiative, a distinctive, irreplaceable personality that controls its own destiny. There is no question here of suicide being normatively permitted, let alone encouraged or commanded. However, this normative pattern indirectly engenders its own suicidogenic current, mainly by isolating the individual and diminishing his personal feelings of solidarity and responsibility for others. As far as suicide is concerned, the individual is unavoidably (though unintentionally) highly "at risk." The social context that obligates and sustains him is too loose, too "thin," to tell him with sufficient authority "Thou shalt not kill thyself." Thus when individuals in this society (through whatever vicissitudes) are tempted to do away with themselves, a high rate of "egoistic" suicide can be expected.

The imagery I have used so far is somewhat misleading, for it simply elaborates without explanation the notion of societal cohesion that Durkheim himself uses—which is, I suggest, a derivative notion. The determining factor of both cohesion and suicide is the amount of normative regulation in a society. This is clear, in particular, from the way Durkheim explains the differing suicide rates of Catholics and Protestants. He argues that Catholics have a lower rate of (egoistic) suicide because theirs is a more cohesive religious grouping; but in fact he ascribes this higher cohesion to the greater volume of regulation issuing from the Catholic Church. A Protestant sect attaches high normative significance to the individual's own judgment in matters of faith, morals, and ritual, and to his own feeling of personal responsibility; necessarily, the framework of normative regulation affecting the individual believer is less detailed and cogent than it is for a Catholic. The Protestant believer is thus more open and free, but by the same token he is more exposed to temptation. Should he ever confront a shattering crisis, he has fewer normative restrictions to dissuade him from suicide.

Finally, the prevalence of metanorm C within a society or sub-society means not that the what and how of action are largely left to the individual (as in the previous example), but rather that the what and how, whatever their origin, lose any normative significance. The striving embodied in action per se has come to be evaluated as morally far more significant than the earnestness with which an individual abides by the what and how of action, however determined. Specific means and ends of action, whether assigned to the individual by the collectivity or chosen by himself, are normatively devaluated, since the predominant metanorm encourages the individual to tamper with them, challenge them, and transcend them. Every attainment is considered only as one step toward a greater attainment, and as meaningless unless it leads to the latter. Every determinate form of action is only valid provisionally, that is, as long as it objectively recommends itself as the best means to a goal. Only the pursuit of continuous improvement is considered morally worthy.

Typically, metanorm C is found in association with metanorm B, and the two together, by encouraging change, have considerable positive effects on the society where they jointly prevail. Norm B allows a certain variation in the ways certain actions are carried out by encouraging each individual to elaborate his own way; norm C allows the resulting collection of relatively differentiated practices to function as a "pool" from which those most suitable to a changing situation can be selected.

Important as these effects are for modern society (and they are characteristic of it), the currency of metanorm C, in particular, can also have considerable negative effects: "One no longer knows what is or is not possible, what is just or unjust, which claims and expectations are right and which are excessive. . . . Consequently, there is no longer anything to which one does not feel entitled. . . . The appetites no longer acknowledge any boundaries at which they must stop" (S 280-81; 253). This is indeed what happens under the conditions of widespread and sustained economic change that modern societies tend to make permanent. "The doctrine of progress at all costs and as rapidly as possible becomes an article of faith" (S 287; 257). Consequently, throughout the society all manner of possessions and privileges hitherto reserved for particular social strata become accessible to others. By the same token, those possessions and privileges lose their cherished significance for the groups who previously monopolized them, and these groups are compelled to attain new possessions and privileges.

Whatever advantages the society may draw from this massive urge toward universal self-advancement, it must also suffer a drastic emotional discoloration. Certain objects and ideas had previously oriented and validated each individual's sense of achievement, allowing him to feel at peace with himself and at ease in his station. Now, metanorm C encourages everyone to attempt more and more, to seek more and more. All men are in a state of constant tension, and nothing they already possess seems to establish their worth or relieve their anxiety. Such relentlessly striving individuals are quite vulnerable in the event of a setback—indeed, sometimes in the event of apparent success. An individual whose conduct reflects the normative priority of metanorm C is out on a limb: he has burnt his bridges, and acknowledges no standard (either his own or the collectivity's) that might establish a balance between his achievements and his desires. He is intent on a pursuit that denies meaning to every concrete attainment and may itself become meaningless. The envy, disappointment, and frustration that these circumstances produce in the society can be expected to generate a distinctively high rate of the suicides that Durkheim calls "anomic."

Let us recapitulate. Discarding as futile and dangerous the various attempts to build up an individualistic social theory, whether utilitarian or not, Durkheim seeks to establish in *Suicide* (and elsewhere) that society is a distinctive realm of reality irreducible to individuals and their relations. The key components of this realm are mental representations, which establish what and how individuals ought to act and think; these are the stuff of social reality. These representations are *not* produced by individuals and later spread through imitation; nor are they primarily characterized by their objective appropriateness as means to private ends. On the contrary, they are external to the individual, and the pressure they exercise on him is a moral pressure. They tell the individual that he *ought* to do something. (This last point will be elaborated in Chapter 8.)

The empirical study of suicide rates leads Durkheim to locate three very important clusters of representations, three metanorms, each producing certain suicidogenic side effects:

> There is no moral ideal that does not combine, in proportions varying from one society to another, egoism, altruism, and a degree of anomie. Social life, indeed, simultaneously presupposes that the individual have a certain personality, that he be ready, if requested by the community, to jettison it, and that he accept ideas of progress to a certain extent. Accordingly, there is no people among whom one cannot find all these currents of opinion, which affect the individual in divergent and even contradictory ways. Where they counteract one another, the [actor] is in a state of equilibrium that preserves him from even thinking about suicide. But let one of them increase its intensity to the others' disadvantage, and it will display suicidogenic effects. . . . The stronger it is, the more subjects it will affect deeply enough to produce suicide; and vice versa (S 363; 321).

The state of normative equilibrium that can minimize the incidence of suicide is not frequently attained or easily maintained. It is attained among the followers of the Catholic faith, since this group attaches enough significance to metanorm *B* to counter the suicidogenic potentialities of metanorm *A* but not enough significance to isolate the individual and put him under serious pressure. It is emphatically not attained in modern society as a whole, according to Durkheim. In fact, the modern predominance of metanorms *B* and *C* is so strong that Durkheim, in this context, qualifies his thesis that deviance is "normal." One sphere of social life that has long—and appropriately—been characterized by the dominance of metanorms *B* and *C* is that of economic-professional activity, which has rapidly gained such ascendancy that the overall moral constitution of modern society is dangerously unbalanced. A general and abrupt increase in suicide rates is both a product and an indicator of this threatening development.

To counter this threat one must engineer large-scale institutional arrangements that can counteract the isolation and demoralization caused by the pervasive significance of metanorms *B* and *C*. Since these two metanorms are very closely associated (indeed, one could argue that Durkheim never establishes a satisfactory distinction between them), the same arrangements may keep both within bounds. The arrangements that Durkheim suggests are similar to guilds, the corporate, publicly recognized groups of producers (both employers and employees) that liberalism had destroyed throughout Europe. Once reestablished with the appropriate modifications, such groups could become the objects of individual loyalty on the part of their members, and would also provide an authoritative regulation of activities. The individual would regain the sense of obligation toward his fellow men and the contentment with his own possessions and privileges that an excess of metanorms *B* and *C* tends to destroy (D Preface).

In this argument, one may note, the distinction between cohesion and regulation is again present. However, Durkheim's reliance on norms as *the* strategic components of social reality reasserts itself, behind the surface of his argument, in the way he construes the operation of these projected institutional arrangements. The corporate groups' ability to produce norms (and back them with effective sanctions) appears throughout as their essential characteristic, and the cohesion they promote is secondary and derivative. The essence of Durkheim's argument, here as elsewhere, is simply: "Let there be norms." Without norms there is no social life, and thus no human life as such.

8. Religion and the Theory
of Institutions

In his Preface to the second edition of *Rules* (1901), Durkheim defined sociology as "the science of institutions, of their genesis and functioning" (R xxii; *lx*). In the same text, however, he stated:

In the present state of the discipline, we do not really know what are even the major social institutions—state or family, the right of property or contract, punishment or responsibility. We ignore almost entirely the causes on which they depend, the functions they fulfill, and the laws of their evolution; we barely begin to perceive some light on a few of these points (R xv; *xlvi*).

From the juxtaposition of these two statements one might suppose that Durkheim consistently focused his own research and writing on the nature of institutions, the variety of forms they assume, and their interrelations. In actuality, the central concept of his work is not that of institutions but that of norms. Institutions are, indeed, "made of" norms, and to that extent they find a place in Durkheim's thought. But he concerns himself mostly with norms as such, with what all norms have in common rather than with the differentiated clusters of norms that make up institutions.

Only in Durkheim's last major work, *Elementary forms of religious life* (1912), do institutions as such receive sustained attention. And even here, as the title indicates, Durkheim adopts only one of the possible strategies of institutional analysis: the detailed discussion of a single major institution. However, in this book and in other writings of his that I have already mentioned Durkheim does sometimes adopt a higher level of generality, discussing the very concept of institution, the "genesis and functioning" of *any* institutions. I will first outline the results Durkheim achieved along this line of inquiry in *Division, Rules,* and *Elementary forms,* returning in the last part of the chapter to the "case study" of religion.

In the writings under discussion Durkheim does not devote much thought to defining the concept of institution. A recent commentator, Guy Aimard, notes:

Durkheim adopted the definition given by Mauss and Fauconnet in their article "Sociologie" in the *Grande Encyclopédie,* and understood by "institutions" all manners of thinking, feeling, and acting sufficiently crystallized that the individual finds them preestablished and quite generally transmitted through education. "An institution," he writes in *Rules,* "is a previously instituted set of actions or ideas with which individuals find themselves confronted and which are more or less imposed on them."[1]

It is easy to detect the circular reasoning in a definition where the same notion occurs in two different forms ("institution" and "instituted") both in the *definiendum* and in the *definiens.* The same flaws occur in another of Durkheim's definitions, according to which institutions are "all beliefs and all modes of conduct instituted by the collectivity" (R xx; *lvi*). This second statement, furthermore, does not distinguish between the concepts of norm and of institution, whereas the definition quoted by Aimard points up the distinctive connotation of the latter by speaking of "a set [*un ensemble*] of actions and ideas." An institution, that is, is a plurality of *manières de penser et d'agir* focused on a distinctive field of social activity; and it is a salient continuous or recurrent concern of society as a whole. These two related points are not elaborated at length by Durkheim, but they emerge from his treatment of specific institutions.[2]

The Genesis of Institutions

Most considerations advanced by Durkheim on this problem can best be formulated in negative terms. They amount, essentially, to a denial that institutions originate as arrangements contrived by individuals in a rational effort to master the contingencies of their own existence. The fact that institutions do sustain individual existence

---

[1] Guy Aimard, *Durkheim et la science économique* (Paris: P.U.F., 1962), p. 25.
[2] See, for instance, F 49, 56; *51, 56.* Also Durkheim, *Journal sociologique* (Paris: Université Française, 1969), pp. 461-62, where a short "Note sur les systèmes juridiques" applies to legal systems a distinction between "practices" and "institutions."

directly and indirectly is no reason for assuming that individuals set about establishing them with that end in view (R 100; *100-101*).

This denial, taken by itself, might be interpreted as another expression of Durkheim's polemic against utilitarianism, which views purposive, instrumental action as a potential threat to the social order, to be guided and restrained by normative considerations. If this were so, we would expect the denial to be complemented by a positive stress on the significance for institution-making of expressive rather than instrumental action, of sentiments rather than rational calculation. And indeed, as a corollary to his negative remarks Durkheim often emphasizes the significance of beliefs, emotions, and expressive behavior (that is, behavior adopted otherwise than as the best available means to a sought end);[3] but his emphasis is on collective sentiments, which find in individuals purely a channel or vessel and not an ultimate source.[4]

The point, as I have previously suggested, is that antiutilitarianism is the major but not the only expression of Durkheim's broader condemnation of individualism per se, which involves a further denial that the individual's private emotions or expressive actions can constitute the source of institutions. Durkheim denies, for instance, that the family should be understood to have originated as an expression of individual affection and attachment, or funerary rites as an expression of the sorrow individuals felt over the death of a kinsman or friend. Such sentiments, as individual sentiments, do not so much generate institutional practices as flow from them. (When felt, of course, they may indirectly reinforce the hold that institutional practices maintain on behavior.)

In sum, Durkheim holds that nothing taking place within the private experience of the individual (be it emotional or intellectual) can be expected to play a significant role in the genesis of institutions. This being understood, one may acknowledge that he addresses his most frequent and explicit condemnation to the utilitarian view of

[3] This point is made in a passage that Durkheim left out of the second edition of *Division*, which is available in the English edition. See D 418.

[4] This point seems to have been missed by Claude Lévi-Strauss, judging from his critique of Durkheim in *Totemism* (Boston: Beacon, 1963), p. 71. The stress on the creative nature of collective sentiments is accompanied, in Durkheim, by an awareness of the derivative nature of individual sentiments.

that genesis. To begin with, he argues that in this context stressing purposive action is poor scientific strategy simply because the subjectively entertained purposes of the actors allegedly presiding over the institution-making activities are not accessible to inquiry.[5] He also suggests that the rational powers of the supposed originators of institutional practices could not afford them much assistance in any case: institutions are extremely complex bodies of practices, whose bearing on the supposed purposes of their would-be originators is mostly indirect and circuitous (D 417).

Within the short sequence of means/ends relations that an individual can actually envisage at any given time, the immediate significance of institutions is mainly that of limiting and often thwarting the pursuit of one's own ends (R 101; *101-2*). Thus any positive payoff of the supposedly purposeful institution-making is in fact undetectable by the institution-makers, whereas the detectable payoffs, if any, are negative. Finally, individual means and ends vary enormously over time and space, as do the possible adjustments of means to ends. Institutions, by comparison, show relatively little variability, not only in their basic structures but even in their detailed configuration. (Social institutions, in fact, often turn up in very much the same form in the most diverse societies.) This dissimilarity is another reason for excluding the possibility of deriving institutions from individual instrumental activity (R 94-95; *94-95*).

This relatively diffuse and explicitly negative treatment of the genesis of institutions is complemented in Durkheim's work by the outlines of a positive treatment. In order to reconstruct the latter, I shall distinguish (somewhat arbitrarily) three aspects of the genesis problem, which I shall label *quis?, quid?,* and *quomodo?*

Durkheim's answer to *quis* (*who* brings institutions into being) is present in the early works but more boldly put forward in *Elementary forms.* Basically, not individuals but societies establish institutions. They do so by giving definite expression (in dogmas of faith, ritual practices, legal norms, broad conceptions of social and natural reality, broad moral principles, etc.) to representations shared throughout the society and held with great, indeed passionate, inten-

---

[5] F 24; *24*. The translation obscures the point by rendering the French *but* as "meaning" and not as "purpose."

sity (F 525; 410-11). In fact (as my previous discussion of the components of society has shown), society not so much *makes* but *is* the universe of these representations. They are the property of the society as a distinctive realm of being—of that "consciousness of consciousnesses," as Durkheim calls it at one point (F 633; 492). At the same time, as purely "mental" entities they must be expressed through the consciousnesses of individuals; they (as it were) think themselves *through* and *within* those consciousnesses, but they are not "thought up" by individuals. *In statu nascendi* institutions are complexes of images that the individuals entertain not in their capacity as individuals but in their capacity as members of the society; not severally as discrete, self-activating entities, but jointly as subservient, "acted on" organs of a greater entity (R 102; *103-4*).

Durkheim's answer to *quid* (which practices become institutionalized) may be derived mainly from *Division* and *Rules*. It emphasizes morphological, or ecological, variables and places a rather deterministic construction on their operation. Many different sets of practices that bear on a given activity may be eligible for institutionalization; but all except one uniquely suitable set are progressively eliminated, and that set is institutionalized. This process of selection ultimately depends on constraints flowing from such "bedrock" variables (R 114; *115*) as the size of the society's territory, the pattern of settlement, and the "material" and "moral" density of the population. More proximately, however, the configuration of any given institution is largely determined by the requirement that it be compatible with configurations previously or concurrently assumed by other institutions of the same society. (This operates both ways, of course; each institution both constrains and is constrained by all others). This, at any rate, is my interpretation of what I regard as the passages most relevant to the selection question in *Division*.

There are certain ways in which two social functions may be related to one another that are more in keeping [than other ways] with the nature of things; these ways are more often followed and thus become habits; then such habits, to the extent that they have acquired greater strength, are transformed into rules of conduct. . . . A body of rules is the definite form acquired over time by the relationships spontaneously established between social functions (D 356-58, 360; *366, 368*).

Elementary forms contains a detailed treatment of the third aspect of the genesis of institutions, which I have called *quomodo* (*How* are certain practices, however selected, institutionalized by the society?). This treatment, of course, only deals explicitly with the genesis of religious institutions (beliefs and rituals); but extending it to the genesis of institutions in general seems warranted, since Durkheim occasionally suggests that this is possible, and since there is a close relationship between religion and other institutions (to be elucidated later).

Durkheim's answer to *quomodo* is closely related to his treatment of *quis*. If the authorship of institutions rests with a plurality of individuals who interact, or rather co-act in unison, then the typical social processes through which authorship is exercised must be such that they sharply restrict the importance of individuality to each participant. Feelings of reciprocal belonging must reach a high pitch; the role played by mundane and private concerns in sustaining each individual's involvement in the activity he shares with others must be minimized; and the process must engender and sustain emotions of an exalting nature. The prototype of such a process, in which enough emotional heat is generated to fuse all those participating into a deeply felt collective identity, is a great orgiastic ceremony like those characteristic of many "primitive" religions.

In this prototype, one may easily identify some of the typical conditions envisaged in Durkheim's answer to *quomodo*. What is required is that a relatively large number of individuals come into close physical proximity, achieving a keen (but chiefly emotional) awareness of each other. They must sustain this proximity and awareness for a relatively protracted period, in settings that physically and/or symbolically separate them from the contexts of their everyday existence. For example, each participant might wear clothing that has nothing to do with his everyday social role and quite literally transfigures him, making him capable of actions and passions that his private self normally does not encompass, which therefore express his submersion in an intensely felt collective identity. When a collectivity gathers under such conditions it acquires the power to "normativize" certain sets of practices, to institutionalize them in preference to all other sets that might apply to the same social concerns.

One may note that these conditions have a distinctly "morphological" character. Essentially, they produce the maximum concentration of a plurality of actors in time and space—that is, a situation of maximum moral and material density. In this respect Durkheim's answer to *quomodo* seems to echo his treatment of *quid*. But this resemblance should not be made too much of, for Durkheim's treatment of the two questions is not really compatible. In *Elementary forms*, particularly, he stresses the emotional incandescence engendered by ritual, and above all the *symbolic* nature of the relationship between specific institutional practices and their ultimate object. These attributes give the process of institutionalization a degree of freedom, of creativity, that contrasts with the deterministic treatment of the *quid* aspect as sketched in *Division* and *Rules*.

In one text (SP 95), Durkheim characterizes the liberty with which the "collective consciousness" operates by paraphrasing a biblical phrase, "The wind bloweth where it listeth." It is hard to see how this mode of operation, applied to the genesis of institutions, can be squared with the view in *Division*: "A body of rules is the definite form acquired over time by those relationships spontaneously established between social functions." The creative liberty of the collective consciousness is, of course, a form of spontaneity, but not quite the *same* spontaneity with which two "social functions" (probably meaning "two flows of social activity") will in the long run adjust to one another in a uniquely apt fashion. Incidentally, as Parsons points out, this solution to the selection question involves the illegitimate transforming of an *is* (the objectively superior suitability of a given "adjustment") into an *ought* (the normative significance attached to that "adjustment," which alone consecrates it as an institution).[6]

The Functioning of Institutions

The term "functioning" (*fonctionnement*), as Durkheim uses it, sets two related but distinguishable problems for the sociological analysis

[6] Talcott Parsons, *The structure of social action* (New York: McGraw-Hill, 1937), p. 321.

of institutions. One is the problem of how institutions affect behavior, which I shall take up in the next section ("The Operation of Institutions"). The other is the problem of which functions institutions perform for society, to the extent that they affect behavior. My presentation of the second problem in this section takes the form of several relatively disjointed points, reflecting the fact that Durkheim did not explore this theme extensively and systematically with reference to institutions in general.

1. Institutions, as we have seen, do not originate from the purposeful pursuit of private interests by individuals. Their usefulness with respect to these interests, however, is closely related to their functioning. "The usefulness of [an institution] is not what makes it come about" (R 96; 97); but "between the notions of tool . . . and of institution there is a close kinship" (F 27; 32). Of course the usefulness in question is not necessarily, or even normally, intended or recognized by the individuals, nor does it bear directly on a given individual existence. Rather, it consists of the *objectively* favorable bearing that a given set of normative practices has upon the needs of the society. Durkheim uses the term "function" to characterize this usefulness because it does not have the psychological connotations that "goal" or "purpose" does. Rather it expresses "a correspondence between the [institution] in question and certain general needs of the social organism" (R 95; 95). "The function of an institution can only be social, that is, it lies in the production of socially useful effects" (R 109; *110*).

2. The very use of terms like "function," "needs," and "social organism" demonstrates Durkheim's acceptance of an analogy between societies and biological organisms. However, he was aware of the limitations of this analogy, and of the dangers involved in failing to recognize those limitations:

[It is] a misconception of the real nature of society . . . [when] society is presented as a system of organs and functions, maintaining itself against outside forces of destruction just like a physical organism whose entire life consists in appropriate reactions to external stimuli. Society is . . . more than this, for it is the center of a moral life. . . . To see society only as an organized body of vital functions is to diminish it, for this body has a soul which is the composition of collective ideals (SP 91, *93*).

3. As we have seen, the functions of an institution are some of its effects, insofar as they correspond to the society's needs; and as effects, normally unintended and unrecognized, they should not be considered as the causes of that institution. However, the functions an institution performs may help to maintain its existence once it has been created by the action of "efficient causes." Unfortunately, Durkheim does not specify how this happens, but only states, quite generally: "If the usefulness of [an institution] is not what makes it come about, it must generally be useful if it is to maintain itself" (F 95; 95). Exceptions are possible (R 91; 91), whereas presumably practices that are positively disruptive, and *only* that, cannot possibly maintain themselves (D 293-94; 306). These two formulations of the same broad principle in fact overlap. Discussing the institution of caste in Indian society, for instance, Durkheim states both that it would not have lasted if it had too often misallocated occupational roles, and that if it did last it did so because it generally managed to place everyone in a suitable position (D 293-94; 306).

4. Again, since the functions of an institution are some of its effects, they do not constitute it. Probably for this reason Durkheim, when defining an institution, avoids referring to its functions (D 395; 399). He asserts as "a proposition equally true in sociology and in biology" that "the organ is independent of the function." This principle yields the following two corollaries:

5. Institutions are *plastic* (Durkheim's term). A single institution may concurrently or successively perform different functions, that is, yield effects that bear favorably upon different needs.

6. Institutions are *fungible* (not Durkheim's term). That is, the same function may be performed concurrently or successively by more than one institution.

7. The principle of the independence of institution from function and its corollaries (Points 4-6 above) apply *a fortiori* to the relationship between an institution and the personal *ends* in view of which individuals comply with the norms making up an institution, avail themselves of the opportunities presented by institutional rules, and so on. These ends vary enormously, since for a given institution they vary not only between one society and another, or between different stages in the history of the same society, but above all between indi-

viduals. The institution of marriage in a given society at a given time may perform a relatively narrow set of functions for that society; but there are a great many different ends that prompt individuals to enter marriage and to comply (or not comply) with the norms making up that institution.

Arnold Gehlen, a German anthropologist and social philosopher, has formulated a general theory of institutions that is probably the most elaborate available today and strongly resembles the one much more tentatively worked out by Durkheim.[7] He states this last point much more clearly than Durkheim, although the latter had already implied it in his notion of the "noncontractual elements of contract." As we saw in Chapter 6, the normatively sanctioned stability and generality of the elements making up the institution of contract allow individual parties to establish contractual relations that are, by contrast, intrinsically impermanent and highly diverse in their concrete configurations. Gehlen is more explicit than Durkheim in pointing out that this very discrepancy between the uniqueness and uniformity of an institution and the multiplicity and diversity of the concrete interests it curbs or supports will help to stabilize the institution itself by establishing its transcendence over the narrowly based, highly contingent interests and motivations of individual actors.[8]

8. The stability of institutions should not be overemphasized. Over relatively long spans of time, Durkheim remarks, institutions appear capable of development, both in the sense that their functions may change without changes in their "nature" (F 386; *305*) and in the sense that the original set of normative practices is often modified and elaborated.

One type of development is merely the expression over time of what we have called the "plasticity" of institutions. By way of example Durkheim suggests that the legal rule *pater est quem justae nuptiae demonstrant*, according to which the legitimate husband of a woman is legally considered the father of all the children she bears during marriage, had under Roman law the main function of establishing who was to enjoy the extensive semiproprietary rights of a

[7] For an overview of Gehlen's theory of institutions, see "Probleme einer soziologischen Handlungslehre," in Arnold Gehlen, *Studien zur Anthropologie und Soziologie* (Neuwied: Luchterhand, 1963), pp. 196ff.

[8] *Ibid.*, especially pp. 218-19.

father over those children; whereas under modern law the same rule is intended mostly to protect the rights of the children themselves.

Another type of development is more significant. Durkheim suggests that institutions have a built-in tendency to become more differentiated and elaborated internally, and at the same time to become self-sustaining and self-justifying; they tend, as it were, to become independent of the "efficient causes" that first brought them into existence. This tendency is rooted in the fact that the component elements of institutions are mental representations and as such possess a unique dynamism (SP 93). The following three related phenomena are the major expressions of the tendency in question.

First, if we assume (as the early Durkheim emphatically did, and the later Durkheim probably did) that basic morphological variables ultimately control the selection from among alternative sets of practices and lead to one set becoming institutionalized in a given field of social activity, we need not also assume that the institutionalized practices will only undergo modifications when those variables change. Once institutionalized, practices often become independent of their morphological matrix and undergo modifications that do not depend on that matrix.

The basic matter of the social consciousness is in close relation with the number of social elements and the way in which they are grouped and distributed. . . . But once a basic number of representations has been thus created, they become . . . partially autonomous realities with their own way of life. They have the power to attract and repel each other and to form amongst themselves various syntheses, which are determined by their natural affinities and not by the condition of their matrix. . . . The new representations are immediately caused by other collective representations and not by this or that characteristic of the social structure. The evolution of religion provides us with the most striking examples of this phenomenon (SP 30-31).

Second, as the institution moves away from its morphological matrix, its originally close affinity with other institutions of the same society tends to become looser. In a relatively developed society, accordingly, different institutional realms need not reveal the same affinity they once did. As a result, the mental frameworks of individuals belonging to two societies that are very different in a number of institutional realms need not be nearly as different from one another as other aspects of the societies are. Indeed, these frameworks are likely to have become very similar, thanks to the process of "intellectualization" and "universalization" that they have undergone in each society. The members of two quite different societies may well operate with exactly the same basic categories of thought (which are for Durkheim *institutional* realities) and thus think very much in the same way (F 635-66; *493-94*).

Finally, institutions may become ends in themselves through the same process of elaboration and autonomization. For instance, "negative" ritual practices (taboos, fasting, etc.), originally carried out solely in preparation for more "positive" practices, may absorb more and more attention, became stylized in more and more artificial and demanding ways, until for some believers at least they become completely independent. The practice of asceticism as a distinctive "road to salvation," according to Durkheim, may often have originated in exactly this way (F 445; *350*). As another example, take the chiefs of "primitive" societies. If they exist at all, they begin as embodiments of the group's superiority over the individual and possess very little initiative; but once established they no longer have to operate merely as mouthpieces of the collective consciousness, and they become progressively independent of the latter (D 172; *195*).

9. The major function performed by the totality of a society's institutions (R 97; *97*) is, and can only be, the keeping of that society "in harmony with itself and with its setting [*dehors*]." This same principle can be given an alternative, equally broad formulation with direct reference to the individual members of the society, who normally benefit from institutions only indirectly. Durkheim suggests (D 336-37; *345*) that institutions make up for the deficiencies in the *instinctual* equipment of the human organism (another conceptualization more fully developed by Gehlen).

But the real task of the functional analysis of institutions lies beyond these generalities. One must specify *which* institutionalized sets of practices serve *which* needs of the society. It follows from what I have said about the mutual independence of institutions and functions that this is an extremely arduous and complex task. Oddly, this very fact has led some contemporary sociological functionalists, notably Talcott Parsons, to undertake that task in the grand manner, by postulating (at a rather high level of abstraction) a comprehensive set of needs (requirements, exigencies, or "system problems") and then locating the institutions, or aspects of institutions, that meet these needs. As is well known, the broad theoretical inspiration of this body of theory owes a great deal to Durkheim. However, he approached the same task in a very different manner.

So far as I know, Durkheim did not attempt comprehensiveness in spelling out needs to be serviced, in listing and classifying institutions, or in relating the latter to the former. Working within the tentative general theory of institutions that I have reconstructed, he undertook only one full-scale attempt at functional analysis, and he focused only on the institution of religion. But to increase the theoretical yield of this undertaking, he chose a group of related religious systems that he considered the most primitive among those accessible to sustained investigation; presumably, the analysis of these "basic" patterns would allow him to reach conclusions applicable to other (indeed, to *all*) religious systems. Moreover, as we shall see, religion was in his view not just one institution among many others, but rather the paradigm, the ultimate support, of all institutions. For all this, Durkheim certainly did not adopt the grand manner. *Elementary forms* is a sustained, empirically based study of religion alone—specifically, of totemic religion.

This strategy, to my mind, has much to recommend it, and I have tried to reflect it in my own treatment here. However, I will depart from Durkheim's approach in two ways. First, I will be discussing religion in general, not totemic religion. Second, I will do as I did when discussing *Suicide* and invert that *démarche* adopted by Durkheim. He proceeds from a close examination of religious practices to the determination of their functions (i.e., the correspondences between some effects of those practices and one or more societal needs). I will start by locating only one societal need, and then indicate how religious practices bear upon it. This approach leads us first to the problem I have previously called the operation of institutions.

The Operation of Institutions

How do institutions operate? That is, how do they affect behavior? In the writings under discussion Durkheim does not explicitly confront this question. I shall therefore examine it in the light of his numerous discussions of the operation of norms, since the basic structural characteristics of the latter have already been considered (see pp. 197-99), and since norms are, after all, what institutions are made of.

Arguments in several of Durkheim's writings (e.g., his critique of "cosmic" and individual/psychological interpretations of differential suicide rates, and his rejection of naturalistic and animistic conceptions of "elementary religion") suggest that social facts as such, and thus norms, should be conceived as alternatives to two extremes: on the one hand, aspects of reality that are purely external to the individual; on the other, aspects that are purely internal. This negative characterization also bears on the question of institutions, except that in this case Durkheim's understanding of the operation of norms does not so much exclude as mediate and "blend" the modes of operation of purely external and purely internal factors that impinge on behavior.

The prototypes of the external factor are the exclusively material constraints that the individual meets in his physical environment and must cope with in physical terms. When the impact of these constraints on behavior is compared with that of normative constraints, the former appear as completely external to the individual: "We cannot directly attain consciousness of physical forces; we cannot even comprehend them as such because they are external to us. When I stumble upon a [material] object, I experience sensations of bother and unease; but the force that causes these sensations lies not within myself but within the obstacle. . . . Its effects are perceived, but the force itself cannot be grasped" (F 522; 408). "Social facts" impinge on behavior quite differently: "They are part of our own internal existence, and consequently we do not simply know the results of their actions but actually see them in action. . . . The constraining and necessitating action that escapes us when it issues from external things can here be comprehended because it takes place wholly within ourselves" (F 522; 408-9).

Nevertheless, it would be erroneous to regard the operation of norms as taking place wholly inside the individual. One might say, following Durkheim, that norms do operate within ourselves, but not *from* within ourselves. Durkheim points out two important non-normative factors that actually operate both *within* and *from within* the individual: instinct, and the utilitarian calculation of advantage. In comparison with these, norms appear to operate on behavior from outside; they are realities *external* to the individual (though not foreign to him) that invoke his *internal* loyalty. Norms are not part of the biological constitution of the individual, nor do they appeal exclusively to his egoism, his greed, and his feelings of uniqueness and isolation from everybody else:

> The collective forces . . . are entirely of a mental nature; they are made up exclusively of objectified ideas and sentiments. . . . Being the product of all, they do not belong to anybody in particular [*Oeuvre de tous, elles ne sont la chose de personne en particulier*]. . . . They have so little to do with the personality of the subjects within whom they operate that they never entirely dwell there. . . . They penetrate man from the outside (F 521; 408).

> The norms orienting our conduct . . . do not determine action from inside but evoke it from outside (D 420).

Except when he had to counter some of the cruder misinterpretations of his tenet that social facts should be viewed as things, Durkheim did not feel it necessary to insist that a norm's operation could not be reduced to that of a material "obstacle"; such irreducibility could be taken for granted once one understood the "extreme immateriality" of social facts (R 90; 90),[9] that is, their existence as mental phenomena. The structural distinction between moral norms and technical rules (the latter being specifically appropriate to the manipulation of material things), which I mentioned in the last chapter, also entails this irreducibility. Neither did Durkheim elaborate the distinction between the respective operation of norms and of instincts. This distinction was largely taken for granted in his own cultural environment, and he accepted it without comment.

Predictably, Durkheim's treatment of the present problem—how norms affect behavior—emphasizes the error of answers that treat utilitarian action, the individual's rational adjustment of means to given ends, as *the* model of social action. It is mainly to oppose such answers that most of his relatively explicit treatments of the problem

---

[9] The English version renders *immaterialité* as "intangibility."

insist almost exclusively on the view that norms affect behavior from outside. According to the arguments already worked out in *Division* (see Chapter 6, pp. 169-72), action construed on the utilitarian model, which evolves as the outcome of purely private considerations, has three flaws that reveal the model's utter inadequacy:

1. It is intrinsically and inescapably egoistic, since it presupposes and engenders no solidarity. It not only fails to solve the problem of order, but makes it insoluble (D 175, 394; *198, 399*).

2. It possesses an intolerably high degree of contingency, of randomness (R 94; *94*).

3. It postulates, at both the beginning and the end of the process, an actor who is inescapably closed within himself, who meets all other actors purely as objects. In Spencerian contractualism, in particular, "The different agents remain extraneous to one another, and at the end of the operation each finds himself anew and perceives himself as wholly unaffected" (D 181; *203*).

A contrario, given a plurality of interacting individuals, each can (1) transcend his private egoism; (2) eliminate in his own behavior actions that might appear arbitrary to others, and (3) break through his own isolation from other individuals, both affecting them and being affected by them. But these things happen only if all actors conduct their individual activity in view of the same criteria. Moreover, it is not enough that criteria be the same merely in that all the individuals singly and severally happen to possess similar or even identical private orientations; in this sense the order-destroying utilitarian principle of "looking after number one" can be the same for all actors. This orientation, says Durkheim, "is common in that it is shared over the community, but it is individual in its object. If it does turn all wills toward the same goal, that goal is not itself social" (D 147; *172*). What is required, instead, is that all individuals draw upon a single *shared* fund of compatible orientations, and do so not severally but by virtue of a common belonging. But if all actors are to be oriented by the same criteria (in this sense of "sameness") then the criteria themselves must be in some sense external to each individual.

The externality of norms is the externality of mental things and they can only affect action by being continually transformed into "internalities" through the mediation of the individual's active subjectivity (e.g., S 115-16, 275; 129-30, 258). This mediation involves an irreducible element of freedom in the relationship between the norm and the behavior that the norm evokes (S 368; 325). It cannot be said, in a strict sense, that the norm *determines* the behavior, although Durkheim's treatment of this point sometimes seems to suggest that it does (e.g., F 296; 237).

To this extent, some degree of "spontaneity" is a necessary element of compliant behavior (D 180; 202-3), but one that Durkheim construes in a rather austere manner. To him, spontaneity always involves a willingness to deploy effort, undergo sacrifice, and let one's better self prevail (SP 98); it is not the wild, self-propelling surge and flow of a vital force; it expresses, so to speak, not so much a *responsiveness* as a *responsibility*. A wholly unrestrained, utterly spontaneous expression of sheer human vitality has social significance, for Durkheim, in only two ways: "upstream" from the norm, it may be an aspect of the creative process through which collective representations (and thus norms) are forged; "downstream," it may be one aspect of compliance with the norms that regulate certain kinds of ritual, playful, and aesthetic behavior. In both cases, however, the significance is attached to particular states of consciousness, which attach, once again, not to private individuals but to collectivities. In its purely individual manifestations, unrestrained spontaneity has for Durkheim the threatening nonsocial or antisocial connotations of mindless instinctual behavior and boundless greed.

Indeed, if an element of spontaneity, however understood, belongs in the relationship between norm and behavior, this element must at the same time be bounded. If human societies run, as it were, on institutional rails, and if institutions never really determine compliant behavior, then in a sense all societies are suspended over the abyss of chaos; they possess a purely conditional existence. This situation is built into their very nature and cannot be changed. But surely some mechanism must operate to restrict the contingency of behavior and maximize the probability of compliance—to establish a safety net between society and the void over which it ultimately hangs. In the structure of norms the basic mechanism is the sanction, which is, as we have seen, a constituent element of the norm. Durkheim's treatment of the norm's *operation*, however, systematically restricts the significance of sanctions as such: that is, the significance of an individual's weighing the probability that a sanction will be applied and estimating its effect on his own gratification or deprivation (S 279; 251-52. F 296; 237-38).

If the consideration of sanctions were too important in the typical individual's subjective orientation toward a norm, the distinction between norms (moral) and rules (technical) would be blurred. Norms would simply be additional factual constraints to be considered when organizing one's action, and would evoke no feeling of individual obligation, no self-transcendence. The norm as such would be "disestablished," and the social order deprived of its most distinctive and critical support. If the consequent fatal destabilization of social relations is to be avoided, the typical subjective orientation toward a norm *must* be a recognition of its "oughtness," a conscious submission to the norm for its own sake, a willingness to grant compliance on no other grounds than that it is authoritatively demanded. This willingness need not in principle exclude calculative considerations, but it must be strong enough to override them when necessary (S 279; 251-52). Typically, the pressure that the norm exerts on the actor must be a "moral" pressure, a self-justifying obligation to perform the prescribed behavior: "The social constraint [characteristic of norms] is due to the prestige attached to certain representations" (R xxi; *ix*).

We might rephrase this point by saying that norms have not only externality but also *superiority*. The second characteristic is what distinguishes a norm's externality from that of material facts—or for that matter from the externality that can be attributed to arrangements worked out by interacting individuals in a purely matter-of-fact way, through the mutual adjustment of claims and the rational settling of differences. In Durkheim's view there can be no such thing as a "horizontal" morality, that is, a morality operating through the reciprocal acknowledgment of spheres of autonomy by discrete, wholly contractual partners, rather than through the common submission of interacting individuals to something that transcends them all. This formulation is a parallel to Durkheim's denial that there can be any such thing as a "private morality" (e.g., D 147; *172-73*).

Thus society is at bottom a "conditional" reality, inescapably dependent on norms that in principle can only be observed freely, and by the same token need not be observed at all. However, this "conditionality" is bounded and controlled by the superiority with which norms are invested: individuals may not be forced to comply with a norm, but if they feel that they *owe* it compliance, it will be effective. But will it? Are we really on safe ground, with a reliable barrier between society and chaos? One may doubt it. The superiority and prestige of norms are not empirically verifiable characteristics, but merely the result of the individual's willingness to submit to them. The transcendence that upholds the validity of norms is "simply the imprint that collective feelings of a certain intensity leave on their objects" (F 343; 273). One may grant that the recognition of a norm's oughtness limits the contingency of compliance with it; but that recognition is itself contingent. Is it not essential to make the oughtness not a property bestowed on the norm by the individuals themselves, but rather the acknowledgment of an objectively superior realm of being?

Of course this acknowledgment must also be expressed through the individual consciousness, taking the form of a set of normative practices. It, too, will ultimately rest on a freely granted compliance with those practices. But individuals may be led to convince themselves that compliance per se does not *constitute* the acknowledged superior reality but simply *confirms* it. If they can, this reality will give to the operation of all norms (and thus of all institutions) a cogency that it would not otherwise possess; normative authority will be accepted as final. Only on this condition will Durkheim's statements about the way in which norms affect behavior acquire empirical validity:

Imperative norms of conduct, by virtue of their origin, are vested with an authority and a dignity that our other internal states do not possess.... Although our moral consciousness is part of our total consciousness, we do not feel that we are on an equal footing with it. In this voice that addresses us only to give orders and lay down decrees, we cannot recognise our own voice. The norm possesses an imperative tone ... and thus, although [the norm] makes itself felt within our own consciousness, we cannot ... consider it as our own thing (F 376-77, 401; 298, 317).

Our moral consciousness, when it speaks to us, impresses us as a power external and superior to us (S 380; 335).

If this is to be the case, there must be norms (both ways of acting and ways of thinking) such that compliance with them fairly directly implies an assertion and celebration (and thus a confirmation) of the existence of an ultimate source and ground of validity of all norms and all institutions. There must be norms that on the one hand reflect the objective existence and superiority of such a source, and on the other compel individuals to testify to its authority through compliance. There must be an institution that directly confronts the individual with the fact of his own inferiority and dependence, and thus persuades him to submit to all norms.

The Place of Religion

We have now, so to speak, located the "functional space" within which Durkheim appears to place religion. The functional significance of the *manières de penser et d'agir* that make up the institution of religion (that is, of religious beliefs and rituals) lies in their expression and reassertion of society's existence as a realm of being superior to the individual and having authority over him. (I speak of "expressing" and "reasserting," and not of "positing" or "generating," because it is essential to the argument that society *is* such a realm, already exists as such a realm.)

As we have seen, institutions *have* functions but are not themselves functions. In particular, they should not be defined in terms of their functions; and a great deal of institutional analysis may take the form of description and interpretation in other than functional terms, dealing with functions only at a late stage or not at all. Indeed, Durkheim's treatment of religion in *Elementary forms* is only functional to a minor extent, and it becomes so only at a relatively late stage. My discussion so far has inverted both the analytical process followed by Durkheim and the ratio of functional to nonfunctional discussion in his argument. At this point, it seems useful to offer at least a partial account of the main body of that argument.

Since every known society has possessed the institution of religion at one time or another (F 343; 273), the empirical material relating to religious life, this "essential and permanent aspect of humanity" (F 2; 13), is vast and extremely diverse. However, all religions "respond to the same necessities, play the same role, and depend on the same causes"; and it is possible to identify quite unequivocally the one central phenomenon of religious life, and to make it the basis of an objective and comprehensive definition of religion:

> What is characteristic of the religious phenomenon is that it always supposes a division of the known and knowable universe into two classes, which comprehend all that exists but radically exclude one another. There are sacred things, which interdictions protect and isolate, and profane things, to which interdictions are applied and which must be kept at a distance from the sacred. Religious beliefs are representations that express the nature of sacred things and their relationships with one another and with profane things. [Religious] rituals are norms of conduct that prescribe how man must behave vis-à-vis sacred things. . . . A religion is a unified system of beliefs and practices pertaining to things sacred—that is, things set aside and protected by interdictions (F 65; 62).[10]

Conceptually, the distinction between sacred and profane is radical: each is defined directly and exclusively by its opposition to the other; the sacred is what is radically *other* than profane, and vice versa. To this formal and minimal understanding of the contrast Durkheim adds the suggestion that although either term can be defined simply by negating the other, implying a relationship of reciprocity, the two should not be conceived as lying on the same plane. They clearly stand in a hierarchical relationship: given any two objects of which one is sacred and the other profane, the sacred is *always* on a higher plane. This feature of the sacred/profane contrast has an obvious bearing on what we have located as the functional significance of religion, although it is posited by Durkheim in a nonfunctional context. The following are three more or less explicit nonfunctional statements of the same feature:

1. As we have seen, Durkheim uses the notion of interdiction in defining both the sacred and the profane. But that notion applies to them asymmetrically: interdictions, in principle, protect the sacred from the profane rather than vice versa (*procul, o procul este profani. Aeneid,* vi, 258).

2. The sacred character of an object, Durkheim states, is *superimposed* on it, added to its empirical nature (F 328, 461; 261, 363). The

[10] I have omitted Durkheim's reference to an organized church as a constitutive element of his definition, since it raises problems that are foreign to my present theme.

fact that no such statement is made for the profane suggests that a profane thing is simply an object, in its matter-of-fact givenness, with nothing added. The sacred, in other terms, involves a givenness plus, the profane only a givenness.

3. Indirectly, the fact that there can be a lesser or greater degree of sacredness in a given case also suggests the existence of a "vertical" relationship between sacred and profane.

The asymmetry in the relationship between sacred and profane can be detected empirically by examining the concrete manifestations of that duality, all of which attach a higher worth to things sacred. Durkheim does not systematically survey the innumerable pairs of items in which the sacred/profane contrast is embodied, but a number of them can be gathered from his discussion of ethnographic (especially Australian) material. Within each of the following pairs, the first item stands to the second as sacred to profane, always with a connotation of superiority:

1. Highly intense and vivid representations vs. low-intensity, "pale" representations (F 297; 238).

2. Mental categories (ideas of time, space, force, causality, etc.) vs. mental constructs with a mainly empirical content (F 21-22; 28-29).

3. Expressive action vs. instrumental action (F 296; 237).

4. Concentrated, periodic, "special" social life vs. dispersed, continuous, routine social life (F 303ff; 265ff).

5. Soul vs. body (F 343ff; 273ff).

6. Properly religious ritual vs. "magical" ritual (F 430; 378-79).

7. Social things (forces and feelings) vs. material things (F 303-4; 243).

8. Society vs. the individual (F 188ff; 154ff).

9. Men and adults vs. women and children (F 196-97; 121-22).[11]

Although many such empirical generalizations can be advanced, they are only that. They state that within a certain ethnographic universe a quality of sacredness has been attached to some objects in preference to others; but they do not contradict the principle that sacredness is arbitrarily bestowed. In principle, anything can be sa-

---

[11] Men and adults stand to women and children less as sacred to profane than as more sacred to less sacred.

cred: rocks, plants, animals, localities, psychological phenomena, and artifacts of the most varied nature. And within any given category, one item may be sacred and others of the same kind profane. Even more arbitrary are the reasons that believers use to justify and establish the sacredness of a given object, the accounts of the events through which an object acquired sacredness, the positive or negative effects ascribed to the use or misuse of sacred objects, and the specific rituals regulating access to a sacred object.

However (and this is of crucial significance to the argument), the fact that societies arbitrarily attach sacredness to objects, and that the sacred objects are themselves indifferent, does *not* mean that sacredness exists only in the eye of the beholder. The given objects that happen to be sacred are arbitrary and ultimately do not matter. But one thing is sacred by its very nature, and is the sole source and ultimate addressee of arbitrary sacredness: this thing is society. The superiority, awesomeness, and power implicit in the notion of sacredness are only fancied to be the properties of given objects and ritual practices; but they reflect the actual objective superiority, awesomeness, and power of society.

Religion, by virtue of concerning the sacred, really concerns society. The intrinsically untenable beliefs and intrinsically nonsensical rituals that make up any religion are but a metaphor; the rationalist mind takes them in their literal sense, is offended by their untenability and nonsensicality, and misses their metaphorical meaning. To the rationalist mind the nonsense and mumbo-jumbo of mythology, dogma, and cult appear at best as manifestations of an immature mentality, and at worst as the expressions of a persistent delirium. But to this conclusion Durkheim objects that if religion is a delirium then it is "a well-grounded delirium" (F 324; 258).

From our own viewpoint, religion ceases to be an arbitrary, unfathomable hallucination and gains a footing in reality. The believer is not deluding himself when he holds that there exists a moral power on which he depends and to whom he owes the best part of his own being. This power does exist, and it is society. . . . Religion is . . . above all the means by which individuals represent to themselves the society of which they are members and the relation, intimate though obscure, that they entertain with it (F 325; 257).

In all its various and complex manifestations religious life is, at bottom, a single and simple thing. Everywhere it responds to the same need and originates from the same state of mind. In all its forms it has the object of lifting man above himself, of making him live an existence superior to the one he would lead if he obeyed only his individual spontaneities.... Rituals are, above all, the means by which the social group periodically reasserts itself (F 592, 553; 461, 432).

Naturally, the relation between religion's outward beliefs and practices and its ultimate goal is not a straightforward one. The *manières de penser et d'agir* institutionalized as religion relate to society only as *symbols*:

Religion is ... the system of symbols through which society acquires consciousness of itself (S 352; 312).

Social life ... is not possible except through a vast symbolism.... Religious interests are but the symbolic form of social and moral interests (F 331, 452; 264, 356).

It is characteristic of symbolic communication that it involves the arbitrary attachment of meaning to otherwise meaningless signs. But one might wonder why the symbolism is needed. Why should an arbitrary system of basically indifferent objects, untenable conceptions, and nonsensical practices interpose itself between the individual and an objective reality that is intrinsically authoritative, superior, and awesome? Why this seeming delirium of the intellect in myth and dogma? Why divert conduct into ritual instead of directly acknowledging and submitting to society? Durkheim does not discuss this problem as directly and explicitly as I think necessary. However, one can derive from *Elementary forms* a discussion of it that also includes elements from arguments not at all related to the central problem. The following are the most relevant points:

1. Society is a reality, but not a physical one; therefore, it cannot normally be apprehended with the directness and matter-of-factness that characterize our understanding of physical reality.

2. The need to which religion responds is that for *attitudes* of submission, *sentiments* of devotion to society and confidence in its protection. Such sentiments and attitudes can be evoked quite as effectively by symbols as by the real thing.

3. From this same functional viewpoint, certain classes of symbols (particularly natural and man-made physical objects) have definite advantages. For instance, although the society can at best only occasionally assemble in its entirety and thus directly evoke the appropri-

ate emotions, physical objects can provide a frequent or indeed constant stimulus to them. Also, a material symbol, through its very facticity, conveys the externality of "social facts" to the individual—an externality that might otherwise elude him (F 330-31; 263).

4. Those situations (ceremonial gatherings and the like) in which the individual experiences the reality of society with particular intensity are not such as to facilitate objective thinking; on the contrary, they presuppose and engender a maximum of emotional involvement, of unrestrained affectivity.

5. Objective as they are, the properties of society that constitute its superiority to the individual—that is, the societal interests that require a sacrifice of the individual's immediate interests—are not perceivable except through arduous and sustained scientific thinking: "The action of society follows devious and obscure routes; it employs mechanisms too complex for its source to be perceived by the simple observer. Until scientific analysis comes and teaches him, he does indeed feel that he is being acted upon, but not from whence he is being acted upon. . . . This leads him to perceive the powers with whom he feels in contact in forms that are foreign to those powers" (F 299; 239-40).

6. A matter-of-fact cognitive approach to the reality of society is *at first* intrinsically impossible, for such an approach can only proceed within a previously established framework of categories and basic understandings of reality. And this framework (according to a very important argument in *Elementary forms* that I must pass over) is itself laid down by religion.

7. The human faculties stimulated by situations in which the reality of society is most directly experienced, besides the emotional-cathectic faculties suggested in Point 4, are faculties of an aesthetic nature. The poetic imagination, the ability to evoke rather than describe and explain, plays a greater role than the operation of cold reason, even in the cognitive aspects of individual reactions to religious experience. Hence the fantastic nature of most myth and the playful nature of much ritual (F 542ff; 426ff).

8. Finally, the process of elaboration and autonomization that religion, like all institutions, must undergo may be partly responsible for the fact that most belief and ritual has only a symbolic relation-

ship to its ultimate referent. One may surmise that at the very beginning every religion involved a much more direct, much less symbolic "confrontation" between the individuals and society; and that it gradually moved away from that directness by embodying in its explicit content increasingly "free-floating" mythological and ritual elaborations at the hands of increasingly specialized personnel.

Religion and Other Institutions

Let us now turn to the question of the relations between religion and other social institutions. The Durkheimian position on this question can be summarized under the following three points:

1. *Religion as the paradigmatic institution.* The nature and operation of the whole normative realm can best be analyzed by a discussion of religion. For instance, the "collective sense of respect" (F *380;* *301*) that attaches to sacred objects closely parallels the "prestige" that characterizes, and typically activates, all norms (SP *48*). The abstention, self-denial, and pain that often appear in ritual performance parallel the self-restraint and renunciation that are always parts of compliant behavior (F 444ff; *350ff*). And the complex, paradoxical relation of mutual dependence that all religions posit between the gods (or *mana*) and the faithful in spite of the transcendence of the former (a relationship beautifully analyzed by Durkheim in his critique of Robertson Smith's theory of sacrifice) exemplifies the voluntaristic nature of compliant behavior and the sense in which the persistence and effectiveness of all institutions are contingent on the very conduct that they regulate:

On the one hand, the individual receives from society whatever is best about himself . . . on the other, society does not exist and live except within and through individuals. Let the ideas of society become extinguished in individual minds, let the beliefs, the traditions, the aspirations of the collectivity cease to be felt and shared by individuals, and society will die. One may repeat what has been said previously about the Godhead: it possesses reality only to the extent that it maintains a place within the human consciousness, and it is we who give it a place there. We may now perceive the profound reason why the gods may no more dispense with the faithful than the latter may dispense with the gods; the reason is that society, of which the gods are a symbolic expression, can no more dispense with individuals than the latter can dispense with society (F 495-96; *388-89*).

In sum, "Religion is the preeminent form, and as it were the short-ened expression, of collective life in its entirety" (F 598-99; 466).

2. *Religion as the proto-institution.* Religion is not only the best avenue to the study of what all institutions have in common; it is also the source from which all other institutions sprang at the very dawn of each society's history. One might say that myth is the proto-type and ultimate source of all knowledge, and ritual the prototype and source of all social conduct. The following is one of many elo-quent passages in which Durkheim stated this point.

Religion contains in itself, from the beginning, but in a diffused state, all the elements which in dissociating, determining, and combining with each other in a thousand ways, have given birth to the diverse manifestations of the collective life. It is from myths and legends that science and poetry have separated; it is from religious ornamentation and cult ceremonies that the plastic arts have come; law and morality were born from ritual practices. One cannot understand our representation of the world, our philosophic conceptions about the soul, immortality, and life, if one doesn't know the religious beliefs which were their first form. Kinship began by being an es-sentially religious tie; punishment, contract, the gift, homage, are transfor-mations of sacrifice, be it expiatory, contractual, communal, honorary, and so on.[12]

This is an early statement (1899) of a position to which Durkheim repeatedly returned; and it is one of the main themes of *Elementary forms*,[13] especially with reference to the role of religion in shaping the cognitive framework within which a society operates and thus lay-ing the foundations for the development of all theoretical and prac-tical knowledge.

3. *Religion as the meta-institution.* We have already functionally interpreted religion as the institution that drastically reduces the con-tingency attaching to the operation of all others (and up to a point, of its own operation) by establishing and sanctioning *manières de penser et d'agir* that specifically confirm the reality of society. In this sense, a religion that successfully operates in a society is the ultimate support of all other social institutions, since it directly cultivates atti-

[12] Quoted by Robert Bellah, "Durkheim and history," in Robert Nisbet, ed., *Emile Durkheim* (Englewood Cliffs, N.J.: Prentice-Hall, 1965), pp. 166-67.

[13] His course "Physique des moeurs et du droit" (P), also contains many elabo-rations of the position.

tudes of respect, devotion, submission, and so on that other institutions must presuppose if they are to operate successfully. (This thesis, incidentally, had already been less explicitly advanced by Tocqueville in his examination of the moral foundations of republican democracy.)

Thus religion not only is the ultimate historical source of the whole institutional apparatus of society, but must remain in operation if that apparatus is to persist. In a statement where "morality" stands for the totality of institutions other than religion, Durkheim argues: "it is impossible to imagine ... that morality should entirely sever its unbroken historical association with religion without ceasing to be itself. ... Morality would no longer be morality if it had no element of religion" (SP 71). In this sense the parallelism between the features of religion and those of other institutions is potentially misleading. Religion is not just a paradigm, a single institution that displays the characteristics of all institutions; nor, for that matter, is it "just" the historical matrix of all other institutions. There is a persistent hierarchy of functional significance among institutions, and in this hierarchy religion alone holds an unchallengeable position of supremacy.

At the beginning of this chapter I remarked somewhat critically on the circularity of two definitions of institution in which Durkheim used the term "instituted" as part of the definition itself. One might speculate that he committed such an elementary mistake because he wanted to make it quite clear that institutions (as against instincts) are the products of action, of human choice—that institutions exist as they are and possess validity only because they are human products. The French verb *instituer*, indeed, conveys very clearly that social things (and institutions are social things *par excellence*) "only realize themselves at the hands of men; they are the products of human activity" (R 18; 17).

This statement may strike one as obvious; yet it is a vital insight into the totality of the social process, of human existence, of history. In fact, the Western dialectical tradition (with which I have previously connected Karl Marx) treats it as the *central* insight. Durkheim, then, shares this insight; and he also shares its all-important corollary

that "men make history but do not know the history they make."
But his interpretation of the corollary is quite different from that
common to the dialectical tradition, as stated, for example, by Hegel:
"In world history, out of the actions of men comes something quite
different from what they intend and directly know and will; they
realise their interests, but something further is achieved which is internally comprised in it, but of which they were not conscious, nor
did they aim at it."[14]

The following formulation of the same corollary by Simmel refers
not to historical action in general but to institution-making in particular: "To the fabric of social life one may well apply the saying:
The weaver does not know what he weaves. The higher social institutions can emerge only among beings capable of purposive action;
except that they arise, so to speak, *alongside* the purposiveness of the
individual, through a formative process that does not lie within it."[15]

Note that in both the Hegel and Simmel formulations the process
in question (the making of history or the making of institutions) goes
beyond the purposive action of individuals but can neither exclude
nor dispense with that action. The process develops *within* or *alongside* action, and to that extent cannot be reduced to it but nonetheless presupposes it. What is involved is a phenomenon whereby the
product escapes the control of the producer, transcends the circumstances of the production process, and perhaps frustrates the very
aims that led the individual to initiate that process. But the whole
phenomenon is still a product, however unintentional, of the purposive action of individuals. The subjectivity of the individual, his
effort to foster his own existence and "realize" himself through his
own activity, is the ultimate presupposition of all sociohistorical
experience.[16]

In Durkheim's interpretation, however, that which transcends individual purposive action does *not* (however deviously) originate
from such action. It lies on a wholly different plane, on which the

[14] Quoted by Karl Korsch, in *Karl Marx* (London: Chapman, 1938), p. 139.
[15] Quoted by Hermann Heller, "Staat," in Alfred Vierkandt, ed., *Handwörter-
buch der Soziologie* (Stuttgart: Enke, 1932), p. 616.
[16] For a recent, persuasive restatement of this view, based on a sound interpretation of the Marxian conception of history, see Helmut Fleischer, *Marxismus
und Geschichte* (Frankfurt: Suhrkamp, 1969).

individual's effort to master the conditions of his existence is not a presupposition but at best a by-product and at worst a hindrance; it expresses the subjectivity of a subject other than the individual. This subject is society, *un sujet qui enveloppe tous les sujets particuliers,* an entity that does not result from the encounter and interaction of individuals but comes into existence and can only persist to the extent that individuality negates itself. Clearly, Durkheim acknowledges the interdependence of society and the individual, and the dialectical nature of the relationship between them (e.g., F 491ff; *385ff*). But he construes this relationship by starting from the societal pole: "Social phenomena come into being not in the individual but in the group" (F 331; *263*). Society, as we have seen (Chapter 6), precedes the individual who can come into being only under the action of society.

Religion, in all its manifestations, represents and reinforces this drastic asymmetry in the otherwise dialectical relationship between society and the individual. Accordingly, the extent to which Durkheim's understanding of the man-made nature of institutions departs from that of the dialectical tradition is particularly clear in his discussion of religion. Durkheim writes at one point that in religion "Man ends up by finding himself the prisoner of this imaginary world, of which he is, however, the author and the model; he comes to depend on these spiritual forces that he has created by his own hand and after his own image" (F 73; *68*). The reader may be forgiven some surprise and unease when he realizes that Durkheim emphatically rejects this understanding of religion (the quote comes from his criticism of an animistic conception of "elementary religion"). However, I would submit, the same understanding is shared by the whole dialectical tradition, and most of us would have difficulty in formulating an alternative understanding that did not entail the acceptance of either religious belief or the theory of the "priestly lie." Durkheim found an alternative by equating God with society, treating the latter as the source of all social reality. Thus religion became for him a well-grounded and indispensable "delirium," arbitrary and fanciful in its selection and elaboration of symbolic objects, but not in its reference to society, the ultimate reality that is being symbolized.

9. Some Critical Remarks

In one passage of *Alice in Wonderland* the following exchange takes place:

" 'Tis so," said the Duchess, "and the moral of that is—'Oh, 'tis love, 'tis love, that makes the world go round!' "

"Somebody said," Alice whispered, "that it's done by everybody minding his own business."

"Ah well, it means much the same thing," said the Duchess.

If for "making the world go round" we read "keeping the society together," Alice nicely summarizes the utilitarian solution to the latter problem. But one may wonder which of the Duchess's statements best describes the Durkheimian solution. On the face of it, the first statement does so. According to Durkheim, "altruism" (surely another name for love) is "the fundamental basis of social life" (D 207, also 90, 140, 174; 228, also *121, 166, 197*); and only on this basis can a situation come about in which people *can* mind their own business. Any minding one's business irrespective of moral considerations threatens the survival of society; and where morality begins "disinterestedness and devotion also begin" (SP 52), so that morality itself ultimately coincides with love.

However, Durkheim did consider the fact that the individual has an interest in what he gets out of existence and can expect returns for his efforts. He was thus led to argue that ultimately "love" and "minding one's own business" must converge, must come to mean "much the same thing." The following are some of his arguments to this effect:

First, the standard behavioral expression of love in social life is compliance with norms, a compliance prompt and generous enough to suggest that it is motivated by a spontaneous, affective devotion.

Structurally the norm is, one might say, a "prophet": it neither describes nor determines behavior; rather, it is a program for behavior, meant to evoke behavior. But it is not a "prophet unarmed," since it includes sanctions (arrangements for the penalizing of noncompliant behavior and/or the rewarding of compliance). Now Durkheim on the whole underplays sanctions, as we have seen, but he never ignores them. However compliance or deviance may be motivated, they typically bring rewards or penalties for the actor. To this extent, it can be said that the actor does himself a favor by complying, and that in his compliant action love and minding his own business converge.

Second, through the socialization process (R 7-8, 103-4; 6, 104-5), individuals acquire a deep psychological investment in compliance.[1] They internalize normative guidelines for thought and action, and as a result even *contemplating* deviance becomes difficult, indeed painful; deviance appears as a threat to their own identity, to their own sense of moral worth. Thus compliance is automatically self-rewarding, irrespective of the rewards or penalties that sanction a norm; the individual, as Tom Lehrer would put it, "does well by doing good." He still needs to exercise effort in order to abide by the norm, needs to strive in order to approach the ideal; but the effort and the striving acquire a charm of their own, and the doing of one's duty becomes a "*sui generis* pleasure" (D xvii; 5. SP 45).

Finally, a situation where everybody minds his own business irrespective of moral considerations is one that closely approximates the war of all against all. Such a condition is, at bottom, psychologically punishing for the individual. "Anarchy is painful to man. . . . [The] sensation of hostility [toward] all about him and the nervous strain involved in resisting it, [the] ceaseless mistrust of one another—all this is a source of pain" (P 24). By comparison a situation where normative constraints operate effectively (and they can only do so through the individuals' willing submission to them) appears psychologically rewarding, for it spares the individual all the strain and suffering that anarchy would inflict upon him.

Through these and other arguments, Durkheim subsumes in the

---

[1] This line of thought has been explored very thoroughly by Durkheim in some writings that I do not discuss here, particularly in those now available as *Education and sociology* (Glencoe, Ill.: Free Press, 1956) and *Moral education* (New York: Free Press, 1961).

tender-minded view—" 'Tis love, 'tis love, that keeps society together"—a tough-minded appeal to "the only individual motive . . . the
desire of increasing one's happiness" (D 231; 251). This analytical operation shows with what thoroughness and profundity, what almost
poetic inventiveness and subtlety, Durkheim treats his chief theoretical theme, the normative elements of social action. No other author
known to me handles this theme with comparable acuteness. However, the very single-mindedness with which Durkheim pursued it led
him, I would argue, to develop a biased view of social life. In his
work, the normative emphasis became so great that he was unable to
produce a truly adequate theoretical framework for sociology. Basically, Durkheim expelled the *non*normative elements from his sociology. Let us see what this omission involved.

At various points in his writings Durkheim persuasively argued—
against individualistic, mechanistic, and supernaturalistic understandings of the source and the nature of morals—his idea that what
is moral is social. Morality, in his view, originates with and from
society, protects social interests, and varies in its content with the
general configuration of society. This point is undoubtedly sound;
but one must object to the idea, implicitly and explicitly echoed
throughout Durkheim's work, that *by the same token* what is social
is moral. That social reality and moral reality are coterminous can
only be granted if a very broad meaning of the term "moral" is
accepted.

Durkheim's arguments on the relationship between moral and social reality, I would submit, fail to differentiate between the following three meanings of the term "moral," which alternate in those
arguments, with damaging logical consequences.

Meaning A. "Moral" here denotes anything that is mental and is
processed through consciousness, anything that involves the operation of specifically human intellectual powers.

Meaning B. "Moral" here denotes a subset of meaning *A*, specifically those mental representations that imply a sense of obligation
and typically evoke the individual's willing submission to the interests of society at the expense of his immediate personal interests.
"Morality begins at the same point at which disinterestedness and
devotion also begin. . . . Moral reality [possesses] a sacred quality

which affects a solution of continuity between morality and economic and industrial techniques, etc., which current utilitarianism tends to confuse [with morality]" (SP 52; 71).

Meaning C. "Moral" here is a further subset of meaning *B*, and consists only of ways of acting rather than ways of thinking (in Durkheim's view, the latter may also possess the obligatoriness that is the basic connotation of meaning *B*). Moreover, it includes only ways of acting that are not backed by the enforcement powers of a political agency (as law is) or by transcendental sanctions (as ritual rules are).

The distinction between meanings *B* and *C* is of secondary importance in Durkheim's work. That between meanings *A* and *B* is extremely important, but Durkheim often ignores it when discussing the relationship between the moral realm and the social realm. In the light of meaning *A* (moral as mental, one might say), all that is social is moral; in the light of meaning *B* (moral as obligatory), not all that is social need be moral. The two meanings are confounded in a number of Durkheim's arguments, which may be summarized as follows.

Human reality as such is continually processed through consciousness; it affects behavior through the mediation of consciousness, and not through the purely mechanistic reactions of physical forces or the operation of biologically given, instinctual determinants of behavior. Typically, the facts of consciousness are representations and images, in particular images *for* behavior, which orient behavior by patterning it and making its course predictable (D 393-94; 398-99): "Collective forces . . . are entirely mental; they are composed exclusively of objectified ideas and sentiments. . . . The social pressure exerts its force in mental ways. . . . Collective movements are not possible unless they are concerted, and thus regulated and defined" (F 521, 298, 527; 408, 239, 412).

So far, the argument can easily be granted. Marx, for instance, would not have hesitated to accept it. The term "relation," which continually recurs in his writings (see Chapters 4-5), on the one hand entails a notion of uniformity and predictability in the behavior occurring between two individuals (or groups), and on the other presupposes the operation of human consciousness.[2] Animals, said

---

[2] This presupposition is emphasized in a sophisticated recent restatement of the Marxian view of history: Helmut Fleischer, *Marxismus und Geschichte*; see, for example, p. 58.

Marx, have no relations; and I have argued that this implies the "representational" nature of relations. We have also seen that in Marx's thought even the bodily aggregations of past labor that are the tools of production acquire a distinctive social significance only to the extent that they are generated and manipulated through relations.

But the Durkheimian argument so far involves only meaning A. In this sense it is true that all social reality is moral. However, this straightforward (and not particularly insightful) generalization often occurs in arguments where, with no warning from Durkheim, meaning B becomes operative. Then, the only facts recognized as "social" are those with a quality of obligation, of "oughtness," attached to them (e.g., F 497; 389-90). In certain passages (e.g., F 453; 316-17) Durkheim recognizes the existence of two sets of mental facts with social significance. But elsewhere (e.g., F 497; 389-90) he implicitly or explicitly adopts meaning B; and, having previously equated moral with social on the strength of meaning A, he "desocializes" all mental facts to which no element of obligation is attached.[8]

For instance, the distinction between moral norms and technical rules (see pp. 197-98) is sometimes used by Durkheim to deny the sociological relevance of a great deal of behavior (or of many aspects of behavior) that on the basis of meaning A would have to be regarded as moral and thus as sociologically relevant. For Durkheim, in fact, to the extent that behavior is determined by expediency (the economic calculation of advantage, technical efficiency, power maximization, avoidance of penalties, etc.) it ceases to warrant sociological attention.

This same tendency to force out of the social field whatever has no obligation attached to it, operates (with rather intriguing effects) in Durkheim's discussion of the sacred/profane distinction. Durkheim, it will be recalled, defines religion as ways of thinking and

---

[8] It may be useful to note that a similar ambiguity attaches to Parsons's understanding of one of the most vital concepts of his own theoretical discourse, the term "normative"; see particularly *Structure of social action*, pp. 44, 56, 75, 81-82, 191, 420. At times, it seems, all is normative that involves intentionality; at other times, only when the standards governing the ends and/or the means within the actor's intentional orientation evoke a feeling of "oughtness" in him may one speak of normativity.

acting that concern the sacred realm. In itself this definition might imply that the profane realm also has some sociological relevance. However, a closer analysis of this treatment of religion (particularly totemic religion, which to Durkheim is as a kind of prototypical religion) reveals two interesting facts.

In the first place, in spite of the above definition, it appears that religion does *not* belong wholly on the sacred side of the sacred/profane distinction, but in fact establishes that distinction and to this extent embraces both sides. That is, the distinction between sacred and profane is itself a "sacred" distinction: it is religion that defines what is or is not sacred.

In the second place, the realm of the profane is elusive, and it seems as if the profane per se is simply sociologically irrelevant. Durkheim produces several pairs of terms, in each of which one term is sacred and the other profane. However, his argument to the effect that religion (to use my own phrasing) is the prototypical meta-institution and his discussion of totemic systems of classification as including the *totality* of experience (F 211ff; *173ff*) both imply that the profane realm is at best derivative and worthy only of peripheral attention; at worst it is simply excluded from any sociological discussion. This second conclusion, the exclusion of the profane from the social, is in my view the actual burden of Durkheim's argument. He makes no place for the profane as such; even the institutions purportedly regulating profane activities are themselves, as institutions, sacred through and through.

In a few passages in *Elementary forms* Durkheim suggests that there is one and only one irreducibly profane activity: labor, or economic activity (e.g., F 439; *346*). He considers such activity as either sociologically irrelevant or relevant only in certain of its marginal aspects that transcend purely economic and technical reasoning. For instance, he argues as follows in a passage comparing the intense social life associated with religious ceremonies to the pace of ordinary existence:

On ordinary days, individual and utilitarian concerns mainly occupy our minds. Everybody attends separately to his personal tasks; for most people it is above all a matter of satisfying the demands of material life, and the prime motive of economic activity has always been private interest. Of course, social sentiments cannot be entirely absent. We retain relations with our fellows; the habits, the ideas, the tendencies imprinted on us by education, which normally preside over our relations with others, continue to make themselves felt. However, they are continuously contradicted and held in check by the antagonistic tendencies aroused and sustained by the necessities of the daily struggle (F 497; *389-90*).

It appears from this passage that for Durkheim labor, i.e., productive activity, is inherently presocial and antisocial; it is socialized only marginally, through the inertia of associations and habits acquired in the properly social realm, which, however, have in principle no direct bearing on economic activity.

This exclusion of the profane reality of labor from the social realm is not explicit and unqualified. However, the typical Durkheimian argument for asserting the sociality of labor consists of asserting that labor itself is *not* (or rather, was not originally) a completely profane activity; that economic value is, at bottom, only another manifestation of the sacred *mana* (e.g., F 598; *466*).[4] Thus the social is once again made coterminous with the sacred (or, as in the previous argument, with moral in meaning B of the term). It follows that the sacred/profane distinction breaks down, for there is no social dialectic between the two. If there is a dialectic at all, it takes place between the social/sacred/moral (meaning B) on the one hand and a residually defined presocial or antisocial realm on the other.

The individual *qua* individual is another casualty of Durkheim's equation of social, sacred, and moral. We have seen that the individual, *uti singulus*, has no bearing on the genesis of institutions. One might then expect Durkheim to introduce him as an element in the functioning of institutions. But this never happens: Durkheim puts individual behavior per se on a wholly different plane from the social plane on which institutions function; it appears as a destructive or at best disruptive element in that functioning. Only by transcending his own individuality, by surrendering to the superiority of the norm and of society, can the individual *correctly* confront the social (that is, the normative) realm. Behavior that does not embody such a "self-

---

[4] This passing remark of Durkheim's is perhaps the prime source of some very interesting empirical and theoretical work by other French social scientists, notably Marcel Mauss (especially in his famous essay on "the gift"), and Charles Le Coeur (particularly *Le rite et l'outil*, 2d ed. (Paris: 1969)).

surmounting" of the individual (such an "ecstasis," as the young Marx would have put it) is not social behavior. Since he is present at the birth of a norm only as part of a collectivity, the individual must also disappear in a collectivity in his capacity as the addressee of the norm.

For Durkheim, then, the basic demand society makes of the individual is selflessness. He does not, of course, hold that this demand is always met, or that meeting it is easy; indeed, the operation of norms continually meets resistance. But once again, Durkheim cannot conceptualize the resisting element(s) as social: since he has equated the social with the normative, whatever opposes norms must be nonsocial or antisocial. This inability to adequately distinguish the resisting elements is apparent in the crucial role that the concept of "normlessness" (*anomie*) plays in Durkheim's understanding of deviant behavior—as though only a normative vacuum could account for the failure of social behavior to be norm-conforming.

In fact, Durkheim is compelled to argue, albeit mostly implicitly, that anomic behavior is not even moral in meaning *A* of the term, that it is mindless, expressing the blind voracity of "the flesh." Noncompliance issues, in the last analysis, from the extent to which that ultimate embodiment of individuality, the physical organism (F 386-87; *305*), breaks through the layer of social/moral representations laid over it by society. In deviance (as Durkheim basically understands it) the beast within man bares its teeth, the lowest, vilest part of man attacks and negates the benevolent and austere superiority of society.

Durkheim contemplates this subversion of the proper order of things with a moralistic shudder, and is led at times (e.g., D 381; *387*. F 389; *307-8*. SP 72-73) to speak of society's mission as that of freeing man from the hold of natural forces, of delivering him from the mindless greed of his senses. A kind of Cartesian mind/body dualism seems to lie behind this imagery; but Durkheim never openly confesses to one, since it contradicts his repeated explicit contention that the intrinsically spiritual, "extremely immaterial" (R 90; *90*) realm of society is itself only one "region" (F 326; *260*) of the all-encompassing realm of nature. An explicit naturalistic monism thus struggles in his thought with an implicit dualism, or perhaps even an implicit spiritualistic monism. The difficulties engendered by this struggle are evident in the following passage from *Elementary forms*, with its half-hearted assertions and cautious qualifications: "The world of representations within which social life unfolds is super-imposed upon its material substratum rather than coming from it; the determinism that reigns within that world is thus rather more supple than that rooted in the constitution of our tissues, and leaves the actor a justified impression of greater freedom" (F 389; 307).

Durkheim's view of labor as wholly profane, individual, and thus nonsocial, and his distaste for the materiality characteristic of the nonsocial realm (e.g., D 340; 348)—these two tendencies bias even his approach to what he considers the proper social realm by mak-ing it difficult for him to deal adequately with social objects. As we have seen, Durkheim treats the *manières d'être*, the concrete, objec-tified traces left on the environment by social activity, as mere pro-jections and indicators of the society's basic norms; and after listing them at first as components of the social realm, he later excludes them from such consideration.

In *Elementary forms* Durkheim deals at length with objects, from artifacts employed in ritual to systems of myth; but these, being re-ligious objects, possess no intrinsic significance, since their relation to God/society (the ultimate addressee of religious beliefs and prac-tices) is entirely symbolic. Unfortunately, this tendency to treat ob-jects as intrinsically indifferent, well grounded as it may be when applied to religion, seems to have given Durkheim a striking lack of concern for *any* objects. He shows little awareness that many classes of objects do not bear an exclusively or even primarily symbolic ref-erence to a wholly spiritual object, but have quite different intrinsic properties—in particular, properties such that the ability to deter-mine the employment of these objects becomes a basis for power over nature, over other objects, or over men.[5]

Another reason why power relations play no significant role in Durkheim's conceptions of the social realm is his inability to con-ceptualize collective units intermediate between the individual and

---

[5] On the significance of nonsymbolic aspects of objects, and their bearing on social power, see Amitai Etzioni, *The active society* (N.Y.: Free Press, 1968), pp. 327ff.

society. This may seem a groundless charge, since Durkheim insistently put forward a strategy for a moral reconstruction of modern society based on occupational groupings that would mediate between the atomized individual and the larger society. However, he consistently visualized those groupings merely as organs of the larger society (e.g., S 275; 249), and the pattern of their relations to one another and to the society was to be markedly hierarchical and authoritarian. His strategy was to provide the larger society with a comprehensive, consistent network of decentralized, functionally efficient, but *not* autonomous agencies for the elaboration and enforcement of norms. These agencies, for the individual, would provide a proximate target for loyalty; they would be "locales" for activities that could express and sustain the individual's intense feelings of solidarity and moral obligation to his society.

Countless passages from Durkheim's writings establish that he regarded only the individual and the total society as significant units of analysis. But if my previous argument that Durkheim expelled the individual as such from the social realm has any validity, it would seem that the larger society is the *only* ultimately significant point of reference in his sociology; "*l'individu écarté il ne reste que la société* (R 101; *102*). For this reason he consistently treated each society as possessing only *one* culture (one might say, as being one culture). Indeed, he argued that intersocietal relations are only possible to the extent that there exists a higher-level culture in which the two different societal cultures can be subsumed (F 409ff; *322ff*).

This Durkheimian conception of society as culture is most clearly (and most damagingly) obvious in Durkheim's treatment of the genesis of norms. His view of the operation of norms, I have argued, implies that norms appeal to the will, affect behavior through the mediation of the will. However, he does not recognize that a will must be postulated not only at the receiving end of the norm but also at its source—that a norm is, after all, a command, and that in a command relation one will attempts to influence and bind another will. There is an intrinsic *partiality* to the will, apparent in Hobhouse's criticism of the Rousseauian "general will": If it is general, it is not a will; if it is a will, it is not general. Durkheim cannot face up to this partiality of the will (and must therefore ignore the willed nature of the norm) because he cannot visualize society otherwise than as a fused entity, admitting of no other subunits than individuals.[6] In his view the norms and institutions, the totality of a society's culture, are as it were "breathed out" by the society in its entirety.

The theoretical sources of this conception of norm-making probably lie in the medieval concept of law;[7] and its limited empirical applicability is probably to be found in small, preliterate tribal societies, such as those Australian tribes that Durkheim once confessed to understanding better than he understood modern France.[8] But there is an alternative concept of law: the Roman concept implicit in the close etymological relationship between *jus* (law) and *jubeo* (to command). Here the process of norm-making typically expresses (and presumably attempts to reinforce) an asymmetry of power between superindividual but subsocietal collectivities. By contrast Durkheim typically conceives norm-making as the sudden blinding awareness of a holy representation, universally shared across a ritual gathering whose intense emotion conquers the individuality of all the participants. The only power relation that can be conceptualized in this process is that of the whole society to the individual; the only conflict is that between the society's spirituality and the individual's mindless organic urges.

A further criticism can be made of Durkheim's treatment of the genesis of norms and institutions. It is hard to see how it can really be applied to the concrete processes through which institutions have been and are being generated in all historical societies; indeed, in his major sociological writings Durkheim never even attempts to discuss these processes (except, perhaps, for some statements to the effect that revolutionary assemblies often develop the same kind of intense emotional heat as "primitive" orgiastic ceremonies). To this objection (if he had viewed it as such) Durkheim would probably have answered that in his view the processes of historical societies

---

[6] For instance, F 296-97; 237-38 contains a rather awkward slip. A statement of the conditions under which norms are obeyed becomes suddenly, and apparently inadvertently, a statement of the conditions under which norms are issued.

[7] For a statement of this concept, and of the contrasting one based on Roman law, see Alessandro Passerin d'Entreves, *The notion of the state* (Oxford: Oxford University Press, 1967), pp. 85-88.

[8] See Bellah, "Durkheim and history," p. 168.

that one might consider institution-making (e.g., legislation) are merely elaborations on, or additions to, institutional frameworks whose origins lie back in earliest history; and that his treatment of the genesis of institutions addresses itself to *those* origins (F 4; *15*) and cannot be falsified by pointing at the calculated, purposeful way in which historical societies actually go about laying down their own specific rules, apparently without the benefit of any blinding self-revelation of the collective consciousness.

In his sociological writings, at any rate, Durkheim always shows a preference (when he is concerned with the past at all) for dealing with the remotest past, with the human actors who were practically at the threshold of history; see, for instance, his treatment of a plurality of institutions in the *Leçons*, or the way he argues that the archaic Roman institution of property had religious roots (D Chapter 13). Persuasive as the latter argument may be, it dwells on the earliest and most obscure phases of Roman history and thus is largely inferential. One can set against it Max Weber's earlier reconstruction of the genesis of the later, classical Roman notion of *dominium*, which appeared in a technical work on Roman legal history. Weber argues that this notion was first developed by a specific socioeconomic stratum within Roman society, whose interests it expressed; this group then entered into protracted struggles with other groups standing for other notions of property, and only thus managed to have its own particularistic notion validated and sanctioned as *the* Roman notion.

Formally, Durkheim's and Weber's arguments are not incompatible, since each deals with a different "stretch" of Roman history. But on the one hand, Durkheim's argument is weakened by the fact that it develops on much less solid empirical ground; and on the other, the two arguments embody different and in fact incompatible *general* understandings of the genesis of institutions. One may suspect, indeed, that Durkheim and Weber had different ideas of the very nature of institutions and norms.

Durkheim occasionally perceives that the genesis of norms may involve a conflict between incompatible views of what the norm's content ought to be; but he views this conflict in starkly idealistic terms:

Society is constituted . . . above all by the idea that it forms itself. And indeed, it may sometimes hesitate over the way in which it ought to conceive itself; it may feel itself drawn in different directions. But such conflicts, when they arise, take place not between the ideal and reality, but between different ideals. . . . Everything unfolds within the realm of the ideal (F 604; 470).

We may perhaps connect with the urge for unity manifested in this view of society the many times that Durkheim emphasizes "essential dichotomies" in his arguments. On close examination, these points seldom turn out to be tenable as dichotomies, in the sense that their two elements do not lie on the same plane; instead one of them stands over the other and, as it were, "envelops" it. In Chapter 6 I have argued the untenability of the mechanical solidarity/organic solidarity distinction found in *The Division of Labor*; only upon the bedrock of a however vestigial similitude of consciousness (mechanical solidarity) can the division of labor begin to operate and go on to produce its own "solidarizing" networks of exchange relations. In Chapter 7 I have argued that Durkheim's distinction between a group's amount of regulation and its cohesiveness is also untenable: the group's norm-making activity is by far the most significant of the two properties, so that cohesiveness can be treated as derivative from it. Finally, in *Elementary forms,* as we have seen, the laying down of the sacred/profane distinction turns out to be itself a sacred activity, and to that extent the sacred subordinates to itself or subsumes under itself the profane (at any rate within the *social* realm, that bounded by institutions).

In my view these unacknowledged breakdowns of purportedly crucial dichotomies express the urgency of Durkheim's moral passion for unity, which consistently although stealthily undermines his analytical commitment to diversity and plurality. Repeatedly, Blake's injunction, "twofold always," yielded in Durkheim's mind to a more cogent and deep preoccupation: *ut unum sint,* "let them be as one."

Predictably, Durkheim's treatment of social stratification, scant and unsystematic as it is, shows traces of his lack of interest in the phenomenon of power. Three characteristics of that treatment bear this out:

1. The normative apparatus of society is seen as the sole determinant of the stratification system (e.g., F 211; *173.* S 275-76; *249-50*).

2. The differential allocation of power is not a determinant of the stratification system but a consequence or a single aspect of it. "It is society that classifies beings as superior or inferior, as masters who command or subjects who obey; it is society that confers on the former the singular property that makes commanding efficacious and constitutes power" (F 522-23; 409).

3. The social tensions resulting from and affecting the stratification system are seen as revolving exclusively around the distribution of rewards (S 275-79; 349-53), not around the allocation of power itself. In Durkheim's view, in particular, the class struggle takes place essentially over the placement of individuals within the occupational hierarchy and over the distribution of income, *not* over the ability of some groups, to the exclusion of others, to determine the employment of the means of production.

All these features of Durkheimian stratification result in the following conception of what is needed to alleviate the tensions resulting from stratification, spelled out in Durkheim's lectures on socialism:

> What is needed if the social order is to reign is that the mass of men be content with their lot. But what is needed for them to be content is not that they have more or less, but that they are convinced that they have no right to more. And for this, it is absolutely essential that there be an authority whose superiority they acknowledge and which tells them what is right. For an individual committed only to the pressure of his needs will never admit he has reached the extreme limits of his rightful portion. If he is not conscious of a force above him which he respects, which stops him and tells him with authority that the compensation due him is fulfilled, then inevitably he will expect as due him all that his needs demand. And since in our hypothesis these needs are limitless, their exigency is necessarily without limit. For it to be otherwise, a moral power is required whose superiority he recognizes, and which cries out: "You must go no further."[9]

This passage suggests one final aspect of Durkheim's first and only social fact: the norm. It is the essence of a norm that it is a constraint, a set of boundaries, a limit; it is its job to restrain the expansive tendencies and centrifugal potentialities of forces that Durkheim

[9] Durkheim, *Socialism* (New York: Collier, 1962), pp. 242-43. The reader will find an excellent discussion of the Durkheimian position on these and other problems in Pizzorno, "Lecture actuelle de Durkheim," *European Journal of Sociology*, IV (1963), No. 1.

treats as intrinsically nonsocial. One may wonder about the wisdom, or even the logical tenability, of a conception in which, to put it metaphorically, the brake comes before the wheel. On the face of it a conception like Marx's, which treats labor and not the norm as the social fact *par excellence*, seems rather more tenable.

It is possible to challenge my contention that for Durkheim the norm is essentially a restraining factor and society itself a set of limits. Durkheim does in fact assert that society is *also* a source of strength, a set of enabling rather than restraining factors (e.g., F 299ff, 402; 240ff, 317). But it seems to me that he views its constraining action as primary and its enabling action as derivative. The relationship between the two resembles that between submission and protection in Hobbes's construction of the relation between subject and sovereign, as in the following Durkheimian passage: "For man freedom consists in deliverance from blind, unthinking physical forces; this he achieves by opposing against them the great and intelligent force which is society, under whose protection he shelters. By putting himself under the wing of society, he makes himself also, to a certain extent, dependent upon it. But this is a liberating dependence" (SP 72).

I have argued that Durkheim's conception of social reality excludes aspects of human experience that I consider fully entitled to sustained sociological consideration. I have also argued that as a consequence the ways in which Durkheim conceptualizes the "social" aspects of human reality present considerable weaknesses. If these arguments have any merit, one may wonder *why* Durkheim so restricted the field of sociology, and why he covered even the territory he assigned to it so inadequately.

I shall merely state one tentative view of how this came about. First, Durkheim accepted a conceptualization of modern society as "civil society," which (as I have argued in my section on Marx) was rather superficial to begin with. Second, unlike the utilitarian proponents of that same conceptualization, he felt a consistent moral and theoretical concern for the problem of order, and judged it to be solvable only if one could devise ways to counter the divisive trends inherent in the civil society; moreover, he constructed his theory as a statement not of the minimal but of the optimal conditions under which that problem could be solved. Finally, he systematically treated his statement of optimal conditions as a statement of minimal conditions. If it can be said that Marx tended to treat as unavoidable those things he considered desirable, then Durkheim treated desirable conditions as indispensable. From this standpoint, the main difference between the two was that Marx wished for revolutionary change and Durkheim for stability, order, and social peace. In Mannheim's terms, Marx was a utopian writer and Durkheim an ideological one.

Along these lines, then, Durkheim constructed a theory that is almost worthless if treated as a set of generalizations about concrete social reality, particularly in modern society. But it has great analytical power, and one might also say great aesthetic and moral appeal, if it is recognized as a single-minded exploration of one, and only one, part of social reality: the normative elements. In this respect Durkheim's thought is an outstanding contribution to the discussion of what makes society possible; and it is valuable if and to the extent that its partiality is recognized.

Index

Index